D1142405

A THEOLOGY OF
THE OLD TESTAMENT

A THEOLOGY
OF THE
OLD TESTAMENT

John L. McKenzie

Geoffrey Chapman

1974

Geoffrey Chapman Publisher

An imprint of Cassell and Collier
Macmillan Publishers Ltd.
35 Red Lion Square, London, WC1R 4SG
and at Sydney, Auckland, Toronto,
Johannesburg
an affiliate of Macmillan Inc. New York

First published in the U.S.A. 1974

ISBN 0-225-66074-1

Printed in the United States of America

To A.E.

Contents

Preface

For Old Testament scholars, the theology of the Old Testament and the history of Israel are the two works which offer them the best chance to summarize their entire work. My project does not have the proportions of the works of Walther Eichrodt and Gerhard von Rad, but neither does any other modern Old Testament theology have those proportions. I make no attempt to work on that scale.

Nevertheless, I did attack the work with some eagerness; I did not yet know of a hidden obstacle. Old Testament theology, as the reader can learn more fully in the Introduction, has no set and accepted structure and style. I knew this. I have some experience in producing books, and I confess that the outline of a book, with one other exception, has never been a problem. To be candid, I have generally worked without one, hoping that the material would develop itself, so to speak. Perhaps the results show this, but one develops one's own style. This proved impossible for Old Testament theology. Before I could write the first section, I had to commit myself effectively to the content of every other section. This has some reference to the works which I mention in the Epilogue. Once the work was planned and partly written, no substantial revision was possible. I could not think of revision; I could only think of throwing it away and starting over again. My fellow authors know as well as I that this must sometimes be done, but they also know that it is only done out of desperation.

Those who have written Old Testament theologies have gone each his own way. I found that once one chooses his own way, one must go it at the peril of falling into the way of another. Hans-Joachim Kraus wrote that it is unnecessary for any one to read all the German biblical theologies, as he did. He is quite right, although I was surprised to learn how many of them, beginning with G. F. Oehler, I have read, most of them with some care and close attention. One must read most of them; but it is a very peculiar form of study the major fruit of which is to know what you are not going to do.

Shortly after I had planned what I was going to do, I happened to read an article by James Barr which I can no longer retrace, in which he said that biblical theology is now out of date; I quote substantially, not verbatim. Such observations do not sit well when they touch a large project which one has just signed a contract to do. I believe that Professor Barr has somewhat altered his stance, since he has produced some opinions on how biblical theology should be done. I am sorry that I was unable to use what he has written, for reasons just given. What the article gave me, of course, was a firm determination to show that Barr is out of date. It has affected my treatment, and that to such an extent that I realize I must offer Professor Barr my amazed thanks.

I must now proceed to the agreeable task of acknowledging the assistance rendered by those—unlike Professor Barr—who knew what they were doing. Mr. John J. Delaney rescued the book from near oblivion and has seen it through the press. His work has been marked by great patience and tolerance, as well as by an almost blind faith in the author; it has been a pleasure to deal with him. Dr. Mary Jo Weaver, as a graduate student at Notre Dame, rendered invaluable editorial assistance for the majority of the work, as well as other aids according to the needs she perceived; possibly I am still unaware of some of them. Miss Anita Weisbrod (since June 1971, Mrs. James M. Robinson) furnished assistance and encouragement in many thoughtful ways for this and for some other literary endeavors. Mrs. Rachel Gibbons typed all the manuscript, which was done in Chicago; to acknowledge this is not to mention the deep and devoted friendship of which I have been the beneficiary. I am grateful to Dan Herr of the Thomas More Association for the kind of advice and counsel which he swears he never gives. I experienced a couple of encounters with infirmity during the writing of this book, which set me back in my work. These were made tolerable by the kindly attention and assistance of more people than I can mention. In addition to those named above, I cannot omit the Reverend Thomas Munson; Louisa and Joseph Cahill; Robert Fox; Joel Wells; Ann and John Coyne; Virginia and John

Burkhart. Of such services is the fabric of life woven, and we too often forget it. I present this book to my colleagues with apprehension, but to my friends with deep gratitude.

John L. McKenzie

Chicago
De Paul University

A THEOLOGY OF
THE OLD TESTAMENT

SYMBOLS AND ABBREVIATIONS

ANEP	ed. James B. Pritchard, *The Ancient Near East in Pictures,* Princeton, 1954.
ANES	ed. James B. Pritchard, *The Ancient Near East: Supplementary Texts and Pictures Relating to the Old Testament,* Princeton, 1969.
ANET	ed. James B. Pritchard, *Ancient Near Eastern Texts Relating to the Old Testament,* Princeton, 1955.
BeitrWissAT	*Beiträge zur Wissenschaft des Alten Testaments*
BeihZATWiss	*Beihefte zur Zeitschrift für Alttestamentliche Wissenschaft*
CathBiblQuart	*Catholic Biblical Quarterly*
D	The Deuteronomist source of the Pentateuch
E	The Elohist source of the Pentateuch
HAT	*Handbuch zum Alten Testament*
J	The Jahwist source of the Pentateuch
JBL	*Journal of Biblical Literature*
Kittel ThW	ed. Gerhard Kittel, *Theologisches Wörterbuch zum Neuen Testament*
P	The priestly source of the Pentateuch
RB	*Revue Biblique*
RSV	Revised Standard Version
ThSt	*Theological Studies*
ZATWiss	*Zeitschrift für die Alttestamentliche Wissenschaft*
+	and
=	parallel passage

Principles, Methods, and Structure

Biblical theology is the only discipline or subdiscipline in the field of theology that lacks generally accepted principles, methods, and structure. There is not even a generally accepted definition of its purpose and scope. The writer is compelled at the very beginning of his task to a choice between some structure already created and to the accompanying duty of meeting the criticisms leveled against the structure, or to the creation of a new structure and the accompanying risk of new criticism.

Biblical theology as a distinct discipline is generally recognized as first appearing in a monograph of J. P. Gabler.[1] Gabler insisted that biblical theology should neither follow the structure and method of dogmatic theology nor receive predetermined conclusions from dogmatic theology. The problem of method and structure will be better seen if we begin, with Gabler, with some idea of dogmatic or systematic theology. Under either name, theology of this kind is an effort to reduce the doctrines of Christianity or of some particular Christian church to a system. Historically no system has been constructed except by the use of the categories of some philosophical system chosen by the theologian for this purpose. In the development of systematic theology the philosophy can in the course of time become altered by the influence of other systems or simply by deterioration; when this has happened, the systematic structure of the philosophy has been loosened. The diversity of philosophical systems, apart from development and deterioration, means that different systems have been devised. More than once the union between the philosophical system and the doctrine has been so close that the system itself approaches the

---

[1] *De iusto discrimine theologiae biblicae et dogmaticae*, 1787.

sacredness of the doctrine, and its language becomes the only orthodox language in which to express doctrine.

It is important to recognize that systematic philosophy in the sense of a comprehensive system began with the Summas of the scholastic theologians of the Middle Ages. Augustine, the most prolific theological writer of the patristic period, never wrote a systematic theology. He did employ the categories of philosophy to set forth doctrine. But he never dealt with any more than particular questions, which could be conceived rather broadly. By the twelfth century theology had become the study of the sacred page (the Bible) without being biblical theology; the professor taught "questions," the study of particular problems, many of which had no reference to the biblical text and were solved by philosophical discussion. The study of particular questions did not demand rigorous consistency in the whole view of theology; there was simply no whole view. When a system was created like the system of Thomas Aquinas, certain basic general principles emerged which were applied to each particular question; the entire system was brought to bear in the solution of each particular problem.

It is not entirely true to say that systematic theology was unhistorical; it is true that it was not historical in the modern critical sense. The systematic theologian was at pains to show that his theological conclusion was in harmony with the traditional belief and teaching of the Church. Systematic theologians made some effort, usually with inadequate tools, to ascertain what traditional doctrines were. With primitive methods they often succeeded in showing that their conclusions had always been taught in the Church, where critical methods now show that manifestly they were not. The systematic theologies of the classical period of theology were weak in the theory of development and haunted by the principle that the entire system of doctrine was found in the Scriptures, if one could interpret them properly.

The progress of theology in the churches has in fact been advanced by the study of particular questions, in modern times by principles and methods not very closely related to the established systems. It is recognized by theologians that a slavish adherence to the principles and methods of the established systems means that many questions are rendered immediately insoluble. It means also that one denies any advance in philosophical methods since the systems were created. Most modern theologians think it is unlikely that a synthesis like the synthesis of Thomas Aquinas could now be devised, and they do not work towards such a synthesis. They are committed to the study of particular questions. Their work is systematic only in the sense that they employ philosophical methods and discourse to present theological conclusions; their method is more like the method of Augustine than it is like the method of Aquinas.

Biblical theology, which has appeared in modern times as a branch or subheading of systematic theology, has not yet been able to break out of the patterns of the older and larger discipline. Roman Catholic theologians have long distinguished between dogmatic or systematic theology and positive theology. By positive theology they mean the study of the written sources of doctrine: the Scriptures; the decrees of the Popes, bishops, and councils; and the writings of the Fathers of the Church. These studies are carried on within the framework of systematic theology; and the purpose of such biblical theology was to produce and criticize "proof-texts" employed within areas of systematic theological discussion. In this method neither the Scriptures nor particular books are studied as a whole for themselves; the entire direction is governed by the theses of systematic theology. Most of the Bible is irrelevant to systematic theology. The distinction between systematic and positive theology is hardly used by Protestant theologians, but Protestant theology has long been familiar with the collection of proof-texts. Older biblical theologies, both Catholic and Protestant, were produced in which the material was arranged according to the divisions or treatises of systematic theology.[2] Even when these theologies were not mere collections of proof-texts, the systematic arrangement was followed because no other arrangement of theological thinking was conceivable.

The nineteenth century saw the rise of the historical and literary criticism which has dominated biblical studies up to the present time. Within the same period systematic theology lost esteem, largely because of the failure of systematic theologians to use or

[2] Franciscus Ceuppens, o.p., *Theologia Biblica,* 5 v. (2nd ed., Turin, 1953).

even to accept historical and critical methods. Theology, traditionally a disciplined expression of religious belief, was regarded as too closely attached to belief ever to achieve the objectivity of historical scholarship. Biblical theologies were not written during most of the late nineteenth and early twentieth centuries because biblical scholars seriously doubted whether the theological method would permit historical and critical scholarship. Instead biblical scholars produced histories of Israelite religion. It was felt that theological method, which had always dealt with eternal verities, would not allow a true presentation of the development of Israelite religion.

Yet it was not noticed that the same reason could be urged against the writing of a Catholic or Protestant theology. Theological Summas have always taken the date of their composition as the high point of theological and credal development. They incorporated a scheme of doctrine which was not known or accepted before they were composed. The apostles would not have understood the Summas of the Middle Ages. The systematic theologians seemed serenely indifferent to development. Walther Eichrodt made an important point when he observed that unless there are certain constant elements in the history of a religion, no theology is possible; and theology can deal only with these constant elements, for they give the religion an identity which can be recognized.[3] It does not follow from this that Eichrodt's "cross section" is the best method to employ in studying the theology of the Old Testament. The problem of any theology, Old Testament or Christian, is that the Summa presents a scheme of doctrine which was never known to more than a few of the believers of that religion. I wish to make the point that no theology has ever found a way to deal with the problem of development of doctrine; the problem is not peculiar to the theology of the Old Testament.

The rehabilitation of biblical theology and the renewal of interest in the discipline date from the publication of the first volume of Walther Eichrodt's *Theologie des Alten Testaments* in 1933. Eichrodt affirmed that a theology should not be a history of religion but a systematic exposition of doctrine. It should not, however, follow the categories of systematic theology but should find its own

[3] *Theologie des Alten Testaments,* v. 1 (8th ed., Stuttgart, 1968), xi ff.

categories based on its own material. Eichrodt chose the covenant of Israel with Yahweh as the central and determining theme of the Old Testament and arranged his material according to its relation to covenant. The work has become a standard classic; it is the best compendium of biblical doctrine, whatever one means by the term, which has been produced. Yet its readers in the last twenty to thirty years have generally agreed that it does not succeed in its effort to create a covenant-centered theology. The beliefs of the Old Testament are simply not that consistent; and if a synthesis cannot be constructed around the word "covenant," one wonders what central theme distinctive of the Old Testament could be found. The covenant synthesis, in the last analysis, is impossible without some artificiality.

Eichrodt also affirmed that Old Testament theology is meaningless in Christian theology unless the relation of Old Testament to New Testament be shown positively. Here we touch again upon an ancient problem which has never been satisfactorily resolved. From the New Testament to the Middle Ages, the relevance of the Old Testament was found either in predictions or in its typology-allegory. Typology and allegory ultimately issue in a hidden meaning revealed only through the New Testament and the Church. Neither prediction nor typology-allegory can be accepted by modern criticism. From the Middle Ages on, the probative value of the Old Testament was the area of interest; as we have seen, this fails to treat the Old Testament as meaningful literature. There is still much uncertainty in modern interpretation concerning the relevance of the Old Testament. Many readers of Rudolf Bultmann think that he leans to the opinion of Marcion that the Old Testament does not contribute to the understanding of Christianity. The problem must be discussed in its proper place at the conclusion of this work. At this point, it is sufficient to notice that the proper function of the interpreter seems to be rather to interpret the Old Testament than to proclaim its value. If he can succeed in making its meaning clear, he will not have to show its relevance for Christian theology.

A response to Eichrodt was produced on the same scale by Gerhard von Rad.[4] Von Rad did not attempt to synthesize the material

[4] *Theologie des Alten Testaments,* v. 2 (Munich, 1957 and 1960).

either in systematic or in his own categories. For him it is a question rather of diverse theologies within the Old Testament than of a single theology; and the structure of the book follows in the main the sequence of the books of the Old Testament. Yet the work is not a history of religion, but a studied effort to write a theology of development. Even here the prophets must be set apart entirely from the narratives, the poems, and wisdom. The major criticism leveled against Von Rad is his extremely casual attitude towards the history behind the Old Testament books, and Eichrodt has asked how a theology without a historical basis can be a genuine theology.[5] Von Rad's position, however, is worth recalling: theology is a study of the beliefs of people, not of their history; and the theological interpretation of their history is independent of the "facts" of their history.[6]

Other Old Testament theologies which have appeared over the same period since 1933 have been studies of particular questions, with no attempt to synthesize either in systematic categories or in any others.[7] These works have their own value as aids to the interpretation and exposition of the Old Testament; and we are permitted to ask whether the idea of "systematic" as applied to the Old Testament has the same meaning as it has when we speak of "systematic theology." I do not imply that one must return to the history of religion. Theology is, by etymology, "God-talk." If one collects all the God-talk there is in the Old Testament, a fairly clear personal reality emerges which is not entirely consistent with itself. Once it emerges, no one could ever confuse it with any other personal reality. Yet, as we have indicated, all the collected God-talk coalesces into a totality which seems to represent the belief of no single Israelite who ever lived. When the biblical theologian puts this God-talk together (let us avoid the word "synthesis" for the moment), he does it by some principle which he deduces from sources other than the Old Testament. When he seeks to reconcile the inconsistencies mentioned, he does so because he experiences

[5] *Theologie des Alten Testaments,* v. 2 (5th ed., Stuttgart, 1964), vii–ix.
[6] *Old Testament Theology,* v. 1 (New York, 1962), 106–12.
[7] Edmond Jacob, *Theology of the Old Testament* (New York, 1958); Ludwig Köhler, *Old Testament Theology* (Philadelphia, 1958); Th. C. Vriezen, *An Outline of Old Testament Theology* (Oxford, 1966).

the totality which the Israelites did not experience. They therefore felt no need to reconcile the inconsistencies. Nor should one forget the capacity of prephilosophical man to accumulate inconsistencies with no attempt to arrange them. This can be seen clearly in Israelite law; and Henri Frankfort pointed out the ability of the Egyptians to think in parallel and sometimes contradictory lines in their mythology.[8] The same capacity certainly appears in the compilers of the Old Testament books. The principles of synthesis deduced from sources other than the Bible are the principles of logical discourse in which modern man is trained. The biblical literature is not logical discourse; and the task of biblical theology may be simply to translate it into logical discourse.

The task of Old Testament theology may become easier and be more successfully accomplished if we remember that it is precisely the theology of the Old Testament, not the exegesis of the Old Testament, not the history of the religion of Israel, not the theology of the entire Bible, which is the object of the study. The religion of Israel included many factors which are not found in the Old Testament; some are unknown, others are poorly known. For the historian of Israelite religion, the temple and cult of Bethel are extremely important, and he is hampered in his task because so little is known of them. To the theologian of the Old Testament the temple and cult of Bethel are important only because of what Amos and Hosea said about them. To their contemporaries Amos and Hosea were not very important.

The interest of the theologian of the Old Testament is not in the religious experience either of Israel as a whole or of the individual Israelites. Any such "experience" is a phenomenon of a particular time and place; as such, it is the object of history, not of theology. The interest of the theologian of the Old Testament is directed to the documents of the Old Testament. It is directed, as we have said, to the totality of the utterances, not to the single items. Presumably something emerges from the totality which does not emerge from any single utterance. If this can be articulated, it is a theological statement concerning the Old Testament which no Old Testament writer ever made or could make. If it is true,

[8] H. Frankfort et al., *Before Philosophy* (Baltimore, 1949).

something is added to the sum of human knowledge. And since the Old Testament theologian is writing for himself and the other students of the Old Testament, he must articulate this in logical discourse, the language which is used in academic discussion. He is not writing for the ancient Israelites and should not use their language nor their thought patterns. What emerges from the totality might be expressed in a poem, a song, a play, a novel; unless the theologian has the literary skill required for the production of these forms, he had better abstain from them; and such a work would not be a theology, which is rational discourse by definition.

We return, then, to our original definition of systematic theology as the expression of belief in the categories and the language of a theological system. No learned man can pretend to write a learned work which would not reflect his philosophy; if he did not have a philosophy, he would not be a learned man. Modern philosophers seem generally agreed that there is no philosophy which is totally true or totally false. It is less important that the writer has a better philosophy, assuming that the word "better" can be used meaningfully, than that he know the virtues and the limitations of the philosophy which he has, that his philosophy would not become a substitute for thought rather than a tool. Much has been said about the imposition of the categories of Greek philosophy upon the Bible, and the consequent distortion of the Bible.[9] This criticism is valid for many works. Yet modern man can hardly open his mouth in rational discourse except in Greek categories; it is important not to avoid them—which is impossible—but to recognize them, to know that what he is saying is not exactly what the Bible says. He is, as I have said, articulating that perception which comes from the totality of the Bible. The articulation is not Bible; it can be true to the Bible, or biblical theology is impossible. As a biblical historian I am a nearly uncritical disciple of Collingwood; I try to rethink the thoughts of the past.[10] As a biblical theologian I try not to rethink the thoughts of the past, but seek new insights which arise from the totality of the thoughts of the past. Let me add that these new insights are impossible

---

[9] Thorlief Boman, *Hebrew Thought Compared with Greek* (London, 1960); James Barr, *The Semantics of Biblical Language* (London, 1961).

[10] R. G. Collingwood, *The Idea of History* (New York, 1956), 210–28.

unless one has rethought the thoughts of the past; to put it simply, one must read the Bible before one writes its theology.

This epistemological excursion seemed necessary before we could define the task of biblical theology, and even more demanded before we could define its principles. The question of synthesis and system remains. I have asked, but not yet answered, whether we can use the word "systematic" of biblical theology in the same meaning in which it is used of systematic theology. The most ambitious venture in this area, the work of Eichrodt, has been successful in spite of the partial failing of the system as such. Von Rad's theology is not systematic in the sense I have already described, the sense in which certain basic principles are applied to each particular question so that the entire system is brought to bear on any particular problem. This type of system seems impossible in Old Testament theology, and we must anticipate a theological statement to explain why. Basic principles emerge in a rational system, which is a thing. What emerges in the Old Testament is not a rational system but a basic personal reality, Yahweh, who is consistent as a person is, not as a rational system. No particular problem is solved without reference to Yahweh, who is not a rational principle.

One seems, then, to be forced into the approach of particular topics; and in these treatments there is order and arrangement, but no system or structure. The topics are usually selected according to the personal studies and interest of the writers; this is not in itself deplorable, but it manifests that biblical theology is an unstructured discipline. Yet there are other factors at work which deserve mention. Up to this time it has been difficult for a Catholic to write a theology of the Old Testament without an explicit section on messianism. A small essay of my own was criticized even in the editorial stage because this topic was not presented with sufficient emphasis. I have been convinced for years that messianism is a Christian interest and a Christian theme; that it is a Christian response to the Old Testament and should be treated as such; that in a theology of the Old Testament, as I have described it thus far, messianism would appear neither in the chapter headings nor in the index. It is not only not a dominant theme, but in the proper sense of the word it is doubtfully a theme of the Old Testament at all. This theme is imposed upon the theologian by theological factors foreign to his area of study. He should be free to make his own selection and to make his own errors of judgment. Yet such a work deserves a title like "Essays in the Theology of the Old Testament," or "Towards a Theology of the Old Testament," or "Prolegomena to a Theology of the Old Testament."

We have already noticed the obvious fact that the principles, methods, and style of theology change, and usually change later than they ought. The change comes because the world and the Church are asking questions which theology is not answering or not even hearing. To illustrate: I have been a fairly convinced pacifist for twenty years. This conviction began with the teaching of the prophets. I do not remember any theology of the Old Testament which dealt with the problems of war and peace. They shall certainly be treated in this work; the purpose is not to promote pacifism, but simply to discern whether in that totality which we have mentioned there emerges some insight into this problem. Those who do not accept my insight are forced either to say that their insight is contradictory or that the Old Testament does not touch the problem at all. Such problems are not simply a question of relevance, but of meeting the development of theology. If this development is not to be met, there is no need for producing an additional theology, now or ever. Those we have are fully adequate. But since it is a biblical belief that whenever man encounters man, God is present as a witness and a party to the encounter, Old Testament theology must deal with such problems as war and peace, poverty, the urban problems, industrial and technological society, and such—not directly, of course, but by stating clearly what principles may emerge from the totality of the utterances. Theology keeps reforming its principles and its contents from the course of the human adventure. This is what gives the theologian the new questions. It is also one of the things, and perhaps the most important, which distinguishes theology from the history of religion.

If any structure emerges from the totality of the God-talk of the Old Testament, it ought to arise from the emphases of the Old Testament. These emphases, which have long been recognized, are simply those themes which occur most frequently and which appear to be decisive in giving Old Testament belief its distinctive identity. The theologian can hardly divert much from his predecessors in his titles of chapters and subdivision. Nor can he avoid personal value judgments in the weight which he assigns to various topics and themes; if he were to present the themes with perfect objectivity, as if they were coins of the same denomination, he would not be faithful to his material. The order in which they are presented is not determined by the Old Testament, but by his own judgment of the most logical and coherent arrangement of material which was never arranged by those who wrote his sources. There is no reason in the Old Testament why biblical theology should begin with creation; in our own theology creation is the belief which is presupposed by all other beliefs. Biblical theology of the Old Testament, we have said, is written for modern readers who are probably religious believers, not for the scribes of Israel and Judaism who produced the source material of biblical theology. Their categories of thought must be of some importance for the arrangement of the material. But in whatever categories the material is arranged, the theologian is not going to escape a topical treatment; his problem is to rise above the merely topical treatment, the disconnected *quaestiones*.

The problem of synthesis is situated in the analysis of experience; the biblical theologian does not have a unique problem. The historian of the battle of Gettysburg is unable to reconstruct the experience of those who were present; strictly, none of those present experienced the totality of the battle. The historian must assemble a large number of individual testimonies. The structure of the presentation will be generally chronological and topographical, for the historian cannot present an intelligible narrative if he attempts to chronicle the events minute by minute. The account will be as confusing as the battle was. He knows, however, better than the participants, better even than the generals, that a pattern was emerging. He must show it even though the commanders did not see it. The pattern led with inevitable logic to Pickett's charge, which becomes not only the climactic action, but the one action of the three-days' conflict which was total. The confusion ends on the third day when the two armies finally confront each other with their entire strength. This analysis of an experience is closer,

I believe, to the task of the biblical theologian, than the analysis of a philosophical complex of ideas. I do not mean that the theology of the Old Testament ends with such a satisfying catharsis as Pickett's charge; it does not, and the theologian of the Old Testament cannot, as long as he limits himself to his material, show that the inner logic of the experience of Israel leads inevitably to the Christ-event. But he is engaged in the analysis of an experience prolonged in space and time. He believes that the experience, prolonged and complex as it is, has a unity which permits him to treat it as one. What is the principle of unity? It can only be the discovery of Yahweh, the God of Israel. I said "discovery," although "recognition" might serve as well. Let us return to the totality of which we have spoken. The discovery of Yahweh was something like the discovery of America; it took several centuries before Israel really began to understand what it had discovered. Yet Yahweh is a single reality. The biblical theologian has to be historian as much as philosopher, perhaps even more so, because the discovery of Yahweh occurs in a series of events like Gettysburg or the discovery of America. It was not the speculative evolution of an idea, not as the Old Testament presents it.

It may appear at this point that the theology is relapsing into the history of Israelite religion; but I have already referred to the pattern which can be discerned even in such nonphilosophical events as the battle of Gettysburg. It is the pattern which gives the battle intelligibility; and the general who anticipates the pattern, as Lee habitually did before Gettysburg, defeats his opponent. Israel's response to Yahweh was habitually a response based on imperfect knowledge at best, on misunderstanding and nonrecognition at worst; and I am speaking of the Old Testament books, not of the superstitious Israelites whom Amos encountered at Bethel. Amos does not recapitulate the supreme insight of the Old Testament into the reality of Yahweh; from some points of view he understood the reality of Yahweh quite dimly. The task of synthesis is to show that Amos has his place in the collective experience with others whose insight is not the same. The totality of the experience makes Amos intelligible—not completely, but better than if he is treated as an isolated and eccentric phenomenon with no ancestor and no descendant. But our interest is not to make

Amos intelligible; it is to make Yahweh not intelligible, but recognizable. Amos is in the pattern; he is not the pattern. He is perhaps the clearest exponent of Yahweh as the Righteous Judge. This is the title of Yahweh; as a total expression of the reality of Yahweh, it is not much better than Prime and Unmoved Mover.

The biblical theologian can scarcely avoid value judgments in his arrangement. Like the military historian, he should be able to distinguish the accessory and the inconclusive from the central and decisive. Not all parts of the Old Testament contribute equally to the total experience. Reviewers of Eichrodt noticed that he had difficulty including wisdom in his synthesis. Yet wisdom is more central in the Old Testament than one could judge from a covenant-centered theology. Wisdom simply has no reference to the covenant; it is older than the covenant, it is so basic to human experience that it has as many nonbiblical contacts as biblical. But it is an important part of Old Testament God-talk and includes themes which are scarcely touched in other books. Some of these themes are permanent in theological discussion and literature. The theologian ought to know that such value judgments are dangerous. But neither he nor his readers can escape their own history. It is difficult to imagine any theological question asked in this generation on which the book of Chronicles is likely to shed any light. But the theologian can write only in his generation.

To what extent are the synthesis and the value judgment determined by the Christian faith of the theologian? We have seen that the question of the relation of Old and New Testaments has been a matter of deep concern to the most important recent Old Testament theologians. I do not think that it is the concern of the Christian Old Testament theologian to explain or to justify the use of the Old Testament in the New Testament; this is the task of the New Testament theologian, for the problems arise in the New Testament. Still less is it the concern of the Old Testament theologian to explain the use of the Old Testament in the postapostolic church. He may deplore its use if he wishes, and he may feel compelled to dissociate himself from certain startling Christian misunderstandings of the Old Testament. As a Christian pedagogue, he may feel it his duty to dispel those misunderstandings which he thinks are serious enough in the contemporary world to deserve notice. But it is the conviction of this writer, reached after some years of discussion, dispute, and vacillation, and not entirely in agreement with some of his previous statements, that the Old Testament theologian will do well if he states the theology of the Old Testament clearly and accurately. Quite simply, I have not found the Old Testament so alien to the Christian faith which I profess that the relations of the two are a serious problem. The one whom Jesus called his father is the Yahweh of the Old Testament. It is here that the totality of the experience becomes vital; for the father is not the Yahweh of any single book or writer of the Old Testament. The task of Old Testament theology for the Christian could be conceived simply as the total description of that being whom Jesus called his father. The Christian Old Testament theologian ought to do at least this; perhaps it is all he can do. This, it will be observed, leaves almost no room for prediction, foreshadowing, allegory, or typology; and these techniques will not be employed in this work.

The Christian faith of the interpreter, however, will be a factor in determining the questions he asks. We have noticed that the biblical theologian and his readers live in a determined period of history and a determined type of culture. The Christian believes that Christianity is a fulfillment of the Old Testament, whatever he means by fulfillment. He reads the Old Testament as a Christian, not as an Israelite. Theology seeks an understanding of faith; it is the Christian faith, not the Israelite faith, which he seeks to understand. The scholar cannot prevent his faith from giving form to the questions he asks: what he can prevent is allowing his faith, instead of the Old Testament, to determine the answers to the questions of the Old Testament theology. We have adverted to the totality of the utterances, and to the insight which ought to emerge from the totality above and beyond what the texts themselves communicate. This insight is the insight of a Christian; but the Christian scholar must avoid reading things into the text. His proper skill is exegesis, interpretation.

This writer has said elsewhere that Jesus is the Messiah of Judaism, and that he can be understood only as the Messiah of Judaism. I stand by this observation; but I do not believe that it obliges me to find faith in Jesus Messiah in the Old Testament, nor to base faith in Jesus Messiah in the Old Testament. Jesus transformed the idea of Messiah when he fulfilled it. The total reality of Jesus Messiah is found nowhere in the Old Testament, not even in its totality. Jesus could have emerged from nothing except Israel and the Old Testament; but the study of the Old Testament does not demand that Jesus Messiah emerge from it.

The task of Old Testament theology can now be summarized as the analysis of an experience through the study of the written records of that experience. The experience is a collective experience which covers roughly a thousand years of history and literature. The experience is one because of the historical continuity of the group which had the experience and because of the identity of the divine being which the group retained as the object of its faith throughout the experience. The analysis must be done in certain categories and not merely by a chronological recital. We seek always the totality of the utterances and the insight which can be gained by assembling them. The theology of the Old Testament has to be a study of the reality of Yahweh. The Old Testament is the sole literary witness to that reality as the record of the experience of Israel, the sole historical witness.

The Israelite Experience
of Yahweh

The Old Testament is a collection of the literary remains of a people of the ancient Near East known generally, but not entirely accurately, as Israel, the ancient name also of the land in which this people lived. The reservation on the name of Israel is due simply to the historical ambiguity of the relations of the people of Israel with the people of Judah, who carried on the religion and the literary and historical traditions of Israel after a people which bore that name had ceased to exist. The solution of this historical problem is not the task of the theology of the Old Testament. The collection of the books does not disclose that Israel and Judah had different ideas and beliefs about their God Yahweh. The literary records were assembled and preserved primarily because they are the records of the experience of this people with Yahweh. This motivation is not valid for all the portions of the books; some of them appear to be nonreligious writing included because of their relevance to the religious experience of Israel.

It is obvious that the record of a religious experience, especially an experience which covers a period so long and so remote and which occurs in a culture so different, presents problems of its own. The theologian of the Old Testament must assume certain literary critical conclusions as valid presuppositions, as far as these conclusions are generally accepted. Theology has nothing to do with establishing or refuting literary critical conclusions. If the critical work is not well done, some of his theological conclusions may suffer erosion. The theologian must also accept a certain amount of historical conclusions. What people think happened is theologically as important as what did happen. It is extremely doubtful that we have a record of the origins of Israel and its religion which is in all details accurate; and the Israelite reconstruction of the account of origins reflects the faith of the time of the reconstruction more clearly than it reflects the events of Israel's origins. But the reconstruction is basic in the theology of the Old Testament, and the theologian is less concerned with the historical task of recovering a more accurate explanation of Israel's origins. It is not unique to Israel that a people should have a legendary account of its origins which is more an utterance of the unity established since its origins than it is an explanation of the origins. The problem of the relation of theology to history is not solved by this brief comment, and it will return in subsequent pages. The faith of the Old Testament reposes on the acts of Yahweh in history; this is a principle which is indisputable. The Old Testament also betrays some ignorance of much of Israel's early history; this is also indisputable. The two terms of the paradox are not reconciled by asserting that Israel believed a number of things about the acts of Yahweh which are not true. The assertion is valid and it is valid for any religion which can be studied; this does not mean that the religion has no theology or that the theology is no more than a tissue of erroneous ideas about the deity. Israel's insight into the reality of Yahweh is not to be measured by its historical knowledge, even the knowledge of its own past.

If we inquire in what ways Israel, according to its literary records, experienced Yahweh, certain categories suggest themselves; and these categories will furnish the structure of the theological analysis which we undertake here. With some brief remarks, we set them forth as a preliminary outline.

I place cult first as the normal and most frequent manner in which the Israelite experienced Yahweh. The importance of cult need not be measured exactly according to the space which is given it in the Old Testament, but the space given it is abundant. That the cult is a ritual encounter with the deity is a universal human belief; we do not have to validate it for Israel, but simply to see what the peculiarly Israelite understanding and practice of cult may have been. In the Old Testament we are almost always dealing with the religion and faith of a people described as such, very rarely with the phenomenon called "personal religion." Cult is by definition the religious expression of a group and not a feature of personal religion. Cult is explicitly or implicitly a profession of faith.

Next I list revelation as the situation in which Israel experienced Yahweh. By this I mean revelation made through authentic spokesmen of Yahweh, and not revelation in an improper sense. One need know little about other religions to recognize that revelation as it was understood in Israel does not appear in other religions except those which claim some continuity with Israelite religion. Israelite revelation is distinguished both in form and content from the revelation known to us in other religions with which Israel had contact. No other religion of the ancient Near Eastern world claimed to be founded on a revelation of the deity which the community worshiped, and on a revelation of a code of conduct imposed by the deity. No other religion exhibits a type of religious spokesman which is more than remotely similar to the Israelite prophets.

In the third place I list history as the area in which Israel experienced Yahweh. The treatment of this area may overlap the treatment of revelation, for the "experience" of Yahweh in history often consisted of hearing the prophetic interpretation of history. Yet the Israelites exhibit a conviction, again without parallel, that their history was the work of the deity whom they worshiped. One sees in the Old Testament a firm belief that Yahweh acts with plan and purpose, that he is not subject to fate, that he is not hindered by other divine beings nor moved by irrational whim.

In the fourth place I list nature as an area where Israel experienced Yahweh. The religions of the ancient Near East can generally, if unsatisfactorily, be classified as "nature religions"; the perception of superhuman power in nature is another universal human phenomenon. Israel again had its own distinctive way of expressing this perception. The question of mythology arises under this heading, as well as the question of creation.

To speak of wisdom as an experience of Yahweh may seem to be stretching our principle more than we ought; yet it is a peculiarly Israelite belief that Yahweh alone is wise and that Yahweh alone gives wisdom. Most of the content of conventional Israelite wisdom can be paralleled in other ancient wisdom literature, but not its religious quality. Similarly, the Israelite critical or "anti-wisdom" literature is not without parallel; but Job and Koheleth are recognized as two of the most original works of the Old Testament. In any scheme of Old Testament theology, wisdom is something of a deviant; it stands in its own category, and it has to be recognized as isolated from other parts of the theological structure.

With some hesitation we then take up a topic labeled the institutions of Israel. During its history the community of Israel appeared in several political forms and with variations in its social structure. The Old Testament writings present each of the developments in these fields as exhibiting theological aspects. The Old Testament is not acquainted with a purely secular politics or a purely secular sociology. One may say that it is acquainted neither with politics nor with sociology as theoretical disciplines; but the materials which we include in these disciplines present theological problems as these materials are presented in the Old Testament. Yet one hesitates to include these elements in a treatment of religious institutions.

Our final heading is a vague title: the future of Israel. This touches the topic of messianism. I have already indicated that I do not think that this topic, precisely defined, is a topic of Old Testament theology. But it is an unparalleled feature of Old Testament belief that it has a simple and impregnable faith in the survival of Israel. As long as Yahweh is, there will be an Israel. This faith is not found everywhere; Amos possibly did not have it. But the majority of the writings exhibit the conviction that there will be an Israel, and the writers are compelled to visualize this future in some way. The variations in this vision of the future are numerous and remarkable, and this is not surprising. Each writer who thinks of the future which Yahweh will grant his people must think of those things in Israel which he believes are vital to its identity. Evidently not all Israelites thought of the same things. Still less did the Christians of the apostolic age think of all these things when they professed their belief that they were the fulfillment of the future which the Old Testament writers had seen.

At this point the theology of the Old Testament must end. The arrangement, it is hoped, will include all the God-talk which students of the Old Testament have found important. It is an artificially unified analysis of a historic experience which has a different inner unity from the unity of logical discourse. A theology is also a theodicy. The experience of the totality, which we have insisted is the objective of Old Testament theology, shows the reality of Yahweh with a clarity which particular books and passages do not have. The Yahweh who was ready to kill Moses—on an impulse apparently—is not attractive, and obscure rather than mysterious (Ex 4:24–26); and it is certainly a pseudotheology which tries to identify this manifestation with the God whose loving kindness is above all his works. Not every biblical experience of Yahweh, not every fragment of God-talk, is of equal profundity; and it is only the totality of the experience that enables us to make these distinctions. Even though the theologian seeks the detached objectivity that modern scholarship demands, he is dealing with a collection of documents that present to those who believe in the documents a God who commands faith. Even if the theologian should not share this faith, he would be less than candid if he ignored the purpose of the literature that he analyzes. There was a time when an Israelite could give his faith to a God who could kill on impulse; many Old Testament writers wrote at length on the impossibility of faith in such a deity. Neither element should be omitted.

I

Cult

Cult means social worship through ritual performance; anything less than this is not cult.[1] It is not private worship and it is not improvised. Some form of cult appears in every religion; and ritual symbolism exhibits certain common features which are found in many religions. These features do not arise from borrowing. Some ritual symbols are almost natural; sacrifice, for example, is a nearly universal ritual symbol. Cult is not the most peculiar feature of ancient Israelite religion; there are many rites and symbols which can be found elsewhere in the ancient Near East, and some borrowing is altogether probable.

Cult is a social experience of the deity worshiped by the group. It is unnecessary for our purpose to attempt to analyze this experience in terms of social psychology. Group exaltation or ecstasy is not an exclusively religious phenomenon, and the fact that certain cultic phenomena are quite similar to phenomena unrelated to cult is not the point. Those who participate in group exaltation are well able to distinguish the religious experience from the secular experience of patriotism, for example. Nor is cultic experience simply the experience of the collective unity of the group. It does not experience its collective unity; but the cultic experience attests the unity of the group with the deity whom the group worships. The group attempts to reach outside itself. The use of religious symbolism is a means of stimulating and heightening the emotional response to the sense of unity, but it does not create the unity. Such highly sentimental hymns as "In the Garden" arise from the situation and the mood which they express.

Modern analogies are misleading, for in the ancient world the

[1] G. van der Leeuw, *Phänomenologie der Religion* (Tübingen, 1956), 420–28.

cultic group and the civic group were one and the same. The modern student of the Bible must simply recognize this fact, even though it is foreign to his own experience. The Israelite group which assembled for the cult of Yahweh was the same group which assembled to defend its land. When the army was assembled, Yahweh was of course invoked. The modern prayer before war and battle is uttered in an entirely different social situation. Most writers who have attacked the question think that the distinction between sacred and secular is not applicable to most of the Old Testament. An interesting book by Adolf Wendel[2] traced the desacralization of Israelite culture under the monarchy. Man desacralizes that which he can control, the thing or the activity for which he feels no dependence on the deity and which he feels the deity cannot or will not help or hinder. The cultic forms of Israel show no change which corresponds to gradual desacralization. The whole of human life and experience is the object of the cult. By ritual symbolism man symbolized his encounter with the deity in the whole of human life and experience.

Cult is a profession of faith older than credal formulae. The worship of a people is the earliest form in which it discloses what it believes the deity to be. It is normal in religion that at least the major cultic rites are believed to be instituted by divine revelation. The manner and style of the cult disclose what the god thinks is important. It is worth our attention to establish at least some brief comparison between Israelite cult and other ancient Near Eastern cults; in some respects the omission of common features is revealing. It should be added that cultic usage is to be interpreted with reservation; it is another normal feature of cult that it retains archaic rites so long that their meaning is sometimes lost. If their meaning were ascertained, they would illustrate an idea of the deity too primitive for later believers.

1. *Festivals*

In all the Old Testament festal calendars we find mention of the three major annual festivals at which all the males are to ap-

[2] *Säkularisierung in Israels Kultur* (Gütersloh, 1934).

pear at the sanctuary. Except for some minor variations, these are all agricultural festivals: the Feast of Unleavened Bread (*Mazzoth*);[3] the Feast of the First Fruits (*Weeks*);[4] and the Feast of the Ingathering (*Booths*).[5] The first two of these occur in the spring, the third in the fall. Each festival has as its central rite the presentation to Yahweh of the produce of the soil. These are clearly thanksgiving festivals and nothing more. The Feast of Unleavened Bread symbolizes the holiness of the grain as it proceeds immediately from the hand of Yahweh. Yeast profanes it and makes it fit for human consumption; but before it is profaned it is to be treated as sacred. All three festivals depend upon the harvest, and they could scarcely have had fixed dates in their earliest form. These appear to be the earliest Israelite festivals; and since they are agricultural festivals, they would seem to have no remarkable feature.

Yet it is precisely what is missing that is remarkable. The elaborate New Year festivals of Mesopotamia and Canaan are now well known.[6] These festivals were the ritual recital and reenactment of the death and resurrection of the god of fertility. Each year the world relapsed into primeval chaos with the death of vegetation. A new creation was necessary; the monster of chaos must be slain anew, and the creative deity fashions a new world from the remains of the monster. Fertility is renewed by sexual intercourse between the god and his consort, ritually symbolized by the priest and priestess. The worshipers share in the new life and the new fertility by ritual fornication with priestesses who represented the goddess of fertility. This brief summary telescopes several of the variant forms of the New Year ritual, and the reader should refer to works which treat the topic fully.

There is no doubt that this ritual was a part of Israelite religion;

[3] See Ex 12:15–20, 13:3–7, 23:15 ff, 34:18; Lev 23:6; Num 28:17; Deut 16:1–8, 16:16; Ezek 45:21; 2 Chron 8:13, 30:13, 35:17; Ezra 6:22.

[4] See Ex 23:14–17, 34:22; Lev 23:15–21; Num 28:26–31; Deut 16:9–12; 2 Chron 8:13.

[5] See Ex 23:16, 34:22; Deut 16:13–15, 26:1–11, 31:10–13; Lev 23:34–36; Neh 8:14–18; Num 29:12–28; Zech 14:16–19.

[6] H. W. F. Saggs, *The Greatness That Was Babylon: A Sketch of the Ancient Civilization of the Tigris-Euphrates Valley* (New York, 1962), 383–89; G. Ernest Wright, *Biblical Archeology* (Philadelphia, 1960), 110–11.

the Old Testament books refer to its practice in Israel numerous times. But the ritual is rejected by the writings of the Old Testament, and this illustrates the difference between Old Testament theology and the history of Israelite religion. To the Old Testament writers, the fertility cult was an abominable superstition entirely unworthy of Yahweh. There is never a suspicion that Yahweh was ever accompanied by a female consort, which the fertility cult demanded. In the Israelite version of the cult, a female consort must have been given him; the name of the consort may appear in the list of deities worshiped at the Jewish military colony at Elephantine in the fourth century B.C.[7] but this can be no more than conjecture. The topic will meet us again when we treat of the Israelite belief in creation, which appears in the Old Testament with no reference to any ritual context. The Old Testament attitude towards Yahweh and nature as expressed in the cult is simply gratitude for the fruits of the soil; his power and his benevolence are acknowledged, but fertility is totally demythologized.

In addition to the three major festivals, others appeared later, or at least they are found only in later books. The most important of these is Passover,[8] presented as a historical feast commemorating the exodus from Egypt. In the ritual of Judaism Passover has long been celebrated together with the Feast of Unleavened Bread, and in modern times the older festival has practically been suppressed. Many scholars have argued that Passover was originally a pastoral festival celebrating the spring yeaning. There is no reference to this in the text, but the hypothesis cannot be judged impossible. The merging of historical with other motifs in festivals is too common a religious phenomenon to permit any *a priori* denials. In later Judaism, both the Feast of Weeks (the promulgation of the Laws) and the Feast of Booths (the sojourn in the desert) developed historical significance. But in the Old Testament, Passover is a historical festival. As such it is the ritual recital and re-enactment of the saving event. It is distinguished from the mythological festival of fertility by the historical charac-

[7] Pritchard ANET, 491.
[8] See Ex 12:1–28,43–49, 5:1, 13:11–16; Lev 23:5; Num 28:16, 9:2–14; Deut 16:1–5; Ezek 45:21; Josh 5:10–11; 2 Kings 23:21–23; 2 Chron 35:1–20, 35:30.

ter of the event. In the historical recital each Israelite in each generation is made to feel that he himself experiences the saving event. Deuteronomy is insistent in its repetition of the statement that the saving event happens to us who are here today and not to our fathers.

Passover is peculiar in its domestic character; it is not celebrated at the sanctuary, but in the home and family. There is no satisfactory explanation of this deviation from the usual pattern; and very few scholars, I fear, would accept the suggestion that the festival is celebrated in the family because it arose in an early period when there was no sanctuary and no cultic assembly. They would more easily accept the suggestion that the domestic celebration is a deliberate archaism; for the cultic legend of Passover locates the institution of the celebration in a period when Israel, according to its own traditions, had not yet established its cultic system.

The Day of Atonement falls one week after the New Year, and it is attested only in later books;[9] it is universally regarded as the festival of postexilic origin. As an expression of collective guilt, the ritual of the Day of Atonement has no parallel either within the Old Testament or outside it. But the ritual expression of repentance is as old as ritual itself; and the Day of Atonement appears to preserve some archaic ritual.

The New Year festival in the Old Testament is lacking in character (see Lev 23:24–25; Num 29:1–6), and this contrasts with the elaborate New Year festivals of Mesopotamia and Canaan. A number of modern scholars have proposed hypotheses of other festivals, some associated with the New Year; these should be briefly reviewed, since it is quite possible that festivals celebrated under the monarchy were never restored after the exile.

The Old Testament has two calendars, one beginning in the spring and the other in the fall. The Bible reader is puzzled by the explicit statement that the New Year is celebrated on the first day of the seventh month, which normally falls about September. Passover and Unleavened Bread are celebrated in the first month, which normally falls about March. The Babylonian New Year fell

[9] Lev 16:1–34, 23:26–32; Num 29:7–11.

in the spring. A fall New Year is more natural in Palestine; vegetation, except for the vine and the olive, is arrested during the dry season from roughly May to late October. Planting is possible after the fall rains begin, and grain is harvested in the spring. Hence the fall New Year is very probably the original Israelite and Canaanite date.

In 1922 Sigmund Mowinckel proposed a fall New Year festival of the enthronement of Yahweh. The thesis is more recently restated with little modification.[10] This festival was later fragmented into the New Year and the Feast of Booths. It was a harvest festival and a New Year festival. Yahweh is enthroned as king creator; the festival contained the mythological element of the annual creation, and we shall treat the mythological idea of creation under the topic of creation. He is also king as the savior of Israel from Egypt. He is enthroned on the ark in the temple of Jerusalem, and the enthronement ritual included a procession which reenacted the establishment of the ark in Jerusalem in the reign of David. The feast celebrated the covenant of Yahweh with David and his election of Zion as his dwelling place. Mowinckel thus combines in a single festival a number of themes which are frequently found in the Psalms, less frequently in other biblical books.

As Mowinckel described the festival, the New Year appears as almost a complete summary of Israelite belief under the monarchy of Jerusalem. It was neither purely a festival of nature nor purely a historical or commemorative festival. The compendious character of such a festival might be adduced among the reasons for doubting its existence. It has to be supposed that the festival was so closely identified with the monarchy that it was completely forgotten during the exile, and that when the ritual cult was reestablished, the enthronement festival was split up into other festivals. This supposition is not impossible. There was no successor to the Davidic king in either his political or his religious capacity. As we shall have occasion to see, the hope of a messianic restoration of the dynasty of David did not include the religious function of the king.

On the other hand, the hypothesis of the New Year festival does

10 *The Psalms in Israel's Worship,* 2 v. (New York, 1962).

supply what is lacking in the Israelite calendar preserved in the Old Testament; and that is a single major festival which celebrates the whole of the religious and national experience of Israel. One is not compelled to postulate such a festival, but one must wonder at the absence from the Old Testament calendar of the elements found in the New Year festival. We noticed that the calendar has no strictly historical festival except Passover and that Passover is a family feast rather than a public feast. The historical significance attached in Judaism to Weeks and Booths can be understood not only as imaginative rabbinical interpretations but also as reminiscences of a festival which was no longer celebrated or remembered.[11] The New Year festival furnishes a *Sitz im Leben* for a number of psalms which are not easily associated with any of the festivals found in the calendar.

In the strict sense, Mowinckel's case cannot be regarded as proved with the kind of proof which historical demonstration demands. It can be proposed only as that hypothesis which best explains the data; it is not directly attested by documentary evidence. But the hypothesis is not based on anything which is known to be alien to Israelite belief and cult. On the contrary, the hypothesis brings together elements attested in the Old Testament which hang loosely without the hypothesis.

Among those who doubt Mowinckel's hypothesis but admit the need which the hypothesis fills must be counted those scholars who postulate a different type of festival. Hans-Joachim Kraus finds that a royal Zion festival fills the need and pulls together the loose literary elements in the Psalms and elsewhere.[12] This festival Kraus explains as the cultic link which justified the transmission of the Israelite covenant from the Israelite amphictyony to David and Jerusalem and which itself replaced the earlier amphictyonic festival. The festival included a historical recital of the Sinai events and a renewal of the covenant. There are a certain number of elements in common with Mowinckel's New Year festival, and according to Kraus, the festival was celebrated at the Feast of Booths,

[11] See Strack-Billerbeck *Kommentar zum Neuen Testament* (Munich, 1965) II, 601, 778–79.

[12] *Die Königsherrschaft Gottes im Alten Testament* (Tübingen, 1951).

in the first month of the fall New Year. Kraus rejects the development of the festival into an enthronement festival of Yahweh.

Aubrey R. Johnson, admitting his own indebtedness to Mowinckel, has developed the hypothesis more fully.[13] He postulates a covenant festival celebrated at Jerusalem. In this festival the covenant with Israel and the covenant with David and his house are merged. The covenant is a manifestation of the sovereignty of Yahweh, which was celebrated in creation and in the saving deeds by which Yahweh delivered Israel; the festival included recitals of both series of acts. Finally, the establishment of the covenant community is a step towards the establishment of the eschatological reign of Yahweh in righteousness; this last element is the most notable development which Johnson has added to the hypothesis of Mowinckel.

These two theories show that the evidence can be explained in other ways; these scholars agree that there is evidence to be explained. This agreement is important; it seems impossible to deny that the phenomena adduced by Mowinckel need some explanation beyond the text itself. One feast, not mentioned in the Old Testament calendar but postulated by these and other scholars, as well as by the very constitution of the Israelite community, is the premonarchic festival of covenant renewal.

A ritual which could be a part of such a festival, and which is assumed to belong to such a festival by most scholars, is found in Deuteronomy 27:11–26 and Joshua 8:30–35. The two passages are evidently related, and one need only suppose that what is represented as a single event is a *Kultlegende* explaining the first instance of a regular observance. Recent studies on the character of the Israelite amphictyony and its covenant basis make such a festival highly probable, even though there is no allusion to such a festival in the Old Testament. Without some such annual festival attended by the delegates of the tribes, one does not see how Israel could have preserved any consciousness of unity before the monarchy. The memory of the tribal covenant-amphictyonic feast was lost when the feast was replaced by a monarchic festival, postulated in some form by Mowinckel, Kraus and Johnson. One

---

[13] *Sacral Kingship in Ancient Israel* (Cardiff, 1967).

must also postulate a corresponding covenant festival in the kingdom of Israel which has left no trace at all.

2. Sacrifice

The sacrificial ritual of Leviticus 1–7 is preserved in the most
recent literary sources of the Pentateuch; this does not imply that
the ritual itself is recent. Sacrifice is a nearly universal phenomenon
in religion, and similarities between sacrificial rituals are inevitable
simply because of the limited possibilities of symbolism. Not
enough is known about the sacrificial ritual of Mesopotamia and
Canaan to permit us to determine what is original and what is derived in Israelite sacrifice. The ritual directions of Leviticus 1–7
are supplemented by allusions to sacrifice in the narrative and
prophetic books; these allusions give little or no information about
the ritual and its symbolism. The conclusion which is suggested
when all the texts are viewed is that the Israelite sacrificial ritual
was not systematized and that several diverse symbolic actions
from diverse sources have been incorporated into the ritual. No
uniform theory of sacrifice can be imposed upon the Israelite ritual.
The one common element which appears in the priestly ritual
is the manipulation of the blood; and the systematization which
can be seen in this rite is probably the work of the priestly scribes.
The blood is always applied to the altar, but the modes of application differ in various sacrifices and either have different symbolic
values or different origins. The altar symbolizes the deity, and
the blood symbolizes the life—in fact, in biblical language the life
is in the blood (Gen 9:4; Deut 12:23). But there is no explanation
of why the blood should in one sacrifice be poured, in another
shed at the base of the altar, and in another smeared on the horns
of the altar. The horns are a symbol within a symbol, for they
symbolize the deity more precisely.
Sacrifice properly is animal sacrifice; meal and cereal offerings,
found in several forms of sacrifice, are accompaniments to the
sacrifice. They make the sacrifice a full meal. Yet the symbolism
of the banquet is not obvious in all types of sacrifice, even though
the slaughtering and destruction of an animal can ultimately sym-

bolize nothing else. The accessory offerings never have a ritual of their own, and thus they appear as accessories. The types of animal sacrifices are four: the whole burnt offering, the peace offering, the sin offering, and the guilt offering. Nothing indicates that any of these types is primary, meaning the original rite from which the others derived.

Most of the literary allusions to the whole burnt offering come from later literature, but it is not safe to conclude that this ritual was a later development. The animal was slaughtered and its blood was dashed at the base of the altar, the carcass was flayed, cut into pieces, and burned. This is the only type of sacrifice in which there is no sharing of the victim at all. The symbolism of the whole burnt offering is obscure. It is not an atonement sacrifice. The total destruction itself indicates that it is a more solemn offering than the other sacrifices; but nothing defines the solemn occasion on which it was fitting. In the postexilic temple the whole burnt victim was offered each day, morning and evening. It appears that it could be a thank offering, a petition, or an atonement offering according to the occasion.

The peace offering is so called from its Hebrew designation *šelem*. "Peace" here signifies good relations between the deity and the worshipers. The sacrificial ritual celebrates them and sustains them. The peace offering is a banquet in which the worshipers and the deity share a common table. The blood of the victim is dashed at the base of the altar. The fatty portions of the entrails and the kidneys are given to Yahweh by burning on the altar; there is thus a twofold symbolism of giving the animal to Yahweh. A third symbolism, less direct, is found in the giving of a breast and thigh to the priests. These portions are "waved" and "heaved" before the altar to signify that they are offered to Yahweh, who then returns them to his representatives, the priests. The remainder is eaten in the sanctuary by the family or group which offers the sacrifice. Since the flesh is holy by consecration to Yahweh, none of it may be eaten outside the sanctuary or on the following day. The rationalism of the twofold offering is that the group offers the entire animal to Yahweh, who then invites them to share it with him at a common meal.

Most of the allusions to the peace offering speak of it as a joyful occasion.[14] The ceremonial banquet is an ancient human way of solemnizing the joys of life. In the ritual of the peace offering, which was a domestic celebration, the deity sits as a member of the family to share its joy. The family are guests in the god's house, but they furnish the dinner. There was no prescribed occasion for the peace offering; it could be offered on any suitable occasion. The priestly ritual distinguished the thank offering, the votive offering for the fulfillment of a vow, and the free will offering for no occasion at all. The peace offering is mentioned more frequently than any other type of sacrifice in pre-exilic literature and may possibly be the earliest Israelite sacrificial ritual.

Both the sin offering and the guilt offering presuppose that good relations between the deity and the worshipers have been ruptured by some fault of the worshipers. The blood of the victim was smeared on the horns of the altar and the remainder poured on the ground; the significance of the difference is not apparent. The portions were given to the deity and to the priests as in the peace offering, but the rest of the animal was burned. There is no ritual banquet, and, as in the whole burnt offering, the symbolism of the meal is somewhat obscured. The differences between the two are not entirely clear, and the sin offering and the guilt offering may be two independent and parallel rituals of atonement. Both rituals have in common that they do not atone for "sins with a high hand," sins committed with full knowledge and malice; the Israelite cult had no ritual atonement for this kind of sin. The sin offering and the guilt offering atone for indeliberate failures to observe the prescribed ritual and for incurring ritual uncleanness. Thus the rupture of good relations is merely a ceremonial rupture; what the offerings repair is not moral unfitness but ritual disqualification for taking part in cultic worship. The sin offering and the guilt offering may originally have been intended only for the priests.

As will appear in several other topics, the individual Israelite experience of Yahweh is neither often nor clearly set forth in the Old Testament. The sacrificial ritual was one of the major cultic experiences of the Israelite. It is worth noticing that except for

[14] Lev 3, 7:11–36, 19:5; 1 Sam 11:15, 13:9; 2 Sam 6:17–18, 24:25; 1 Kings 3:15; Num 6:14; 1 Kings 8:64; Ezek 46:2, 45:17; Deut 7, 12, 18.

the whole burnt offerings, the sacrificial ritual is intended for the family and for individuals. The family experience of the peace offering is "rejoicing with Yahweh." The sacrificial ritual has no real ritual of repentance; indeed, no such penitential ritual is found in the Old Testament, although some of the psalms contain confessions of sin. But these confessions are rather occasions for petition for deliverance; it is assumed that the petitioner has sinned, for otherwise why should he be afflicted? We shall return to this problem under other headings. Our point here is that the main elements of the cultic ritual, its festivals and sacrifices, express thanksgiving and joy rather than other sentiments.

3. Temple and Sanctuary

The idea of the holy place is pervasive in religion, and it is remarkable that early Israelite religion deviates from the common pattern.[15] A holy object symbolizing the divine presence appears in the traditions earlier than the holy place and the holy building. The temples of Mesopotamia and Egypt had no counterpart in Israel before the monarchy.

The holy object was the ark, called the ark of the covenant, the ark of the testimony, the ark of Yahweh or of *elohim,* and some similar titles. This was a wooden box, described in the postexilic source P (Ex 25:10–22) as three feet nine inches by two feet three inches by two feet three inches. One tradition affirms that the ark contained the two tablets of the law inscribed by Yahweh for Moses. This was a portable shrine symbolizing the presence of Yahweh; and such a portable shrine would be at home in a nomadic tribe which lives in tents, not houses. The ark was housed in a tent until the reign of David and then was permanently installed in the temple of Solomon. Some scholars have suggested that the ark and the tent were two holy objects originally independent of each other. The tent was called "the tent of meeting," signifying the meeting of Yahweh with Israel; it was the place of revelation through oracular utterance. Like the ark, it was

[15] Van der Leeuw, op. cit.

a portable symbol; and it is curious that there was no permanent holy place during the period of the amphictyony, when Israel was settled on the land. No explanation of this somewhat foreign usage is available except the Israelite tradition that the worship of Yahweh came into the land with an immigrant tribe. The unreal tent of the priestly source (Ex 26), constructed according to the dimensions of Solomon's temple, is a product of scribal imagination; but the tradition of the premonarchic tent is solid. It must be conceded that the symbolism of the ark and tent overlap somewhat. Both symbols exclude the idea of a sacred area (*temenos*); the deity is present where the portable symbol is set down, and he leaves the area when it is moved. He really dwells "in the midst of his people" and not on holy ground. The ark was carried at the head of the column when the tribe moved from place to place and at the head of the battle column (Num 10:33–35, 14:44; 2 Sam 11:11).

The precise quality of the symbolic presence is ambiguous and very probably shows considerable development. Yahweh is said to be enthroned upon the cherubim when the reference is to the ark (1 Sam 4:4; 2 Sam 6:2; Ps 80:2); and in the temple of Solomon the ark stood between the images of the cherubim, winged figures of guardian genii. But the configuration of the ark does not suggest a throne, and it is possible that the ark was not a chair but a footstool. Yahweh, who cannot be represented by image, stands invisible upon the footstool. A similar explanation of the calf of the temple of Samaria as an invisible footstool has been proposed.[16]

There is no parallel in ancient Near Eastern religions to the prohibition of images.[17] The prohibition touches images for worship, but in Israel and Judaism it has been understood as a general prohibition with a few exceptions like the cherubim in the temple of Solomon and the wall paintings in the synagogue of Dura-Europos. Palestinian archaeology has disclosed nothing which could be called an image of Yahweh; it has disclosed hundreds of images which are evidently representations of non-Israelite gods

[16] William Foxwell Albright, *From the Stone Age to Christianity* (2nd paperback ed., New York, 1957), 299–301; H. Th. Obbink, "Jahwebilder," ZATWiss 58 (1929), 264–74.
[17] Ex 20:4–6; Deut 5:8–10; see also Lev 26:1; Deut 4:15–23.

and goddesses, in particular female figurines of the fertility god-dess.[18] These images illustrate biblical references to superstitious cults in Israel. The god Ashur was represented by an archer within a winged disk, and the Egyptian Aton as the solar disk with rays terminating in hands;[19] these are schematic, not representational, but they would fall under the Israelite prohibition.

The prohibition is comprehensive, covering anything that is sus-ceptible of representation—that is, anything which is visible. Yet to say that the Israelites conceived of Yahweh as spiritual in the sense of immaterial says more than the texts will support. The anthropomorphisms of the Old Testament speak of Yahweh's eyes, ears, hands, arms, nostrils, mouth, and feet; yet while they may be spoken of, they may not be represented in art, and were not. Yahweh was not properly conceived as invisible; the sight of him was fatal to mortal eyes, which is not exactly the same thing as invisibility.

The implication of the prohibition is the statement that Yahweh is like nothing in the heavens above, the earth below, or the waters under the earth. These are the boundaries of the universe as the Israelites thought of them; Yahweh can be assimilated to nothing in the universe. He is "wholly other," to use the phrase of Rudolf Otto. One may find a theoretical inconsistency between the pro-hibition of images and the anthropomorphisms of biblical language. One may even find a theoretical inconsistency between the image-less Yahweh and the location of Yahweh symbolically where the ark reposed; the Old Testament neither sought nor achieved theo-retical consistency. The prohibition of images went far towards preventing the assimilation of Yahweh to the deities of other an-cient Near Eastern religions. The books of the prophets attest that the danger of assimilation was real. The god who cannot even be symbolically represented by anything in nature is above and outside nature.

Neither the throne nor the footstool suggests the covenant; and the tradition of the tables of stone very probably reflected the historical reality that the ark contained a document stating the

[18] William Foxwell Albright, *The Archeology of Palestine* (Harmonds-worth, 1951), 107.
[19] Pritchard, ANEP 536, 408, 409.

terms of the covenant. We shall see in dealing with the covenant that the treaty documents on which the covenant is most probably modeled were stored in the temples. This association, however, must be a later reinterpretation of the ark, which has in itself a satisfactory symbolism of presence with no reference to covenant. As the ark of the covenant, the ark symbolizes not only the presence of Yahweh among his people but also the union of the tribes with Yahweh and with each other. It was as the symbol of Israelite unity that it was brought to Jerusalem by David and finally installed in the temple of Solomon.

The ark and the tent, which certainly came together in premonarchic Israel, whether they originally belonged together or not, were authentically Israelite symbols of the presence of Yahweh. The temple of Solomon was an imitation of non-Israelite symbols; and there is no reason to differentiate between the temple of Solomon and the temples erected at Bethel and Dan in the kingdom of Israel. The temple was the symbolic palace of the deity; like the tent, it was his residence. The ancient temple was not built for the assembly of the worshipers, who assembled in the outer courts; it was the palace of the god, and his privacy was protected by the holiness of the place. The god lived in his temple as the king lived in his palace. Both in Mesopotamia and in Egypt the temple was a symbol of celestial reality; in Egypt the temple symbolized the world in which the god reigned, and in Mesopotamia the temple was the earthly counterpart of the heavenly temple. It was a point of contact between heaven and earth; the idea is echoed in the Old Testament story of the tower of Babel (Gen 11:4) and probably in the ladder of Jacob (Gen 28:12); Jacob recognized that Bethel (the site of an Israelite temple) was the house of God and the gate of heaven (Gen 28:17).[20]

The temple of Solomon was such a deviation from traditional Israelite cult that it had to be authenticated by an oracle of Yahweh. This is found in 2 Samuel 7, pronounced by Nathan to David; the oracle had to be given to the founder of the dynasty and of Jerusalem, not to his son. The oracle clearly states that the temple was not built because Yahweh "needed" a house, and implies

[20] Cf. "The Significance of the Temple in the Ancient Near East," *The Biblical Archeologist* 7 (1944), 41–63.

that the temple is not only the house of Yahweh but also a symbol
of the "house" (dynasty) which Yahweh will build for David. The
selection of the site of the temple is also attributed to revelation
(2 Sam 24). There is no doubt that the site is the modern Haram
esh Sharif, occupied since the ninth century A.D. by the Dome
of the Rock. There is very little doubt that this was the site of a
sanctuary in pre-Israelite Jerusalem, but the narrative of 2 Samuel
24 ignores this.

Few parallels have been found to the structure of the temple
of Solomon; the narrative itself states that the temple was designed
and built by Phoenicians, and almost no Phoenician temples from
this period have survived. Compared to the great temples of Egypt
and Mesopotamia, the temple of Solomon was quite small. The
inner chamber, which elsewhere enclosed the image of the deity,
housed the ark. In the earliest temple there is no doubt that the
ark was visible through the main door as the image was visible
in most other temples. Entrance, however, was prohibited to others
than priests; this was normal. The altar stood in the outer court,
and there the sacrificial ritual was performed.

The courts of the temple contained some symbols which are
still not understood. These included the two free standing columns
named Yakin and Boaz, and the enormous bronze vessel of water
called the "sea." The character of these objects suggests that they
were cosmic symbols—more precisely, symbols of Yahweh's cosmic
dominion. It has been suggested that the names of the two columns
were the first words of inscriptions. It has also been suggested
that they were fire pillars, but the description seems to make them
somewhat impractical for this purpose. As symbols of the pillars of
the world they are perhaps more easily understood. The "sea"
could hardly symbolize the monster of chaos, but rather the sea
as subdued by Yahweh. This ornamentation can easily be related
to the New Year festival in which Yahweh was celebrated as king
and creator. Indeed, the act of creation may have been identified
with the building of the temple-palace, as it was in both Mesopotamia and Canaan; the building of the temple was the climactic
act of sovereignty asserted in creation.[21]

[21] *Enuma Elish,* Pritchard ANET 68–69; Baal of Ugarit, Pritchard ANET
134.

Less explicit in the texts but implied in the architecture is a Davidic-messianic symbolism of the temple. The temple must have been notably smaller than the rest of the palace complex of which it was a part. Many find the term "royal chapel" improper for the temple of Solomon, but in spite of the uncertainties of the total design it is clear that the temple was incorporated into the buildings and courts of the palace. The description does not suggest that the temple courts had an entrance distinct from the gates of the palace courts. The covenant union of Yahweh with the house of David was effectively symbolized by the union of the temple with the palace. Furthermore, the covenant of Yahweh with Israel stood with the covenant with David. Zion, the temple mountain, was the residence of Yahweh. It will become the tallest of all mountains to which all peoples will stream (Is 2:1–4; Mic 4:1–4). It becomes the mythological mountain of the north, the residence of the gods in Canaanite mythology (Ps 48:1–2). These are echoes of the ancient Near Eastern belief that the earthly temple is the counterpart of the heavenly temple; it is also the residence of the king of Judah.

The law of Deuteronomy 12 prescribes that the cult of Yahweh shall be carried on only at the sanctuary which he has chosen. Historians associate this law with the cultic reform of Josiah (2 Kings 22–23), instituted in 622–21 B.C. Before this reform, according to numerous allusions in the books of Kings, the people of Judah worshiped at the "high places." These high places were local shrines in towns and villages. If the name "high place" is correctly translated, they were located on hilltops and can be compared to the "high place" preserved at Petra, which is not only on an elevation but is difficult of access.[22] If cultic worship had been limited to the temple of Jerusalem, most Israelite males could not have been present, and this must have been the effect of the reform of Josiah. These allusions recommend the opinion that the temple of Solomon was a royal chapel and that it was a center of worship for the palace community, identical with the population of Jerusalem. The cultic experience of Israel and Judah was not

[22] G. Lankester Harding, *The Antiquities of Jordan* (New York, 1959), 117–20.

situated in the Jerusalem temple but in the local shrines of the towns and villages. Very little trace of this cult has been left in the Old Testament, in which the cult of the second Jerusalem temple has become the model of Israelite cult. There are numerous allusions to cultic abuses in the local shrines; not all of them were unfounded, it seems, but under the monarchy the standards of the Jerusalem cult were not established as normative. Indeed, it is quite clear that during the Assyrian period (735–640) the cultic abuses of the Jerusalem temple were as deplorable as any abuses elsewhere.[23]

4. Priesthood

The history of the Israelite-Jewish priesthood is obscure and uncertain; and it is not the task of biblical theology to study the history of the institutions.[24] At one end of the Old Testament stands the domestic priesthood of the patriarchs, which is instituted by no authority. At the other end of the development is the postexilic priesthood, authenticated by a somewhat fictitious genealogical derivation from Aaron. The functions of the priests are described according to postexilic practices. It is clear that the Israelite priests, like the priests everywhere, were authorized mediators between the worshipers and the deity. A hereditary priesthood is more common than any other kind. The major offices of the Israelite priests were the offering of sacrifice, the rituals of purification, and the rituals of blessing. As they were sacred persons, certain restrictions were laid upon their conduct, particularly when they entered and left the sanctuary.

Clear in some older texts (Deut 33:7–11; Judg 18:5; 1 Sam 14:41, 28:6), but not mentioned in the priestly code, are the priestly functions of giving oracles and instruction in the torah. Of these the second is surely a development of the first. As late as David's time a priest still wore the mysterious devices called Urim and Thummim which could answer questions by a symbolic

[23] Roland de Vaux, *Ancient Israel* (New York, 1961), 322.
[24] Ibid. 361–66.

Yes and No. This was certainly a primitive oracle, and it is not mentioned after David, certainly because it fell into desuetude. In the priestly code the Urim and Thummim have become merely a part of the ornamentation of the high priest (Ex 28:30). There may have been earlier forms of priestly oracular speech which have not been preserved. The explanation of torah, on the other hand, was the explanation of the revealed will of Yahweh concerning matters of cult and morals. The priest could not only explain torah, he could pronounce; a priestly decision in matters which fell under his competence had the authority of the torah.

The number of priests and the specialized duties assigned to them are notably less than the number and duties of priests in Mesopotamian temples, and they may suggest a somewhat different position of priests in the Israelite social structure from their position both in Mesopotamia and in postexilic Judaism. One of the older sources (Ex 19:6) describes the entire people of Israel as a kingdom of priests and a holy nation. The Israelite traditions have no professional priests before Moses and Aaron. Quite possibly priests were not as important in the cultic experience of premonarchic Israel outside of the royal sanctuaries as they were in the royal temples and in the postexilic temple. The genealogies of Ezra and Nehemiah suggest that a remarkably high percentage of the population of Judah were of priestly descent (Neh 10:39 [cf. Neh 12:1–7,12–21]; 1 Chron 24:1–9). The existence of a large number of professional priests with highly specialized duties has the effect of removing the worshipers more and more from active participation in the cultic actions. The ritual of sacrifice described in 1 Samuel 2:12–17 had no counterpart in the ritual books of the Pentateuch. There the priest does nothing except send a servant to exact the priest's portion of the victim and burn the fat, the portion which belonged to Yahweh. The worshiper himself "sacrifices." In the sanctuary of Shiloh, the scene of the narrative in 1 Samuel, there were no priests except Eli and his two sons. The type of worship implied in the narrative is much simpler and much more directly the act of the worshipers than the solemn cult of the great temples in which the worshipers were screened from the deity and the cultic action by great crowds of priests.

5. *The Holy*

In the cult the Israelite experienced the holiness of Yahweh.
Rudolf Otto defined the holy as the numinous, the "wholly other,"
the attribute of the divine which combines the fearful and the
fascinating.[25] The idea of the holy is found in all religions, but
the Israelite understanding of the holy has its own distinct character. When Yahweh's holiness is seen, his identity is seen; he is
manifested as divine, as Yahweh: "You shall know that I am
Yahweh." This identity can be seen in his speech and in his acts,
in his power and in his character. It is not primarily a moral attribute, but it becomes moral when the identity of Yahweh is contrasted with the sinfulness of man. The holiness of Yahweh can
be compared to a burning fire; the sight of Yahweh is fatal to
those who see him (by paradox he is invisible; Deut 4:24, 9:3;
Is 33:14; Ex 33:20). The idea of holiness is not entirely rational;
the nearness of Yahweh is both fascinating and terrifying, and
man does not respond to his near presence as he responds to
anything else. The cultic rules of holiness insure both reverence
to Yahweh and protection of the individual and the community
from the greatest of all powers, motivated by a morality so superior
to man's morality that it is incomprehensible. The holy does not
exclude from Israelite cult the possibility of "rejoicing in the presence of Yahweh." But the theme of holiness, if it becomes dominant, tends to emphasize the fearfulness of divinity rather than
its fascination.

The entire area of cult symbolizes the holy. The quality of holiness is derived from Yahweh to all that belongs to him. In the
first place the world belongs to him, but the world is not thought
of as holy. The people of Israel belongs to him and is called holy,
but this also lacks the specific holiness of the cultic area. Holiness
seems to admit degrees. The focus of holiness is the place of
Yahweh's symbolic dwelling. This was the ark; and the indiscreet
Israelite who touched the ark even with good intentions was struck

[25] *The Idea of the Holy* (New York, 1958), 6–7, 25–30.

dead (2 Sam 6:3–8; 1 Chron 13:7–11). The ark may be touched and the place of its residence entered only by those who have been consecrated, who have themselves been rendered holy. Holiness is a quality of place, of persons, and of objects; in each of them the degree of holiness is determined by their proximity to the focus. The ultimate fringe of holiness is the worshipers themselves, who must have the lowest degree of ritual holiness in order to take part in the cult. At this point the ideas of holy-profane and clean-unclean impinge upon each other.[26] Probably they were originally unrelated, and the Levitical laws are an early effort to rationalize them. For reasons which lie outside analysis, birth and death and related activities make one unfit for worship and demand rites of purification. The vessels and tools of worship are also holy. Places and objects can be reserved for sacred use. Persons, on the contrary, must pass from the area of the holy to the area of the profane, and the passage is governed by rules which are intended to guard against the profanation of the holy. Again one finds that these rules cannot be entirely rationalized; why should the high priest be allowed to marry only a virgin, while priests of lesser rank may marry widows (Lev 24:14)?

Ritual holiness could go with two attitudes. One attitude was that moral integrity was not enough to prepare one for the cultic encounter with Yahweh. The other attitude was that moral integrity was not required for the cultic encounter. We shall see in the prophetic criticisms of the cult that the second attitude was indeed found in Israel. The "Holiness Code" (Lev 17–26) shows that the first attitude was also found. This code associates a number of moral precepts with holiness conceived as the condition in which one is ready for cult. The existence of the two attitudes shows an ambiguity towards holiness and morality which the Israelites did not resolve. The symbolic holiness of the cult did not assure that the cultic encounter was a genuine revelation of the identity of Yahweh.

[26] De Vaux, op. cit., 460–61.

6. Prophetic Criticism of the Cult

Cult is generally accepted in the Old Testament as the normal means by which the community encounters Yahweh. One needs little acquaintance with the history of religion or little experience with cultic worship to know that cult is open to many abuses which have often made people wonder whether cult is a legitimate approach to the deity. To many of our contemporaries cultic worship is superstition by essence. There are also some discordant voices in the Old Testament which show that the attitude of the Israelite towards cult was more complex than simple and naïve acceptance.

Criticism of the cult in varying severity is expressed in Psalm 50:7–15, Amos 5:21–25, Isaiah 1:10–17, Jeremiah 7:1–15 and 21–22, and Isaiah 66:1–4. Psalm 50 cannot be dated with any precision. Amos 5:21–25 is accepted as original by all critics. Isaiah 1:10–17 is not certainly from Isaiah, but it is very probably pre-exilic. Jeremiah 7 appears to be original with Jeremiah. Isaiah 66:1–4 belongs to the postexilic period. The criticisms come from different periods and they are not all of the same character.

Psalm 50 is the easiest to handle. The poet rather gently and ironically speaks in the person of Yahweh and tells the Israelites that he does not accept sacrifices to satisfy his hunger. It is very doubtful that any Israelite really believed that sacrifices satisfied Yahweh's hunger; they may very well have believed that Yahweh wanted sacrifices more than anything else or that they did something for Yahweh by offering sacrifice. The poet makes Yahweh prefer vows, prayers of thanksgiving, and sincere confessions of need. The Israelite liturgy did contain these elements; and the rebuke touched no more than a kind of naïve and pardonable superstition about sacrifice. The other passages are less kindly.

Both Amos and Jeremiah are thought by some scholars to express an acquaintance with a tradition of early Israel which had no institution of the sacrificial ritual as we now have it in the Pentateuch. In fact most of the liturgical passages of the Pentateuch come from the priestly source, which attributed the entire cultic system of the second temple to Moses. The older sources J and E are much less explicit concerning the institution of the cultic system by Moses; and it is possible that both the prophets knew traditions which had no ritual institutions. The Israelite sacrificial system actually does not show any sharp difference from other sacrificial systems. There is, as is well known, considerable ambiguity concerning the knowledge of Moses and his work exhibited in the prophetic writings. The point is that nothing either in the criticisms of the Pentateuch or the prophetic writings imposes upon us the existence of a tradition in the eighth and seventh centuries concerning the institution of the sacrificial system by Moses.

To be more specific than this with the rhetoric of the two prophets is dangerous, but one can hardly evade the danger. Amos seems to deny not only the institution of the sacrificial system but even the offering of sacrifice during the desert sojourn. Jeremiah, on the other hand, rather speaks of the absence of any commandment of sacrifice. Amos adds a difficulty which Jeremiah does not have. Yet it seems scarcely possible that Amos could have had a tradition in which sacrifice was not mentioned, and one must suppose that he pushed it for all it was worth.

The common element in Amos, Jeremiah and Isaiah is that Yahweh speaks as rejecting sacrifices and not merely as criticizing abuses. The reasons for the rejection are the same in all the prophets: the offering of sacrifice is not joined with righteousness within the community. Both Amos and Jeremiah elsewhere announce the total destruction of all institutions, both religious and secular.[27] For Amos and Jeremiah there is no reason to take the rejection in any other sense than absolutely. Jeremiah predicts the destruction of the temple of Jerusalem in the same context. Isaiah is less precise in his predictions of a future destruction; but there is no reason to take his rejection as conditioned by something which he does not utter. None of the prophets speak of a reform of abuses as a way of solving the problem which they present. One need not suppose that they look to a noncultic religion of the future; they simply look to the abolition of the cultic system which they knew.

[27] Amos 2:13–16, 3:12, 5:2–3, 6:1–3, 8:1–3, 9:8a; Jer 7:1–15 (the temple), 8:8–9 (the law), 22:29–30 (the monarchy), 23:33–40 (prophecy).

Whatever be the ambiguities of the pre-exilic prophets, there is no ambiguity in Third Isaiah. The prophet spoke in the cultic community of postexilic Jerusalem, the community which produced the priestly code and the elaborate ritual of P. He does not speak of a distinction between legitimate and superstitious cults, not even expressly of the moral corruption of the worshiping community as the pre-exilic prophets spoke of it. He simply enumerates several ritual actions and identifies them all as superstition. Heaven and earth are Yahweh's throne and temple, not the temple of Jerusalem. The prophet clearly repudiates the temple, the cult, and the priesthood.

These passages do not surprise us by their awareness that hypocritical worship is possible; they do create something of a problem by indicating that their authors seem ready to abandon cult without replacing it. In the same book of Jeremiah, a new covenant is presented with no intermediaries between Yahweh and the individual worshiper (Jer 31:31–34). Critics have often doubted that this passage came from Jeremiah, but it is in the same line of thought with the rejection of the cult; from both there seems to follow a religion without social structure. Jeremiah and Amos both faced the possibility—indeed, the expectation—that the people of Yahweh as such would cease to exist; there would be no worshiping community of which the believer could be a member. Such a worshiping community did arise after the exile, but this was not within the vision of the prophets. In actual fact these prophets have very little to say to the Israelite who found himself uprooted from the community of his faith. These would have to find their hope and their encouragement elsewhere. For Amos and Jeremiah the judgment of Yahweh fell with the same totality upon the cult as upon the monarchy and the nation. No institution they knew would return in the form in which it disappeared. Third Isaiah expressed a rare disapproval of the restoration which was ultimately instituted. The future of Israel was not conceived as a mere revival of institutions which had failed to do their work. Yet to say that the cult had simply failed is again to say more than the texts permit. This will concern us in the sections to follow. The conclusion from the prophetic criticism is that cult did not have a sacramental *ex opere operato* validity as a means of approaching Yahweh.

7. *The Cultic Community*

The postexilic community of Jerusalem was effectively and almost formally a cultic community. It was not founded as such, although one of the motives alleged for the restoration of Jerusalem was the restoration of temple and cult (Ezra 1:2–4, 6:2–12). But this restoration was not immediately accomplished, and indeed until the reforms of Ezra was not firmly established. Until these reforms the community struggled to survive as a small ethnic group in a sea of foreigners. After Ezra the community felt it had achieved the ancient ideal of Yahweh dwelling in the midst of his people. For this it needed no political institutions. As we shall see elsewhere, the postexilic community saw itself as a kind of messianic fulfillment, the saved remnant.

One cannot without reservations transfer this idea of the cultic community to Israel before the exile. At the same time, it is difficult to assess the importance of the cultic ritual in the formation and preservation of the Israelite faith and community. We have observed certain prophetic criticisms which reveal massive failures in the cult. These should be balanced against certain values, which have been well set forth by Sigmund Mowinckel.[28] In the ancient world we cannot assume that religious community was instituted and supported by doctrinal instruction. What the people believed and accepted as obligations was professed only in cultic ceremonial; as we have pointed out several times, this was the community's collective experience of the deity. The individual person could not think of a purely personal experience; ritual performances for private persons were still ritual and fulfilled through the cultic and sacerdotal system. The Israelite prophets deviate sharply from the universal patterns, but even the prophets should not be taken outside of the cultic system in which they lived and in which they formed their basic ideas and beliefs about Yahweh and in

[28] *The Psalms in Israel's Worship,* 2 v. (New York, 1962), I, 97–105.

terms of which they addressed the Israelites. The hymns, as Mowinckel points out, are the best summary of what the Israelites thought Yahweh was; the hymns have their limitations, but they show the cultic system at its best.

In modern times a comparison between the cultic systems of Israel and its contemporaries is possible.[29] The comparison is most revealing when one observes a number of highly developed rituals which had no place in Israelite cult. Such are the rituals of divination which have left such extensive remains in Mesopotamia. The Israelites had certain oracular practices; the references to these are few and disclose no extensive apparatus for discerning the future by occult means. The Mesopotamian lived in a world where demons constantly threatened his fortunes and his health. The priestly offices and functions by which demonic attacks were averted matched the divining priesthood in their numbers and complications. Mesopotamian religion cannot always be distinguished from magic, which is really anti-religion; Israelite religion was liberated from this type of superstition. What the Mesopotamians expected from the rituals of divination and incantation the Israelites expected from Yahweh or did not expect at all. The Old Testament cultic experience of Yahweh left no room for divination or demonology. Here, however, it is necessary to recall the distinction between the history of Israelite religion and the theology of the Old Testament. There is ample evidence that superstitious rites flourished in the Israelite community; the belief in Yahweh which is expressed in the Old Testament repudiates these superstitions.

Mowinckel has pointed out that the limitations of the religion of the hymns lies precisely in their exclusively Israelite character. In the cult Yahweh is experienced as the God of Israel rather than as the God of the world and mankind. His saving power was celebrated mostly in the recital of his saving acts in behalf of Israel, whether in the past of the exodus and the possession of the land or in more recent victories. One does not find expressed in the hymns the prophetic awareness of judgment. Having said

[29] Cf. Saggs, op. cit., 299–358.

this, one perhaps has not gone beyond the prophetic criticisms of cult.

One returns, then, to the essential nature of cult as the rites by which the believing community recognizes and professes its identity and proclaims what it believes about the deity it worships and the relations between the deity and the worshipers. The Israelite cultic system did not succeed in professing the totality of Israelite belief. It failed to maintain Israelite faith in crisis. The prophetic criticisms are not the whole truth concerning Israelite cult. Cult was also the factor which sustained the framework of Israelite belief. Many modern critics believe that the cult was the most important source of the literature of the Old Testament. One must avoid premature and sweeping judgments, but the results of recent work suggest that earlier interpreters seriously underestimated the importance of cultic worship in the formation of Israelite belief and Israelite literature.

II

Revelation

1. The Idea of Revelation

The idea of revelation, an intelligible communication from the deity to man, runs through all religions.[1] Indeed, it is the idea of a revelation as constituting the religion which distinguishes religion from philosophy. We use the term "intelligible communication" so that it can include vision, hearing, or other sensible experiences from which meaning can be derived. Thus intelligible communication can include the simple awareness of presence, the "prayer of quiet" of which Teresa of Avila spoke. The intelligible content here is the recognition of another, whether as a strange and hitherto unknown presence or as the return of a known presence. It allows also for the awareness of experiences which can be distinguished no more clearly than pleasure is distinguished from pain, fear from courage, joy from grief; these emotional experiences can be distinguished from each other and to that degree are intelligible, even if the causes which elicit the experiences are only obscurely recognized. The common element in revelation is that the agent who communicates is recognized as superhuman and as deserving of that response which men agree is given only to the divine.

The analogy between revelation and interpersonal communication is clear and obvious. It is the only analogy which man has for his experience of the deity, whether his experience of the deity is authentic or not. If the deity does not communicate with us as persons, he does not communicate at all; and this communication means more than eliciting a personal response. I respond person-

---

[1] G. van der Leeuw, *Phänomenologie der Religion*, 640–46, and Gabriel Moran, *Theology of Revelation* (New York, 1966), 22–56.

ally to nature or to objects. The beauty of nature can elicit the feeling of joy or of awe, the power of nature can elicit fear. The animal which attacks me elicits fear and anger. I need not personalize those objects in order to feel pleasure, fear, or anger; yet I am well aware that my response to them differs from the response which I give to beauty, power, or hostility in another person. This is precisely the interpersonal response, the response which is lacking in the soldier who shoots the enemy or is shot by the enemy. In the popular phrase, nothing personal was intended. The impersonal encounter can easily be personalized. So likewise the encounter with nature can be personalized; and the history of religions is very largely the history of how man has personalized nature and objects and turned them into gods and demons. Man sometimes continues this personalization even after he has learned that it is based on an error of judgment; he continues it simply because he still believes there is a personal reality there to which a personal response is due, even if he has not identified that personal reality correctly.

The study of revelation in religion is the study of the response to the divine communication, not of the communication itself. The response is the only thing that falls within the area of phenomena. The divine communication is known only by the response except by those who receive the communication directly. No demonstration is necessary to show that those who receive the communication are unable to share it; they are able only to declare their response. If one wishes to describe an encounter with a second person to a third person who does not know the second, he can describe it by the use of analogy; the listener has met persons. Unless the listener has met gods he has no analogy for a divine communication. Revelation in religions is the experience of a few who communicate their responses to other members of the religion. Quite literally, the others believe in the god on their word and not because of their own experience, inverting the saying in John 4:42. As we have seen in dealing with cult, however, the experience of revelation develops into a cultic experience which is a social reality. The deity is experienced in the cult, but in virtue of the revelation which the cult commemorates, preserves, and communicates.

The objects of revelation by definition include things which are hidden. The "hidden" is defined in relation to the knowledge possessed by the receiver of revelation. It is not simply the unknown, but the unknown which can become intelligible when it is revealed. One cannot imagine the revelation of television to a people ignorant of electricity; one can imagine the revelation of electricity, since electricity, for all except the scientists who discovered it, is known by revelation. The proper object of revelation is the deity; revelation in the first place is self-revelation. What is of most interest in the deity is his attitude towards men and his relation with men. These presumably cannot be known without revelation, at least not well enough known to justify important decisions. Men feel that they can deduce whether the deity is angry or pleased with them by the way the deity conducts himself towards them; but they can be sure of the reasons for his anger or his good pleasure only by his attestations.

"The meaning of human existence" is not a problem which troubles all mankind. The world exists and man exists in it; this is not a problem to be solved but the basic fact by which other problems are solved. Nevertheless, the "hidden" which is revealed usually includes objects which must be presumed to lie outside the scope of human knowledge in any hypothesis of development, and in particular the knowledge of origins and of ends—protology and eschatology. These are the major concerns of myth, which is conceived as a revelation and not as a result of human thought and investigation. The myths of origins explain why the world is constituted as it is and why the human condition in the world has the character it has; naturally the mythological explanation of the human condition is concerned with the people or the culture in which the myth belongs. Eschatology explains the direction in which the world and man are moving; it is not without interest that not all religions exhibit eschatological myths and that the human condition is not everywhere understood as something which needs eschatological resolution. It is conceived as going on forever, like the world in which man exists.

It is, however, of supreme importance to man that he know the will of the gods for himself. In some way the important precepts and prohibitions are revealed or validated by revelation. Matters of such importance include cult, as we have seen. Law and morality are also included. In most of the ancient Near East the gods did not reveal law but lent their authority and their sanction to the law of the king (Pritchard ANET 159, 165, 177–80). Such assurances did not remove occasional doubts that man could really know what is pleasing to the gods.[2] Further assurance was sought through occult revelation, obtained through the skills of divination. These skills enabled man to interpret the present and forecast the future. They disclosed the intentions of the gods in events. Divination was understood as a regular and authorized means of revelation for a particular situation and a particular problem. It enabled men to form their decisions in accordance with the course of future events as disclosed by the gods.

Divination was less frequently practiced through oracular speech and much more frequently by the interpretation of phenomena. According to the phenomena studied, these skills are classified into belomancy (lots or arrows), rhabdomancy (rods), physiognomy (human behavior and facial expression), cheiromancy (palms), oneiromancy (dreams), teratology (unusual or monstrous parturitions), hepatoscopy (animal livers), ornithomancy (birds), ophimancy (reptiles), dendromancy (trees), empyromancy (flames), kapnomancy (smoke), lecanomancy (oil in water), astrology (heavenly bodies and meteorology). The theoretical basis of these skills is that the gods signify their intention in almost the whole realm of nature, but the signification is symbolic. Divination is a traditional skill based both on revelation and on the compilation of experience. The Mesopotamian literature shows that the diviners constantly enlarged their stock of observations and conclusions. The literature also shows that the revelation which men ultimately seek most eagerly is the revelation which discloses the course of future events and gives them an advantage over their competitors.

The forms of divination, we observed, rarely include the oracular speech delivered by an oracular spokesman; oracular speech was not a regular and routine form of divination. We have mentioned among intelligible communications seeing, hearing, and other sen-

[2] H. W. F. Saggs, *The Greatness That Was Babylon: A Sketch of the Ancient Civilization of the Tigris-Euphrates Valley,* 320–25.

sible experiences which are believed to be direct experiences of the deity. The vision is rarer in the Old Testament than it is elsewhere in the ancient world; the visionary could more easily see a god whose form was known in images than a god who is not represented by image. The visions of the Old Testament are visions of symbols of the deity or traces of him, such as the skirts of his robe, or objects in nature which, like the objects of divination, need interpretation (Is 6:1; Jer 1:11–13; Am 7:1, 8:1). Yahweh was also experienced sensibly in other manners less easy to define, such as the hand of Yahweh laid upon one. These allusions may be included among the experiences which we call awareness of presence. The characteristic experience of revelation in the Old Testament is the hearing of the word.

The spoken word, according to a pattern which can be traced elsewhere in the Old Testament and in the ancient Near East, is an extension of the personality of the speaker.[3] It becomes a subsistent entity laden with power, able to accomplish that which it signifies. These qualities, found in the word of man, are found pre-eminently in the word of the deity. The word of Yahweh is the charism of the prophet. This is the word which creates and destroys, which demands its fulfillment once it is uttered, which is the hinge upon which history turns. The word of Yahweh is not a regular and routine manner of revelation. It is under the control of no one and is not available upon demand. When the prophet hears it, he must speak it; when he does not hear it, there is no way in which he can produce it.

The authentication of revelation is a modern problem; ancient sources seem unaware of the problem or indifferent to it. On the hypothesis that the deity does communicate with man, the communication furnishes no more of a problem of identifying the speaker than human speech furnishes. One may mistake the human speaker, but such a mistake will not last long nor is it difficult to correct. The gods, it was assumed, spoke through normal channels such as those which existed in all organized religions. It was not assumed that they were interested in deceiving their worshipers or were

[3] John L. McKenzie, "The Word of God in the Old Testament" ThSt 21 (1960), 183–206.

amused by deception. The modern man will find this attitude incredible and altogether naïve in its attitude towards the possibility that man might use the word of God for his own purpose. The ancient would respond that the gods are able and willing to protect their word against those who would abuse it and that divine communication, like human communication, cannot exclude all possibilities of deception. When man hears the word of God, he is expected to use the same intelligence and discernment with which he hears the word of man.

2. Covenant Law

The Israelite religion was based upon a tradition of covenant law which is altogether without parallel in ancient religions. The revelation of covenant law is attributed to Moses as the mediator; and covenant law determined the character of Israelite belief, cult, and society. As we shall see, the monarchy was something of a deviation from covenant law and needed a justification of its own.

The patriarchs—Abraham, Isaac, Jacob, Joseph—are precursors of Israelite religion rather than its founders. Except for one late narrative concerning circumcision (Gen 17), no Israelite institution was attributed to them or even known to them. The name Yahweh in one literary tradition was not known to them; and the other traditions were aware that the name Yahweh was not known before the revelation of covenant law. Thus the patriarchs are presented as heroes of faith, but not as models of Israelite life and observance. The necessity of incorporating these precursors into Israelite tradition involves a problem which lies outside of Old Testament theology proper; but they do furnish a link between Israel and the land, which was a factor in the covenant.

As the revealer of covenant law, Moses stands alone, without predecessor, associate, or follower. To place Moses precisely in history is not the task of Old Testament theology; we must notice that it is not a simple task, but that no modern scholar doubts the historical reality of Moses nor his close association with covenant law. The reconstruction of the events by which Israel came to be a community of covenant law is a complex problem which has not been entirely resolved.[4] The narratives of the Pentateuch, which come from different oral and literary traditions, agree that Moses was the spokesman for Yahweh in a unique manner. Strictly speaking, the traditions of Moses as savior and leader of the exodus and Moses as spokesman of covenant law need not go together; but, as we shall see, the traditions of the deliverance are included in covenant law.

No other revelatory figure in the Old Testament has experiences of revelation like Moses. Some of the extraordinary qualities of Moses are due to the compilation of the Pentateuch. All Israelite law which is preserved in writings has been brought into the collection of covenant law. It is not a question of how much of this law is due to Moses, but whether any of it is due to Moses. The growth of attribution can be traced in the law of the division of the spoils in war, attributed to Moses in Numbers 31:27 but with much more historical probability to David in 1 Samuel 30:24, and in fact it may be a much older and more general practice which, as so often happens with ancient customs, was attributed to some ancient hero as its founder. The compilation of the Pentateuch really reflects less the idea of covenant law, to be explained below, and more the later idea that no law was permanently valid in Israel unless it had been spoken to Moses by Yahweh. The compilation makes Moses the speaker by dictation from Yahweh of every law in the Pentateuch; and rabbis of the postexilic period counted 613 laws in the collection. Even so, it should not be thought that the compilation is a complete collection of Israelite law; if it is, then some remarkably large areas of civil and criminal practice were left with no explicit legal determinations. The compilation is meant to attribute all the laws which survived in writing to the promulgation by Moses of the words he heard from Yahweh.

This was certainly not the oldest form in which Moses appeared in the tradition; and we shall see what can be said about the original stipulations of the covenant. All the traditions again agree that Moses retired from the Israelite assembly to hear the words of

[4] Martin Noth, *The History of Israel* (2nd ed., New York, 1960), 53–138; John Bright, *A History of Israel* (Philadelphia, 1959), 110–51; George E. Mendenhall, "The Hebrew Conquest of Palestine," *The Biblical Archeologist* 25 (1962), 66–87.

Yahweh in solitude. The tent of meeting (see above) in one tradition may have been the place where Moses heard the speech of Yahweh. In other traditions it is the summit of a mountain called Sinai and Horeb; the two names are not an indication that the mountain had two names but of the uncertainty of its location. All the traditions locate the covenant experience south of Canaan, not necessarily in what has been called since the fourth century A.D. the Sinai Peninsula. This mountain certainly in the oldest traditions was a place where the presence of Yahweh was localized. Elijah went to Horeb and there encountered Yahweh again; Horeb, which was reached by forty days and forty nights of uninterrupted walking (1 Kings 19:8), was located in a region unknown to the author. As we have observed, the location of Yahweh in a certain place was not characteristic of Israelite belief in Canaan. Yet this was the mountain to which the ancestors of the Israelites in Egypt had to go to worship their god (Ex 5:3) and from which Yahweh came to aid Israel against its enemies (Judg 5:4); and most modern scholars interpret Judges 5:5 as a title, "He of Sinai." No doubt the compilers also thought Sinai was the mountain of Exodus 3. Very probably the earliest traditions which located Yahweh at Sinai were only imperfectly synthesized with the traditions of his movable presence in the ark and his final settlement in the temple of Zion. Zion becomes in the Psalms the place from which Yahweh helps (Ps 14:7, 53:7, 110:2, 128:5, 134:3).

There is no other mountain of revelation in Israelite traditions. Comparisons between holy mountains where the gods resided can easily be adduced from Canaan (the mountain of the north, where the gods dwelt) and Greece (Mount Olympus). Neither of these were mountains of revelation; and the theme is not borrowed by the Israelites from any known source. The theme is echoed of Zion in Isaiah 2:3 and Micah 4:2: *torah* shall proceed from Zion. Now *torah* is just what proceeded from Sinai in the exodus traditions, and in the messianic age found in this passage common to two prophets, Zion will be the new Sinai. The passage does not indicate a new Moses.

The mysterious character of the mountain is portrayed through the use of elements which are best called mythological. The smoke and flame which envelop the mountain are not to be reduced to simply storm or earthquake, although the description is based on natural phenomena; these elements belong to the theophany, to be treated later, and are not as a rule elements of the experience of revelation; they rather belong to the representation of Yahweh as savior. The revelation of Sinai is the only revelation which is given in such an atmosphere of awe and terror. In such an atmosphere the impossibility of a general communication with the deity is obvious (Ex 19:21–25, 20:18–20), and the wonderful and exceptional character of the mediator of revelation is manifested beyond doubt; Moses is the only man to whom Yahweh speaks face to face and mouth to mouth (Ex 33:11; Num 12:7). Yet this singular privilege is directly contradicted in Exodus 33:17–23 in favor of the general belief that the sight of Yahweh was fatal to the beholder. This passage must have arisen as a corrective to an older view which excepted Moses from the general law; the synthesizers maintained the unique position of Moses as the hearer of revelation, but limited his intimate converse with Yahweh to hearing.

The original revelation in the story of Moses is the revelation of the name (Ex 3); this was a revelation by vision and by speech. Flame is a common sign of the presence of the deity both in the Old Testament and in other religions; and flame is associated with the covenant revelation of Sinai, as we have noticed. Yet the burning bush remains singular and the symbolism somewhat obscure. Yahweh renders himself visible not directly, for that would kill the viewer, but in a phenomenon which attracts attention. It is possible that the story retains an older account of a manifestation of a deity in a marvelous flame which has been assimilated into the Israelite traditions.

The revelation of the name was of supreme importance. Unless the name of a god were known he could not be invoked or recognized. The narrative arose in a world of polytheism where gods and goddesses, like men and women, had to be distinguished from each other by personal name. "To know the name" in biblical language was not merely to have the identification tag; it was also to experience the reality of the thing named.[5] The name was not

[5] Johannes Pedersen, *Israel: Its Life and Culture I–II* (London, 1959), 245–59.

a mere tag but was a manifestation of the reality. The self-revelation of Yahweh begins with his name.

The identification of Yahweh with the god of the fathers was a later theological reasoning. The history of the rise of Israel is obscure and is not within the scope of Old Testament theology; but the identification of the group who first recognized Yahweh as god is not certain. It cannot surely be identified with groups who recognized Abraham or Jacob as their ancestors. The group which Moses led was not yet known by the name of Israel; and no other name has been preserved. The traditions indicate that the name was not known to the ancestors and imply that the reality of Yahweh was not known to them either, according to the ideology of the name.

Unfortunately the significance of the name cannot certainly be derived from the existing text. The name *yahweh* is constantly used in the Old Testament; the pronunciation of the name has been reconstructed in modern times, since the vowels were not written in the original Hebrew script; and Jews did not pronounce the divine name from a reverential fear after a date sometime in the last centuries before the Christian era. Etymologically the name suggests the Hebrew verb *hayah,* to be; this was understood by the Greek translators (ὁ ὤν, the one who is) and the Vulgate (*qui est*, he who is). But this etymology is not itself sure; and even if the name is derived from the verb *hayah,* this does not imply that the Septuagint and the Vulgate have explained it correctly. The reader of the present text can see that Moses' question in Exodus 3:13 is answered directly and without complication in 3:15. The attempted explanation in 3:14 is disturbing; it really does not explain the name and must be regarded as an early but secondary effort to connect the name with the verb *hayah.* According to this explanation, the name was not Yahweh but Ehyeh—or more fully, *Ehyeh 'ašer ehyeh,* which defies translation. It can be rendered only as "I am what I am" or "I will be what I will be." William Foxwell Albright ingeniously reconstructed the phrase into *yahweh 'ašer yihweh,* "he brings into being what comes into being";[6] but it is difficult to explain why this phrase should have

[6] *From the Stone Age to Christianity* (paperback ed., New York, 1957), 261.

been modified. The phrase in Hebrew suggests that the name is denied; this denial is on all accounts unlikely. One has to be satisfied with conjectures; Exodus 3:14 cannot be the original text, and there is no way of restoring the original.

A number of recent studies have thrown new light on the formulation of the covenant and covenant law.[7] There was never any question as to whether the relationship of Yahweh and Israel as a covenant had any parallel elsewhere in the ancient world; no parallel existed. The covenant of Yahweh and Israel was formed after the analogy of agreements between men and in particular after the analogy of agreement in societies which do not depend on writing for the execution of agreements and the preservation of their records. In such societies the spoken word has a solemnity and a kind of subsistent reality which it does not have in more sophisticated societies; it is surrounded by ceremonial and attested by witnesses and sanctioned by imprecations. The unparalleled quality of the relation of Yahweh and Israel was that it was founded on mutual agreement, election of Israel by Yahweh, and acceptance of Yahweh by Israel. No other ancient religion conceived the relation of deity and worshipers in positive terms founded upon a collective act of the people which could be located in space and dated in time. There is still no parallel to this positive relation, but certain literary parallels to the formulation have been found.

George E. Mendenhall has shown that the elements of Old Testament covenant formulation are all found in a type of treaty preserved in Hittite documents from 1450–1200 b.c.,[8] a period slightly earlier than the rise of Israel and the covenant. In remarking above that the event could be placed in space and time, we should have added that it is still impossible to place it exactly. The fact that these treaties are known in Hittite is merely acciden-

[7] George E. Mendenhall, "Law and Covenant in Israel and the Ancient Near East," *The Biblical Archeologist,* 17 (1954), 26–46, 49–76; Klaus Baltzer, *Das Bundesformular,* Wissenschaftliche Monographien zum alten und neuen Testament Series (Neukirchen, 1960), no. 4; Walter Beyerlin, *Herkunft und Geschichte der Ältesten Sinaitraditionen* (Tübingen, 1961); Albrecht Alt, "Die Ursprünge des Israelitischen Rechts," *Kleine Schriften zur Geschichte des Volkes Israel* (Munich, 1959), 278–333; Dennis J. McCarthy, *Treaty and Covenant,* Analecta Biblica Series (Rome, 1963).

[8] Mendenhall, op. cit., 24–46, 49–76.

76 A THEOLOGY OF THE OLD TESTAMENT

tal; the form was used throughout the ancient Near East, and no direct contact between Israel and the Hittite Empire need be postulated. Some Aramaic treaties from the first millennium B.C.[9]—and therefore notably later than the Hittite Empire and the rise of the covenant in Israel—show close affinities with the Hittite treaties and indicate that the form survived substantially. This has not altered the conclusion accepted by many scholars that the literary parallels strongly indicate an early date for the Israelite covenant.

The type of treaty in question is called the "suzerainty treaty," imposed by an overlord in opposition to the parity treaty, negotiated by two independent and presumably equal powers. V. Korosec was the first to set forth the formal elements of the suzerainty treaty with no intention or awareness of biblical parallels.[10] These formal elements were six: (1) preamble, identification of the suzerain with a recital of his titles; (2) historical prologue, a recital of the benefits conferred upon the vassal by the suzerain; (3) stipulations, the obligations imposed upon the vassal; (4) provision for deposit in the temple and public reading; (5) the list of gods as witnesses; (6) curses and blessing formula. Mendenhall suggests that there must have been other elements not found in the written texts, and he identifies three: (7) formal oath of the vassal pledging obedience; (8) solemn ceremony accompanying the oath; (9) form for initiating procedure against a rebel.

The entire structure is reflected in no particular covenant passage of the Old Testament, and this has been noticed by those scholars who hesitate to accept the parallel; but their presence in a disjointed form has to be recognized, and if one does not believe in the relationship between the covenant formula and the suzerainty treaty, one is forced into the disagreeable hypothesis of coincidence. By the time the compilers did their work, the literary parallel of the suzerainty treaty was not known. In Exodus 20 and Joshua 24 the parallels can be shown thus:

1. Exodus 20:2; Joshua 24:2.
2. Exodus 20:2; Joshua 24:2-13.

[9] Joseph A. Fitzmeyer, *The Aramaic Inscriptions of Sefire,* Biblica et Orientalia Series (Rome, 1967), 121-25.
[10] *Hethitische Staatsverträge,* Leipziger Rechtswissenschaftliche Studien Series (Leipzig, 1931), as quoted in Mendenhall, op. cit., 27.

3. Exodus 20:3–17; Joshua 24:14–15.
4. Missing in Exodus; Joshua 24:26.
5. Missing in Exodus; Joshua 24:22,27 (and see below).
6. Missing in both (Mendenhall mentions the ceremony of Deuteronomy 27–28 and Joshua 8:30–35).

The first commandment, the prohibition of the worship of other gods, has its parallel in the treaties; the vassal is forbidden to change his allegiance or even to deal with another sovereign. The treaties provide for an annual appearance of the vassal at the court of the suzerain; one is reminded, although the parallel is not exact, of the stipulation that Israelite men are to appear before Yahweh three times during the year (Ex 23:17, 34:23). Joshua 8:34 provides for the public reading of the stipulations; both this and the ritual of cursing are treated as a single event and not as a regular occurrence, but we have already noticed that a covenant renewal ceremony is postulated for many reasons. As we have seen, the tradition that the tablets of the law were kept in the ark of the covenant has a historical basis. The invocation of gods as witnesses was of course impossible; in Joshua 24:22 the people themselves are witnesses, and in 24:27 a memorial stone serves as witness. Mendenhall has pointed out that heavens and earth are invoked as witnesses (Deut 32:1, Is 1:2).

We can return now to the question mentioned earlier: what was the original content of covenant law, which in the treaty hypothesis can be reckoned as treaty stipulations? The entire mass of Israelite law cannot be included; most of it is obviously later than Israel's appearance as a settled people in Canaan. From the earliest period of interpretation the Decalogue (Ex 20:1–17; Deut 5:6–21) has held a peculiar position as the foundation of Israelite law, in spite of the fact that Jews and Christian churches have never reached an agreement on how the ten commandments are to be counted. Apart from the strictly religious commandments ("the first tablet"), to be discussed below, the Decalogue contains extremely basic moral precepts, so general that most of them need extensive exegesis. Yet these general moral precepts and prohibitions have a great importance in the history of religion for the simple reason that never before had the will of any deity been so clearly and expressly affirmed as standing behind basic moral law. There is no good reason why this distinctively Israelite belief should not have appeared at the very beginnings. It gives the God of Israel a unique character at any time it appears.

Yet the stipulations could have hardly been limited to moralism; religion, we have seen, is cultic by its history if not by its essence. The first tablet does have cultic precepts and prohibitions, but they are much fewer in number and smaller in scope than Israelite cult. One may project the interpretation that these were the distinctively covenant stipulations of cult and that things like the festivals and the sacrificial system were either practiced in common with other religions or developed later in Israelite history than the covenant stipulations. These distinctively covenant or Israelite stipulations are the worship of Yahweh alone, the prohibition of images (already discussed), the vain use of the name, and the Sabbath observance.

The monotheism of Israel is incontrovertible, and it is impossible to show that polytheism was ever accepted in Israel on an equal footing with Yahwism. Here we must again recur to the distinction between the history of Israelite religion and Old Testament theology. The history of Israelite religion has to include the clear evidence of polytheism found both in the text of the Old Testament and in archeological remains. The Yahwism of the Old Testament is everywhere intolerant of polytheism; and it is impossible to show that the religion of Israel in the proper sense of the term was ever anything but Yahwism.

Strictly speaking, the first commandment does not impose monotheism as a belief; it forbids the worship of other gods, and this is further explicated by the second commandment, the prohibition of images. If one must distinguish between speculative monotheism, the affirmation of the existence of one and only one god, and practical monotheism, the worship of only one god, not only the covenant stipulation but by far most of the Old Testament exhibits practical monotheism.[11] A hymn which affirms that Yahweh is greater than all gods (Ps 135:5) or asks who is like Yahweh among the gods (Ps 86:8) is not speaking in terms of speculative monotheism. It is very probable, as almost all critics say, that the express

[11] William Foxwell Albright, *From the Stone Age to Christianity*, 247–52.

denial of the reality of other gods was made in no Old Testament writing earlier than Second Isaiah (Is 40:18–20, 41:21–24,29, 43:10–13, 45:5,6,14,22,23, 46:9). But practical monotheism should not be dismissed as hardly more than educated polytheism. The first commandment obliges the Israelites to ignore other gods, to have no dealing with them. The Israelites are not vassals of other gods, who can do nothing for them or against them. The Israelites cannot help themselves by dealing with other gods, and they anger the god with whom they are in covenant. In terms of the suzerainty treaty the gods become like rivals of the suzerain; they are ineffective rivals.

The vain use of the name is not free from obscurity. We have already adverted to the ideology of the name in the ancient Near East. The name of Yahweh partook of holiness, like the ark or the temple. But the use of the name "for nothing" or "for vanity" is not entirely clear. The word in some contexts means false speech, and most probably vain use is the invocation of Yahweh to attest something which is not true. The Old Testament abounds with such phrases as "As Yahweh lives," and it seems that the ancient Israelite was ready to invoke the deity to attest almost any statement which was thought important. The commandment, then, is more a commandment of truth in speech than of respect for the divine name. Disrespect lay not in frequent use but in its use to attest falsehood. The hypothesis has been proposed that the vain use of the name is the use of the name in magic;[12] but the word *šaw* does not obviously have this meaning.

The Sabbath is certainly a distinctively Israelite observance; nothing like it is known elsewhere. But the Sabbath is rarely mentioned in certain early texts; a few passages mention it in the period of the monarchy, but by far the majority of allusions are postexilic. There is also some uncertainty about the nature and purpose of the observance. One may say at once that the rigorous Sabbath observance which began with the priestly code in the postexilic period and was developed with even greater rigor in the rabbinical period did not appear in the monarchy. There is no evidence that the Sabbath observance included any cultic act before the post-

---

[12] Sigmund Mowinckel, *Psalmenstudien*, v. 1 (Kristiania, 1921), 50.

exilic period. One of the early testimonies (Amos 8:5) speaks of the abstention from trade. It appears that the oldest Sabbath observance was the abstention from profane activity; this is defined in Exodus 20:9–11 and Deuteronomy 5:13–15 as "work." The expansion of the Sabbath commandment in Exodus and Deuteronomy, however, is almost certainly an expansion in the style of the priestly code. It is impossible to determine what the original character of profane work was understood to be. Rabbinical interpretation was much occupied with defining with ultimate precision the thirty-nine types of forbidden work; and Christian moral theology in later centuries did not lag far behind the rabbis in its search for an exact practical definition of "servile work."

If the Sabbath in its earliest form was the consecration of one day out of seven to Yahweh by the abstention from all profane activity, then it was a peculiarly Israelite institution with no parallel. It is a novel concept of sacred time, which elsewhere, in the Old Testament too, means festal time. Earlier efforts to assimilate the Sabbath to unpropitious days of Mesopotamian religion (paralleled in other religions) have foundered;[13] the description of the Sabbath leaves no implication whatever that the Sabbath was considered an unpropitious or unlucky day for business. The recension of Deuteronomy adds the humanitarian motive of rest. This is missing in the expansion of Exodus and is very probably a more recent development from a period when the idea of setting aside time by consecrating it through destruction, like the destruction of the whole burnt victim, had become somewhat elusive in the Israelite-Jewish community. The Sabbath rest is also reflected in the P creation account; Yahweh himself rests on the seventh day after six days of work and makes his rest the model of the rhythm of work and rest for man (Gen 2:2–3). The early Israelites needed no such rationalization; and if the Sabbath is originally understood as the mere abstention from profane work and the consecration of time by not using it, the Sabbath may easily be included among the earliest and the distinctly Israelite covenant institutions.

Against the antiquity of the Sabbath it has been urged that

[13] Hugo Gressman, *Altorientalische Texte zum Alten Testament* (Berlin, 1926), 329; Roland de Vaux, *Ancient Israel,* 476–77; Kittel ThW 7:2–3.

the nomad is unable to spend a day in idleness. Strictly speaking, this is no more valid for the nomad than it is for the peasant or the modern churchgoing Christian. The modern version of the Sabbath rest demands the employment of a large number of people in profane business. One may postulate for the ancient Israelites the rationalization of Jesus concerning the ox which falls into a pit on the Sabbath (Lk 14:5) and the watering of the ox and the ass on the Sabbath (Lk 12:15). Even more telling in this connection is the solid doubt that early Israel can be simply described as a nomadic community.[14] In fact, there has hardly been any society in human history in which the Sabbath repose would not have been a serious inconvenience. It is this very inconvenience which recommends it as one of the observances of early Israel.

As we shall see in more detail, the premonarchic Israelite community in Canaan is now, after the studies of Martin Noth, most frequently understood as a tribal league; to this league Noth gave the Greek name of "amphictyony," which in Greece indicated a league of cities that owned and administered a central religious shrine.[15] This league was bound by the covenant agreement to Yahweh and to each other; the covenant included the acceptance of the treaty stipulations, which became covenant law. Early in the history of the tribal league there developed a peculiarly Israelite way of life, indicated by such phrases as "It is not done so in Israel" (2 Sam 13:13) or "to do folly in Israel" (Gen 34:7; Deut 22:21; Judg 19:23–24, 20:10). The Israelite way of life was shared among the tribes by their common acceptance of covenant law; this, in addition to the central shrine (see above on cult) was one of the links which held the league together. Noth and others have argued very plausibly that the original stipulations of the covenant became principles by which Israelite law was expanded to cover questions raised in the urban-agricultural communities of which Israel was composed, and Noth has argued that the "minor judges" were amphictyonic officers whose duty it was

[14] Albright, *From the Stone Age to Christianity*, 164–66; George E. Mendenhall, "The Hebrew Conquest of Palestine," *The Biblical Archeologist*, 25 (1962), 66–87.

[15] "Das System der zwölf Stämme Israels," BeitrWissAT 4 (1930), 1.

to study the law and promulgate answers to questions.[16] When
the monarchy arose, it came into existence in a community with
an extensive and fairly well defined tradition of common law. It
does not appear that this growing body of covenant law was
understood as the law which Yahweh had revealed to Moses or
any other mediators; it was the interpretation and application of
the covenant stipulations. The will of Yahweh was understood to
be that Israel should be a law-abiding community. The lawbreaker
was a threat not only to his neighbors and to public order, but
also to the relationship of the community with Yahweh. The ancient penalty of stoning for certain offenses was not simply adopted
because of the abundance of stones; the modern Bible reader thinks
of the ancient penalty as soon as he first sees the Holy Land. It
is rather unusual that a community does not delegate the execution
of criminals to an individual officer. Stoning was literally as well
as symbolically execution by the entire community; no single person was responsible for the death, and the community demonstrated that it rejected the offender and the offense. One would
like to trace more closely those obligations and offenses which in
some way seemed to touch the covenant or the Israelite way of
life more closely, the offenses which were "folly in Israel" or, in
the language of Deuteronomy, the Holiness Code, Ezekiel, and
Proverbs, became "abominations." Where that word is used, it
seems most frequently to signify idolatry or offenses against sexual
morality.

The period of the monarchy seems to have been a period of
setback for covenant law. In ancient monarchies the king was the
source of law and its enforcer. The Old Testament actually says
little about royal law, more about the king as judge and the institution of royal judges. The prophets appealed to tradition without
actually invoking covenant law; and we can deduce that the king
was never recognized as being superior to covenant law, whatever
the kings themselves may have thought. The tension between monarchy and the popular tradition of covenant law is reflected in the
prophets (see below) and in some narrative passages such as the
rejection of Rehoboam (1 Kings 12) and the trial of Naboth (1

[16] "Das Amt des 'Richters Israels,'" *Festschrift für Alfred Bertholet* (Tübingen, 1950), 404–18.

Kings 21). The episode of Naboth reflects the early covenant law which prohibited the alienation of land outside the family:[17] the law should more properly be called a custom, since it is nowhere explicitly stated. But the texts quoted by De Vaux justify the commonly accepted conclusion that the idea of the donation of the land from Yahweh was valid both for Israel as a whole and for the individual owners. It was an attack upon Yahweh himself to take another's land.

When a Jewish community was re-established after the exile, the community showed a strong sense of guilt; the prophetic teaching of judgment had apparently made a deep impression on the survivors, and the fall of Israel and Judah was attributed to the violations of the law of Yahweh.[18] According to the narrative of Ezra-Nehemiah, Ezra was sent to Jerusalem with royal authority to promulgate the law under which the Jewish community should live (Ezra 7:7–26). The law was produced by Jewish scribes in the Persian Empire; and it seems unlikely that the production of the law was done by the initiative of the Persian king. The document of the law was largely identical with the Pentateuch source known as P; and it became the basis of the Jewish way of life.

In the postexilic Jewish community of Judea, and still more in the Jewish communities which arose outside of Palestine (the Diaspora), many of the laws of the Pentateuch were unrealistic. After the prophets and the wise men came the scribes, who were the copiers and the interpreters of the law. By a peculiar type of interpretation they extracted from the text of the Pentateuch an answer to every moral or ceremonial problem which arose; and by a peculiar but not unique ability to deal with the unreal they also answered a large number of questions which had never arisen and would never arise. Thus the Law, the Torah, became what it had never been before, a complete and comprehensive guide for conduct, founding not only a way of life but a lengthy catalogue of detailed precepts and prohibitions which were far more extensive than the 613 commandments counted in the Pentateuch. The Law and its observance more than anything gave the Jewish com-

[17] De Vaux, op. cit., 166–67.
[18] Ezra 9:6–7; cf. Jacob M. Myers, *Ezra and Nehemiah*, Anchor Bible (Garden City, N.Y., 1965), 61–63.

munity its permanent identity; ultimately covenant and law became synonymous. This had not been the original meaning of the words.

It is of some importance whether the elements of the suzerainty treaty were recognized as such in the earliest forms of Israelite religion. If they were recognized, then the basic relationship of the community to the deity was the relationship of vassal to sovereign. This in turn touches upon the question whether the idea of the kingship of Yahweh was earlier or later in Israelite belief and in Old Testament literature. In several passages the institution of human kingship is called an infringement on the kingship of Yahweh (Judg 8:23; 1 Sam 8:7, 12:12). The anti-monarchic passages cannot be called late simply because they are anti-monarchic; and of the passages cited here Judges 8:23 appears to be the earliest, although all three no doubt reflect anti-monarchic sentiments which arose under the monarchy. Yahweh is called king in Exodus 15:18, Numbers 23:21, and Deuteronomy 33:5. Modern critics are now inclined to date these poems early, even earlier than the monarchy, although Exodus 15:18, the closing line, may be a doxology added to the original. Other allusions, frequent enough, are clearly later. Thus the psalms of the kingship of Yahweh (Ps 47, 93-100), assigned by Mowinckel to the New Year festival, attest the kingship of Yahweh both in creation and in his saving acts on behalf of Israel. These psalms are not early but they can be witnesses of an early theme.

It seems most likely that the suzerain-vassal relation was the original and fundamental relation of Israel and Yahweh, as opposed for instance to such relationships as creator-creature (which no one has suggested) or father-children; and the relation of suzerain-vassal is not the same as the relation of king-subject. Israel, the vassal, is bound to the suzerain by the saving acts which the suzerain has performed. The suzerain has saved the vassal people from extinction and has given them the land in which they are settled. On condition of fidelity they can count on the assistance of the suzerain against their enemies. The relationship is a stable condition which looks forward to no substantial growth or change, and in that sense the Israel of the premonarchic period represented "realized eschatology." The alternative to fidelity according to the curse formulae of Deuteronomy 28 is extinction. The curse formulae of Leviticus 26 conclude with a possibility of restoration after judgment; very probably the original formula, like the formula of Deuteronomy 28, had no such hopeful element. The experience of Yahweh in history and prophecy would enlarge the horizons of the suzerain-treaty-covenant of Yahweh and Israel.

3. Prophecy

A. Origins

In most modern biblical interpretation since the eighteenth century the prophetic books have been esteemed as the high point of revelation, of the Israelite religious experience and of Old Testament theology. It is curious that it is so difficult to trace the origins of prophetic revelation. What is known of earliest prophecy indicates that the high point of biblical revelation came from humble, even somewhat undignified beginnings. Samuel the seer was a village wise man who for a small fee could tell where to search for strayed animals, presumably also for other lost articles (1 Sam 9:6-8,20).

Antecedents of the Israelite prophet elsewhere in the ancient Near East have only a remote resemblance at best, and limited to form as opposed to content.[19] The prophets of Mari spoke to the king in the same messenger formula employed by the Israelite prophets. The messenger formula is the formula used by the royal courier who memorized the message and then after a formal introduction, "Thus says X king of Y; speak to A king of B and say to him: Thus says X king of Y . . ." the message was then given in the first person, the courier speaking in the name of the king. Both in form and in content the Israelite prophets differ clearly from diviners and oracular spokesmen.

The Hebrew word for prophet, *nabi'*, is of uncertain meaning and etymology. Albright explained it as a passive derived from Akkadian, meaning "one who is called."[20] The word does not explain the character of the class to which it was applied. The

[19] Cf. Herbert B. Huffmon, "Prophecy in the Mari Letters," *The Biblical Archeologist,* 31 (1968), 101-24.
[20] Albright, *From the Stone Age to Christianity,* 303-5.

earliest sure appearance of the word designates groups which appeared at the beginnings of the monarchy. Similar groups appear later under the monarchy in the time of Elijah, called "sons of the prophets." The plural "prophets" probably indicates the plurality of the group; the title is not like the title "sons of Israel," which designates the eponymous ancestor. Modern scholars often translate the phrase as "band" or "company of prophets," implying that any individual member of such a group would be called a *nabi'*. There is no reference to an individual member except in 2 Kings 9:1, where the individual is called "one of the sons of the prophets." The character of these groups differs, but not to the extent that no continuity between them can be affirmed. The earlier group can be identified as a cult group whose specific cult form was an ecstatic worship of song and dance (1 Sam 10:10–12, 19: 20–24). The later group are less clearly a cult group; they are rather associates, companions, disciples, or assistants of the prophets Elijah and Elisha, who receive the name *nabi'*. The erudite gloss of 1 Samuel 9:9, which identifies the *nabi'* with the earlier "seer," cannot come from a very intimate acquaintance with either *nabi'* or the seer. The association of both the early and the later group permit the affirmation that they represented religious and political conservatives in Israel, meaning that they adhered to cultic and social traditions and were opposed to the monarchy and its innovations. It is altogether likely that this group, which is described as composed of strong and healthy young men, was a political force of some significance.

Yet there is no obvious connection between such a group or even their leaders (supposing that the leader was called *nabi'*) and the kind of spokesman to whom the title of *nabi'* is given in the prophetic books. Other groups of prophets appear who can be described as royal or court prophets. These were oracular spokesmen, but they retained some of the ecstatic character of the earlier groups. The fact that they appear to have been regularly consulted has led a number of scholars to conclude that the title "prophet" was borne by some cult officers. This type of prophet speaks the word of Yahweh and has this in common with those whom we shall call "classical prophets," meaning by this term the prophets whose words are preserved in the prophetic canon.

The cult prophet of Yahweh is not surely mentioned anywhere in the Old Testament; this is said in contrast to the prophets of Baal, who are clearly described as engaging in cultic acts (1 Kings 18:17–40). The cultic prophet by definition is a cultic officer with a regular appointment to a cultic function; his capacity to perform the function comes from his appointment. Such cultic prophets, it is supposed, uttered responses to questions and petitions in the cult; they spoke for Yahweh (Ps 2:6–10, 20:6–8). Aubrey R. Johnson has suggested that the "prophets" of 1 Samuel 9–10 and 19 had their correspondents or their successors in the cult of the temples who formed temple choirs and worshiped with song and dance.[21] These were the predecessors of the Levitical choirs of the chronicler.

The type of prophet mentioned so far does not appear as a uniform type; but all members of the type raise the questions of "professional" prophecy. The term is used in opposition to the classical prophets, none of whom clearly show membership in any professional group. Amos denies that he is a prophet or a son of a prophet (Amos 7:14–15); he "prophesies" (that is, speaks and acts like a prophet) at the direct command of Yahweh. The text is both revealing and difficult. The words "prophet" and "son of a prophet" can only mean denial of membership in the groups designated by that name. Amos neither affirms nor denies that the "prophets" of whom he is not one also spoke by a command of Yahweh. Is it speaking by such a command that makes him call his own speech "prophesying"? The only common element of which we can be sure is not in content or in commission, but in this, that the speech of Amos, like the speech of the prophets, is the word of Yahweh. The word of Yahweh was the charism of the prophets as *torah* was the charism of the priest and counsel the charism of the wise (Jer 18:18); in this line Jeremiah admits a conflict between himself and others who are called prophets.

The professional prophet was one who was possessed of a certain skill which distinguished him from others who did not have the skill, whose only or main support in life was his profession.

[21] *The Cultic Prophet in Ancient Israel* (2nd ed., Cardiff, 1962), 69–75; cf. also Alfred Haldar, *Associations of Cult Prophets Among the Ancient Semitics* (Uppsala, 1945), 90–160.

The skill in question is the skill in speaking the word of Yahweh, a skill which in our terms is better called a charisma. The professional character of the charisma implies that it could be acquired by membership in a group of fellow professionals and by training. It is indicated not only by the enthusiastic worship attributed to the prophets in 1 Samuel 10 and 19 but also by the conduct of the court prophets in 1 Kings 22 and from the musical inspiration sought by Elisha in 2 Kings 3:15 that a group discipline of ecstasy was practiced by the prophets. The descriptions do not suggest (except for Elisha) that speaking the word of Yahweh was the normal and expected result of group ecstasy; but it would not be improbable if this result were expected. We can project that the professional prophet was one who belonged to such a group and who mastered the techniques of ecstasy sufficiently well to speak the word of Yahweh, either as one of the group or—presumably more rarely—as an individual spokesman. The theory behind such a professional attitude was simply that Yahweh was ready and willing to speak to those who would listen and that those who were willing to submit to the proper discipline could open their ears to hear the word which most men were unable to hear.

The court prophets appear in the reign of David. Gad is associated with David even before David became king (1 Sam 22:5). Both Gad (2 Sam 24) and Nathan (2 Sam 12) are credited with characteristic prophetic utterances, characteristic meaning moral rebukes addressed to the supreme ruler. Gad is credited with assuring the selection of the site of the temple of Zion (2 Sam 24), Nathan with the oracle assuring the permanence of the dynasty of David (2 Sam 7). Nothing is known of the origin of these prophets; they appear to be professional prophets in the sense defined above, and they may have come from the group of prophetic worshipers. In the question of Solomon's accession, when a prophetic oracle might have been expected, Nathan's share in the transaction was not prophetic utterance but simply court intrigue (1 Kings 1). The selection of a successor to David was not made by the word of Yahweh but by the word of David, and this was understood. Both Gad and Nathan seem to be royal officers, but they are not included in the lists of officers of David (2 Sam 8:15–18, 20:23–26; 1 Kings 4:1–6). At other times we find kings consulting prophets with no indication that these were court prophets (1 Kings 14:1–16) and sometimes with clear indications that they were not (2 Kings 3:11–19, 23:14–20). Among the classical prophets both Isaiah and Jeremiah were consulted by kings, but it is highly improbable that Isaiah was a royal prophet, and Jeremiah certainly was not.

The position of Samuel has to be treated as ambiguous. It is doubtful that any of the narratives of Samuel preserve his original character. It is doubtful that the *nabi'*, even in the most primitive form, appeared in Samuel himself or in the period of Samuel. The importance and influence of Samuel, reflected in the narratives, is best explained on the assumption that he was the head of "the sons of the prophets" and thus exercised an influence wider than local or tribal.[22] In a later period of the transmission of the traditions no corresponding figure was known in Israel and Judah, and the role and mission of Samuel were then seen in the *nabi'*.

There is a certain consistency in the prophets who appear in the books of Kings; the consistency is found in the character already described as conservative, representing the traditional religious, political and social forms in Israel. Not every dynastic change occurs with the word of a prophet, but where the word is spoken it is a conservative word. The word of Shemaiah to Jeroboam, giving him a mandate to rebel against Solomon, is a product of the Deuteronomic historians and charges Solomon with patronizing the worship of other gods. The narrative of 1 Kings 12 affords other information concerning Solomon; here the principal objection against the monarchy is the institution of forced labor, the very kind of slavery from which Yahweh had liberated the ancestors of Israel in Egypt. The same Shemaiah further authenticates the revolt (1 Kings 12:22–24) by an oracle forbidding Rehoboam to attempt to suppress the revolt by war.

It is curious that the subsequent narratives are concerned much more with prophets in Israel than with prophets in Judah. No prophet is mentioned in the kingdom of Judah between Rehoboam and Isaiah, an interval of nearly two hundred years. (The books

[22] John L. McKenzie, "The Four Samuels," *Biblical Research,* 7 (1962), 3–18.

of Chronicles supply the missing prophets. One cannot be sure that these prophets existed.) It is quite unlikely that there were no prophets in Judah; and it is possible that the Judahite monarchy and the Jerusalem priesthood left little room for the prophets to operate. In the palace insurrection in which Joash succeeded Athaliah (2 Kings 12) the leading role was played by Jehoiada the priest. In Israel prophets were active, or at least prophetic utterances were recorded. The word of Ahijah predicted the downfall of the dynasty of Jeroboam (1 Kings 14:1-6); the words of the utterance are Deuteronomic in style. Jehu predicted the fall of the house of Baasha (1 Kings 16:1-4); the words attributed to Jehu seem to have reference to the fall of the house of Omri, but exact quotation is not our interest here. Our interest is the recurring tradition by which prophets were associated with the dynastic revolutions of Israel.

This association is most clearly perceived in the fall of the house of Omri. The exegesis of 1 Kings 19 presents certain problems; but the narrative, combined with the narrative of 2 Kings 9:1-13 is clearly intended to identify Elisha and the prophets with the *coup d'état* of Jehu and even to make Elisha the inspiration of the *coup.* The narrative of 1 Kings 19 is with equal clarity intended to associate Elijah with the conspiracy and assassination. Modern historians are not all willing to accept this association with Elijah.[23] There is no reason to question the part of Elisha in the affair nor to doubt the political activity of the prophets in Israel. As they appear in these narratives, they are seen to be anti-monarchic in the sense that they claimed the right to denounce the king and to call for his deposition. In the politics of the time this meant his assassination and the extermination of his family and supporters.

Elijah and Elisha are more fully described than any other pre-literary prophets. The narrative is not certainly free from legendary accretions and modifications; on the other hand, the portraits of Elijah and Elisha are not drawn after the image of any of the writing prophets nor indeed after the image of any other Old Testament character. Neither of them is described as a speechmaker;

[23] James A. Montgomery, *The Book of Kings,* International Critical Commentary (New York, 1951), 314–15.

the prophetic sayings which they utter are brief; were they collected under the titles Elijah and Elisha, as the writings of the minor prophets were collected, they would not much exceed the book of Obadiah in length. The sayings of Elijah, with the exception of the story of Naboth (1 Kings 21), are all warnings against the worship of the Baal. The narrative makes Jezebel, the princess of Tyre who was Ahab's queen, the patroness of the cult of the Baal. In all probability the situation was more complex. Albrecht Alt proposed that the city-state of Samaria was the Canaanite capital of the dynasty of Ahab. Ahab, Alt supposes, ruled a dual Canaanite-Israelite monarchy as David and Solomon had ruled a Judahite-Israelite dual monarchy.[24] Elijah and the seven thousand who had not bowed the knee to Baal (1 Kings 19:18) represented the conservative Yahwists of Israel who did not believe that the state could combine the worship of Yahweh with the worship of another god. In Alt's interpretation of the position of Samaria in Israel, the prophetic revolution was directed not only against the cult of the Baal but also against a Canaanite ruling aristocracy and a legal-social system which was in direct opposition to the traditional legal-social system of covenant law.

The traditional designation of Elijah and Elisha as "prophets of action" as opposed to the classical "prophets of the word" is well justified, as long as one remembers that the type of action meant included intrigue and revolution. In fact, both Elijah and Elisha are described as wonder-workers in a series of stories which, especially for Elisha, exceed the limits of credibility. The wonders credited to Elijah are all associated with the three years' drought which was the great sign of Elijah's career; he announced its beginning and its end in the ordeal of Mount Carmel, and the story of the widow of Zarephath (1 Kings 17:8–24) is located within the same period. Compared to Elisha, the wonders of Elijah are rather modest; by far most of the anecdotes of Elisha are concerned with unrelated wonders operated by the prophet for various unrelated persons. The classic character of the prophet did not include thaumaturgy among his typical traits, and the stories of

[24] Albrecht Alt, *Kleine Schriften,* II[3] (Munich, 1964), 33–65, III (Munich, 1959), 258–302.

Elijah and Elisha in this respect are eccentric. Yet that the word of the prophet is a word of power is said in such passages as Jeremiah 1:10; the power of the prophet to build and to tear down lies in his power to predict the rise and fall of nations. It is seen in a more primitive manner in the question addressed by the elders of Bethlehem to Samuel (1 Sam 16:4). They ask, trembling, whether his coming is peaceable; the powerful word of the prophet could wreak harm. Yet this surely ancient belief in the power of the prophetic word has not produced thaumaturgic legends for most of the prophets mentioned in the Old Testament and in particular for the prophets of the literary canon. On the other hand, a small group of revolutionaries who could overthrow a powerful dynasty and, according to Alt's understanding, its aristocratic supporters was sufficiently remarkable to evoke legends of its thaumaturgic powers. These stories do not establish thaumaturgy as one of the characteristic qualities of the prophet.

The prophets of Baal whom Elijah encountered on Mount Carmel (1 Kings 18), mentioned also in the purge of Jehu (2 Kings 10:19), may have a title which they did not have in Canaanite religion; there is no Ugaritic correspondent to Hebrew *nabi'*. Their behavior indicates that they were an ecstatic cultic group quite similar to the Israelite "sons of the prophets"; and such ecstatic cultic worship is not specifically either Israelite or Canaanite. Such cultic groups in Israelite and Canaanite religion might be expected to exhibit similarities and even mutual borrowings. If the title was used in the Canaanite cult of this period, it was probably borrowed from the Israelites.

Interspersed in the Elijah-Elisha stories are some other anecdotes of prophets which seem unrelated to Elijah and Elisha. The court prophets appear at the court of Ahab (1 Kings 22) and predict his victory over the Aramaeans—falsely, as the event showed. The prophets who predicted an earlier victory (1 Kings 20) were more accurate. These men instance in their own way the conservatism which is characteristic of the early prophetic groups; the enemy of Israel is the enemy of Yahweh and is doomed to defeat. They exhibit neither the conservatism of Elijah and Elisha, which was ready to risk the military power of Israel in order to remove the Canaanite cult and its accompanying Canaanite social implications, nor did they exhibit the later prophetic interpretation of foreign enemies as the agents of Yahweh's judgments on Israel. It is worthy of notice that even Elisha appears as a prophet of victory in several anecdotes. This is more easily understood when the anecdote is located in the reign of Jehoash of the dynasty of Jehu (2 Kings 13:14–19); but similar anecdotes are related in the reign of an unnamed king of Israel who in the narrative antedates Jehu (2 Kings 6–7). But when Elisha incited Hazael to assassinate Benhadad of Damascus (2 Kings 8:7–15), the story implies that Hazael's vigorous wars against Israel would weaken the dynasty of Omri. One need not suppose that the prophet himself was any more consistent in his thoughts and actions than the stories about him. Whenever politics are invoked in support of a religious cause, it is difficult to maintain consistency in either the politics or the religion. It is not surprising that Elisha should in one context have spoken like the patriotic court prophets, in another as he spoke to Jehoram during Jehoram's campaign against Moab (2 Kings 3:13–14); yet even in this episode the oracle was favorable.

It seems that Micaiah ben Imlah (1 Kings 22:13–27) must be classified among the professional prophets; yet he prophesied no good for Ahab but only evil (1 Kings 22:8) and thus can hardly be considered a court prophet. He seems to be in the same line with Elijah, yet there is no relation between the two; nor is Micaiah represented as the uncompromising Yahwist which Elijah was. The story does not reveal the motive of the mutual hostility of Ahab and Micaiah. Micaiah's explanation of the court prophets is that they were deluded by Yahweh himself. In a more sophisticated culture this might be taken as irony; in the Old Testament it is in the same line of thought as the hardening of the heart of Pharaoh (Ex 7:3) and the dullness inflicted upon Israel by Yahweh (Is 6:10, 29:9–10). Both Micaiah and the court prophets were prophets of Yahweh; the opposition between them was not the opposition of Yahweh and Baal. Nor do the words of Micaiah show any trace of Elijah's intolerance of Ahab's compromise with Baalism.

B. Inspiration

The problems of prophetic inspiration have usually been treated as univocal for all the prophets. Perhaps we should allow for the possibility that the question should be treated separately for each individual prophet; the text of the Old Testament does not afford material from which the theologian can form a general concept of "prophetic inspiration" which is valid for each of the prophets. Most of the literary prophets say nothing about the manner in which they were inspired. The few who do speak of it exhibit individual differences. We have adverted to the professional prophets, who very probably had techniques for educing the word of Yahweh; but these techniques are not described. It is difficult to erect an elaborate theory of professional techniques on Elisha's use of a minstrel to induce what appears to be an ecstatic trance. Possibly music and other devices were in normal use and are not mentioned more frequently simply because they were normal. The court prophets of Ahab (1 Kings 22) seem to be inducing group ecstasy. The sons of the prophets in 1 Samuel 10 and 19 induce group ecstasy but do not utter the word of Yahweh.

The literary prophets who give some evidence of the nature of their inspiration are Amos, Hosea, First Isaiah, Jeremiah, Ezekiel, and Second Isaiah. When the experiences are compared, the differences are more striking than the likenesses. All speak the word of Yahweh, but no two are moved in the same way to speak the word of Yahweh. First Isaiah (6), Jeremiah (1), and Ezekiel (1) are credited with "inaugural visions." Possibly Amos 7–8 should also be called an inaugural experience; the visionary element is missing. The brief reference in Second Isaiah (40:4–6) is also an inaugural experience with no visionary element.

The much discussed saying of Amos 7:14–15 must mean that Amos does not accept the identification with the professional prophets implied in the words of Amaziah (7:12–13). He also denies implicitly that he speaks with any professional technique. It seems therefore that his claim of a mandate to prophesy distinguishes him from the professional prophets. The phrase does not necessarily express disapproval of professional prophets; as far as the text of Amos goes, he may have been as ready to accept their legitimacy as any other Israelite or Judahite of his time. He claims a personal mandate; the professional prophets did not make such a claim and did not need to make it. It was Amos who had to validate his prophetic commission, not the professional prophets. The manner in which his call came will be discussed below in connection with the call of Jeremiah and Hosea.

The inaugural vision of Isaiah is located in the temple, which for Isaiah was clearly the place where one encountered Yahweh. Yahweh, of course, is not clearly seen; and the prophet fears death because he is so close to the lethal vision of Yahweh. It is something of a paradox in Old Testament imagery that the voice of Yahweh is not fatal, although the vision of Yahweh is. The key word of the experience is the word "holy"; and the word is more frequent in Isaiah than in other books. The prophet's commission (6:9–13), it has been noticed, is not entirely in harmony with the words of First Isaiah, whatever be one's critical hypothesis of the words of First Isaiah; the commission is quite as grim as the message of Amos, as we shall see.

A reconstruction of the experience is not possible in the sense that one can determine what Isaiah really saw when he thought he saw the skirts of the robe of Yahweh. The experience falls under the heading of mystical, which at the minimum must be defined as a perception of the nearness of the divine so much more vivid than the ordinary awareness of the divine that it can be compared to the experience of sensation. Isaiah's awareness is more prosily described as a sudden frightening insight into the holiness, the "wholly other" character of Yahweh. From this awareness comes a further insight into the relations of Yahweh with Israel and Judah and a perception that this relation has become a critical relation of judgment. His awareness of this relation imposes upon him the obligation to declare it; he can only declare it because his insight gives him no directions as to what can be done about it. The inaugural vision includes no commission to invite to repentance and to offer forgiveness. The content of the inaugural vision does not preclude further experiences; and for this reason one should not, simply on the basis of the inaugural vision, deny that Isaiah was capable of saying anything of promise. It is possible, however, that a prophet could do no more in the entire collection of his sayings than give expression to the one experience of the type called "inaugural."

The inaugural vision of Ezekiel is so packed with symbolism and imaginative detail that interpreters generally despair of describing the "experience" which is behind it; and perhaps the entire vision of the chariot is imaginative writing with no mystical "experience" such as we can easily suppose for Isaiah. Furthermore, most of Ezekiel 1–3 can be described as "inaugural visions" or "inaugural experiences" in the sense that the content is the prophet's mission rather than any particular saying about the concrete situation in which the prophet speaks to the people. It is a problem of literary criticism and not of biblical theology to explain the presence of this embarrassing fullness of inaugural visions in Ezekiel. But the symbolism of the visions is not subtle. The vision of the chariot signifies the presence of Yahweh with the exiles in Babylon, and this is of considerable importance; it was never considered that Yahweh had traveled with the Israelites exiled by the Assyrians in 721 B.C. The commission of the prophet is to speak to a rebellious house; the emphasis makes it clear that the exiles have not interpreted the disasters of Judah as the judgments of Yahweh. The obligation and the responsibility of the prophet are expressed with singular clarity in 3:16–21, which has a doublet in 33:7–16. In spite of the comparative richness of "inaugural" material in Ezekiel, the mission of the prophet is not known with greater clarity and precision than the mission of any other prophet. The commission of Ezekiel, like the commission of Amos and Isaiah, suggests no element of promise. The oracles of promise in Ezekiel are all collected in chapters 33 to 48, and possibly another inaugural experience is signified in the release of the prophet from dumbness at the news of the fall of Jerusalem (33:21–22); but the content of the prophet's words is not mentioned.

While literary criticism is not the business of theology, it should be a help to theology; and one should notice that most critics believe that the compilation of the book of Ezekiel is not the simple arrangement which the book itself suggests.[25] The problem

[25] Otto Eissfeldt, *The Old Testament: An Introduction* (New York, 1965), 367–81.

REVELATION   97

of the unity of the book cannot be regarded as solved in one way
or the other. But in the broad general outline of the book the
compilers have presented an entirely credible prophetic experience.
They describe a prophet who, like Jeremiah, actually experienced
the judgment which they and others before them had pronounced
upon Israel. Critics sometimes seem to forget that the disappear-
ance of one's own nation can be a shattering experience. When
the nation is also one's religious group, the experience can be
more shattering, if the comparative is possible here. In Ezekiel the
compilers present a prophet who sees restoration only after the
accomplishment of the judgment. Possibly the early Ezekiel saw
no future for the people of Yahweh. The prophetic insight was
based on the fall of Jerusalem, which opened the realization that
Yahweh had a purpose for Israel which went beyond judgment.
One may compare the insight of Second Isaiah (40:2); Jerusalem
has received due punishment and has served her sentence.[26]

This leads us to the call of Second Isaiah. The insight mentioned
above is not, however, the basic content of Second Isaiah's call
and mission. This has to be the realization that the rise of Cyrus
of Persia means the fall of Babylon. One may guess that Second
Isaiah did not mention the seventy years of Jeremiah 25:11–12
only because he had never heard of them. Why should the fall
of Babylon mean the restoration of Jerusalem? Nothing in the
probabilities which we know could have suggested this to the
prophet; and one may suppose that Second Isaiah thought in terms
of service to the king of Babylon, a service which was not to be
transferred to another conqueror.

I have mentioned above that the visions or calls of Amos, Hosea,
and Jeremiah can be grouped. The common element is present,
although the inclusion of Hosea may seem to be a trifle subtle.
The common element is that in each of these prophets the prophetic word arises from something seen or experienced in the
world of nature and man, as contrasted with the chariot of Ezekiel.
The series of visions in Amos 7:1–9 and 8:1–9:1 include locusts,
fire (possibly a figure for drought), a basket of fruit, and the

26 On the double punishment, cf. John L. McKenzie, *Second Isaiah*, Anchor Bible (Garden City, N.Y., 1968), 17.

temple and the altar. These are not visionary objects. The character of the vision is best illustrated in the basket (*ḳayiṣ*), which suggests the end (*ḳēṣ*). The words may both have been pronounced *ḳēṣ* in eighth-century Israel. This would be a pun in our speech; but we do not think of the power of the word as the Israelites did. When Amos heard or said or thought, "Here is the *ḳēṣ*," the full impact of what he had said struck him with prophetic inspiration. Without a word play, the locusts and the fire are agents of destruction and the temple is the object of destruction. The sight of the object suggests the word, and the word suggests the prophetic utterance.

The inaugural "visions" of Jeremiah are found in Jeremiah 1, although the word "inaugural" applies clearly only to 1:1–10 and the word "vision" only to 1:11–13. But both "visions" are objects of experience which symbolize the prophetic word. "Almond" (*šakēd*) leads to "awake" (*šōkēd*), and this in turn to "Yahweh is awake." As for "basket" and "end," the pronunciation of the two words may have been identical in Jeremiah's time. The second object is a boiling pot set over a fire. The spilling of the pot is the execution of the threat upon Israel.

I have said that the inclusion of Hosea in this classification may be subtle. It is not the task of biblical theology to solve the complex problems of Hosea's matrimonial experience;[27] it is sufficient for our purpose that within all the disagreement in details, all interpreters agree that Hosea's matrimonial experience led him to the insight which, in modern colloquial language, would be expressed thus: "Israel, like my wife, is a tramp." I believe this well illustrates a possibility raised above, that the whole of a prophet's utterances may arise from a single prophetic experience or insight. Nothing is needed to interpret any saying of Hosea beyond the fundamental insight that the relations of Yahweh and Israel are analogous to the relations of husband and wife.

It is quite probable that we have many prophetic sayings without the key word or the key object of vision which is given in these passages. A thorough investigation of a book or an extended section of a book could establish this with greater probability.

[27] Harold H. Rowley, *Men of God* (London, 1963), 66–97.

Certainly in these passages we have explicit examples of a prophetic utterance, "Thus says Yahweh," which arises from a normal experience of seeing or hearing. These sayings include no ecstatic element whatever.

In some instances the prophet himself produces the object of vision. The symbolic actions of the prophets do not all surely have the same purpose. Nothing indicates that they are intended to have magical value, and it seems a bit alien to Israelite thought patterns to regard them as "visual aids." They are better understood, it seems, as efforts to produce the "word-thing" of the prophetic utterance in more than one dimension. Isaiah could say, "You will walk naked like captives"; he could walk naked like a captive with or without saying it. Jeremiah's symbolic actions produce the key words "rotten" (ch. 13), "smash" (ch. 19), and "yoke" (ch. 27). The symbolic actions of Ezekiel 4–5, according to the scheme of the compilers, were performed with no verbal explanation.

We have observed that no single idea of prophetic inspiration can be found in the prophetic books, and it is not intended to make the catchword or the object seen such a single explanation. But the word heard and the object seen are the occasions of prophetic utterance more frequently than any other single source. We still do not learn how Amos heard that Yahweh wished him to prophesy to Israel, and we understand even less why Amos, a Judahite, was commissioned to prophesy to Israel and not to Judah. Isaiah was the first to prophesy in Judah. Interpreters have not yet learned what it was in the experience of a prophet which made him say with assurance, "Thus says Yahweh." Perhaps no one can explain this unless he has shared the assurance.

Of all the prophets, Jeremiah is not only the most candid about his inner feelings, he is the only prophet who mentions them. In the inaugural experience, Jeremiah expresses doubt about his ability to fulfill the commission (1:6). He is bewildered and despondent at the delay of judgment upon the wicked (12:1–6). He feels that Yahweh has deceived him by compelling him to pronounce threats which are never executed; he has become ridiculous and the object of enmity (18:7–11). His despondency is so great that he wishes he had never been born (18:14–21). In a collection of sayings about prophets, Jeremiah examines the difference between what we call true and false prophets. He knows no difference except that he has an overwhelming and a compelling awareness that he has to speak, even though he himself dislikes the content of the message. Prophets who speak "peace" have no such compulsion; they cannot distinguish between their own words and the word of Yahweh (23:9–40). In his encounter with Hananiah he has no response except that the truth of the prophecy of "peace" is ultimately attested only by the event (29:5–9).

It does not follow from the fact that only Jeremiah discloses such doubts and uncertainties that only Jeremiah had them. At the same time we must be careful here also not to impose a rigid pattern upon the different prophets. Jeremiah reveals a fear based upon personal inadequacy, a revulsion against the enmity he elicits by his prophecies of doom, a sympathy with the people whose destruction he announces, and some uncertainty about the authenticity of his message. His problems are resolved—to the degree to which they were resolved—by what he presents as a dialogue with Yahweh. As a result of these conversations, he received at least a temporary reassurance which enabled him to maintain his firmness; I say at least temporary, for the text does not indicate that we are dealing with a single episode in the life of the prophet. His insight into the reality of Yahweh contrasted with the reality of the collective wickedness of Judah brought him recovery from the fits of weakness to which he was subject; indeed, the recovery sometimes led him to vindictive expressions of assurance that his message was true and of desires that it be accomplished (11:18–23, 15:15–18, 17:14–18, 18:19–23, 20:11–12). One can see how the formulation of the word of Yahweh by Jeremiah was influenced by his personal experiences and his temperament. Each prophet was an individual spokesman, and differences in their thought and style can easily be recognized. Jeremiah has a harsh word for prophetic plagiarists (23:30).

Jeremiah may also warn the student not to be careless in distinguishing "true" from "false" prophecy. He implies rather clearly that his own assurance was not entirely free from doubt at all times; and he too had some difficulty in distinguishing the word of Yahweh from his own words. The prophets who promised Ahab victory over the Aramaeans (1 Kings 22) were proved false by the event; Ezekiel also promised Nebuchadnezzar victory over Tyre (Ezek 26:7–14), a promise which he or a scribe had to retract (Ezek 29:17–20). It has taken a great amount of ingenious symbolic exegesis to bring Second Isaiah's restoration into harmony with the events.[28] Thus one cannot even say that the canonical books are a collection of the prophetic sayings which have survived the test of Jeremiah (Jer 28:8–9): "The prophets who preceded you and me from ancient times prophesied war, famine, and pestilence against many countries and great kingdoms. As for the prophet who prophesies peace, when the word of that prophet comes to pass, then it will be known that the Lord has truly sent the prophet." Jeremiah here establishes a presumption in favor of oracles of judgment. Given the human condition, one does not need to demonstrate the truth of an oracle of judgment; one must doubt on principle an oracle of peace. Yet the canonical books, including Jeremiah, do include oracles of peace. We readers of the Bible, especially we Roman Catholic readers, tend to treat the prophets with a reverence which combines divine veracity, biblical inerrancy and papal infallibility. We do not deal with the possibility that the preserved words are those which stood the test of time and history. It is extremely difficult to explain the position attributed to Isaiah with reference to the invasion of Sennacherib and to reconcile it with the prophetic speaker who can be identified in Isaiah 1–12 and 28–33. What is the test of time and history? It is not merely the fulfillment of prediction, a test which would be irrelevant for almost all of the prophetic canon, but a recognition by the scribes who have preserved the books that they heard in these sayings the word of Yahweh. One cannot say simply that the professional prophets and the court prophets were liars or self-deceived; neither can one say that the canonical prophets were infallibly accurate. Jeremiah says clearly that the prophets of his time were largely corrupt, uttering statements which they knew would be accepted by their listeners. This has certainly been a very common type of corruption both in politics and religion; and Jeremiah was indignant not so much because men

[28] McKenzie, *Second Isaiah*, 140.

adapted the message to the audience, but because they did it in the most critical moment of Israelite history, when there was no hope except in facing the truth.

c. The Message of the Prophets

The individual character of the prophets of the canon makes it necessary to deal with each one in order to summarize the Israelite experience of Yahweh in the word of the prophets. The treatment is a very general summary of topics which can each be discussed on the scale of a book, and the student should pursue the study of these topics in depth by consulting the specialized works in which the prophets are treated individually.[29] It should also be noticed that the prophets spoke to different audiences in different situations, with the possible exception of Isaiah and Micah. One should not expect the sayings to show uniform emphasis and entire agreement in content. It is just these inconsistencies arising from differences in persons and situations which explain the richness of the prophetic revelation of Yahweh.

The type of writing called "apocalyptic" is not included in this summary treatment. It belongs in Chapter VII, "The Future of Israel," and will be discussed there.

AMOS

There is a general critical consensus that Amos 9:8b–15 are an addition to the original collection of the words of Amos.[30] This seems entirely probable especially since 9b is a direct contradiction of 9a. If the critical consensus is correct, then Amos is the only prophet who is entirely a prophet of doom with no hope of restoration after judgment. Sayings like 5:6,14–15 and 7:3,6 are the only elements of the book which can be adduced as im-

[29] Eissfeldt, op. cit.; Martin Buber, *The Prophetic Faith* (paperback ed., New York, 1960); Curt Kuhl, *The Prophets of Israel* (Richmond, 1960); Gerhard von Rad, *Old Testament Theology* (New York, 1965); Eric Heaton, *The Old Testament Prophets* (Harmondsworth, 1958); Adolphe Lods, *The Prophets and the Rise of Judaism* (London, 1937).

[30] Eissfeldt, op. cit., 400–1.

plying a possibility of forgiveness; and Amos clearly does not regard this as a real possibility. His prophetic commission is to announce the reasons why Israel must submit to judgment; he does not make it clear why the judgment is annihilation. If he addresses Judah, it is only by indirection—again, if one accepts the critical consensus that the "Judahite" glosses are the work of scribes who made the application of the threats to Judah explicit. This totality of judgment does not mean that Amos denied the possibility of restoration; he simply does not mention it.

As the book is structured, Amos first deviously leads to the statement that Israel, like other peoples, is subject to a special judgment because of revolting crimes against humanity. The crime of Israel, which has the climactic position in the enumeration, is the oppression of the poor by the wealthy, who in Israel were identified with the court and the royal official aristocracy. And if one can sum up a book of such depth so briefly, this national vice of Israel is the theme of the book.[31] Like the other prophetic books, Amos is a compilation of sayings delivered on different occasions and consequently seems repetitious when it is read at one sitting. The dominant theme of admonition for social oppression is interrupted by threats of total destruction, already mentioned. In 4:6–11 Amos enumerates a series of natural disasters which should have been understood as punishments designed to correct the delinquent. They were not so understood, and in 4:12 Amos announces the final and supreme punishment, described simply and mysteriously as "meeting your God." What we miss in the enumeration is the prophet who is to interpret the natural disasters as judgments. Amos does not seem to think that such an interpreter was necessary; the Israelites knew Yahweh and his law well enough to recognize the signs of his displeasure. This is notably different from the Mesopotamian complaints that the gods have inflicted misfortune for reasons unknown to man.[32] Amos allows no excuse for uncertainty concerning the motives of Yahweh's anger.

[31] One of the most unfortunate comments in the history of exegesis was Jerome's remark that Amos ". . . as a peasant was unskilled in speech." *Commentariorum in Amos* (PL, v. 25 [Paris, 1884], 990).

[32] ANET 435.

Amos does not mention the covenant of Yahweh with Israel. It would have suited his message very well to treat the judgment as a fulfillment of the conditions of the covenant to which Israel had been unfaithful. Instead, he speaks of Yahweh's "knowing" Israel alone of all peoples (3:2), which must mean to recognize as his own; and this becomes a motive not of privilege but of punishment. While the exact words are not found, the thrust of the sayings of Amos, particularly 8:12, 9:4,7–8, is that the relation between Yahweh and Israel has been voided. This may be connected with the absence of any future hope for Israel. In Amos' understanding of history, there is nothing on which such a hope could be founded. There is no Israel; Amos did not have Ezekiel's vision of the valley of dry bones (Ezek 37). Since Amos was a Judahite, this did not mean for him that there was no longer any people of Yahweh. The crisis of Judah in the sixth century presented a more acute problem, and later prophets did not respond to this problem with the totality of Amos.

HOSEA

Hosea, like Amos, addressed the people of the kingdom of Israel; and these are the only two canonical prophets who spoke to the northern kingdom. The book presents an unusual number of textual and exegetical problems; the sayings have been collected with very little effort to find a principle of arrangement, and indications of date and occasion are entirely lacking. Hence it is more difficult to sum up the thrust of the sayings of Hosea.

It is clear, however, that the entire prophetic message of Hosea is dominated by his own unhappy matrimonial experience. His insight was that Yahweh's experience of Israel was the experience of a man whose wife is faithless. In Israelite law, as in all ancient Near Eastern codes known to us, adultery was punished by death; but the laws as well as other literary indications show that the supreme penalty could be evaded if the husband did not wish to press the charge. Hosea represents Yahweh as the offended spouse whose love is not extinguished by the offense. Hence Hosea in the dominant image of his prophetic speech exhibits what is missing in Amos, a hope of forgiveness and escape from judgment. As the compilers have arranged the sayings, a certain dramatic order appears in a collection which, as we have seen, shows no principle of arrangement. The effect produced is a portrait of Yahweh experiencing a conflict of emotions, torn between his sentimental love of an unworthy Israel and his own righteousness in judgment. In this emotional conflict righteous judgment finally prevails (13:9–16), and the decision to destroy Israel is as grim and uncompromising as the conclusion of Amos.[33]

As far as one can define the thrust of the sayings of Hosea, it is determined by the parable of marriage. The cardinal sin of Israel is infidelity to Yahweh, that is, the cult of other gods. It is somewhat remarkable that Amos has very few allusions to this (e.g., Amos 5:26, 8:14). Certainly Hosea seems to echo Elijah and Elisha; but the type of compromise religion patronized by the dynasty of Omri perished with that dynasty. One may speak of a "Baalization" of the worship of Yahweh, and indeed many writers have spoken of it. The words of Hosea about the unfaithful wife suggest something more than the cult of Yahweh with some of the attributes of the Baal. On the other hand, Hosea does not say or imply that the Israelites abandoned the cult of Yahweh for the cult of the Baal. Nothing is left but the introduction of polytheism into Israel; and it is impossible for us to determine the extent to which polytheistic cults were practiced. One would think that the royal sanctuaries of Bethel and Dan were sanctuaries of Yahweh; Amos speaks with some contempt of both of these, but Hosea does not mention them. His references to the "calf" are all located in Samaria (8:5–6, 10:5–6) except 13:2; and this verse does not locate the calf in any other place. Hence we have here a recrudescence of the Baalism of Samaria patronized by the dynasty of Omri in the royal city for its Canaanite population.

Hosea does not share the emphasis of Amos on the oppression of the poor and the weak. Since he spoke a generation after Amos, whose probably brief career is to be located late in the prosperous and orderly reign of Jeroboam II, he reflects the much more dis-

[33] John L. McKenzie, "Divine Passion in Osee," CathBiblQuart, 17 (1955), 287–99.

orderly conditions of the period which followed Jeroboam. He hints rather broadly at a general breakdown of law and order as well as of public morality (4:1–3, 7:1). These allusions can be quite easily placed in the dynastic conspiracies and feuds which are reported in 2 Kings 15:8–31 (Hos 10:3, 13:10–11). Hosea does not draw an explicit connection between the polytheism of Israel and the breakdown of public order and morality.

Hosea's final chapter discloses a dim vision of the future; this chapter, brief as it is, will come up for discussion in Chapter VII, "The Future of Israel." We have pointed out that the highly personal character of the relation of Yahweh and Israel as Hosea conceives it almost demands such a dim vision. Amos does not demand a restoration. Hosea's future lies entirely outside the field of history. There is no imaginable series of events which could bring to pass the reconciliation which he sees, and in this sense his vision of the future is eschatological.

MICAH

Even among the prophets the book of Micah is remarkably impersonal and reveals nothing about him except that he was a Judahite and contemporary of Isaiah. The central message of Micah is somewhat obscured by some critical problems;[34] there is a growing consensus among modern critics that very little need be regarded as secondary in the book. Micah charges both Israel and Judah with polytheistic cults, the oppression of the poor, especially by the acquisition of large holdings of land, the perversion of justice, dishonesty, and a breakdown of public order. The threats of Micah are quite vague; like the threats of earlier prophets, they predict invasion by foreign nations. Micah (3:12) has a singular and unparalleled threat of the total destruction of Jerusalem, so rare in early prophecy that it was remembered and quoted in favor of Jeremiah when he uttered a similar threat over a hundred years later (Jer 26:17–19). The sacred character of Zion as the place which Yahweh had chosen for his dwelling seems to have become a commonplace in Judah, particularly after the fall of Samaria.

[34] Eissfeldt, op. cit., 409–12.

We shall meet it again in the message of Isaiah, who has left no threat as uncompromising as Micah 3:12.

Chapters 4 to 7 contain rebukes and threats interspersed with promises of victory. Critical questions have been raised concerning the originality of these promises.[35] The discussion of these passages appears in Chapter VII, "The Future of Israel."

ISAIAH

While the dates generally assigned to Isaiah put his career between 740 and 700 B.C., it is difficult to be sure of the date of any of his sayings outside of the first few and the last few years of this period. The sayings which can be dated with some assurance refer to the Syro-Ephraimite war of 735 and the invasion of Sennacherib in 701. These were two political crises for Judah, and Isaiah speaks more to the political situation than any of the prophets who preceded him. Here, as in other prophetic books, there are critical problems. Without treating these in detail, we can limit ourselves to the major portions of Isaiah 1–12 and 28–33 and the narratives of Isaiah 36–39 (= 2 Kings 18:13 to 20:19, with some variations).

The political direction of many of the sayings of Isaiah can be explained by a reference to the political situation in which he lived. The Assyrian expansion which began with the accession of Tiglath-pileser III in 745 had nearly reached its ultimate limits with the campaign of Sennacherib in 705–701.[36] In this expansion the kingdom of Israel perished in 721 and became an Assyrian province. Judah became a vassal of Assyria when Ahaz invoked the aid of the Assyrians against Israel and Damascus in 735. The rebellion of Hezekiah in league with other small states in 705 issued in the reassertion of Assyrian overlordship, which continued with no relaxation until about 630. Hence Assyria was the most powerful influence on Judahite life and religion, and it appears clearly or dimly in the background of almost everything Isaiah said. Assyria

[35] Ibid.
[36] Noth, op. cit., 253–69.

was a secular power of a strength and magnitude greater than anything Israel had experienced since its appearance in Canaan.

We have already noticed that the inaugural vision of Isaiah does not entirely correspond with his collected words (6:9–13). The moral rebukes of Isaiah are well summed up in the woes of 5:8–24 and 10:1–3. These rebukes echo Amos and Micah; they are directed at land monopoly, drinking and carousing, unbelief, perversion of morality, bribery, perversion of law and justice. Isaiah says little of polytheistic cults in Judah, although he does advert to superstitious rites of a character which cannot be determined (1:29, 2:8,18,20). Like Amos 4:1–3, he speaks with unexpected harshness against frivolity, especially against frivolous women (3:16–17, 24–26, 22:12–14). This frivolity becomes particularly revolting when it is combined with careless wickedness or unbelief. The threats which correspond to the rebukes are also the standard threats of natural and political disasters. These threats, however, are not uttered with the certainty of Amos and Hosea. Isaiah calls to repentance and offers a program by which Judah may escape the judgment which it has earned by its infidelity.

The response of Isaiah both to the threat of Israel and Damascus in 735, a threat elicited by the approach of Assyria, and to the invasion of Sennacherib in 701 was the same; it was a recommendation of faith (7:9) and trust in Yahweh with no political or military action, neither the invocation of Assyrian aid in 735 nor an alliance with Egypt in 701 (28:7–29, 30:1–17, 31:1–3). No politician could find such a recommendation anything but unrealistic, and the national vice against which Isaiah speaks most frequently and most severely is the refusal to believe that the posture of Judah before Yahweh had anything to do with its political welfare. Isaiah does not promise military victory or a restoration of the empire of David, but simply survival in a crisis. Unbelief in this crisis was a denial that Yahweh was interested in saving Judah or that he could save it if he were interested.

Isaiah never clearly speaks of Assyria as the power which will destroy Judah, and here he is in sharp contrast with Amos and Hosea. No total fall of Judah can be found in his words. Assyria is a threat which can punish Judah severely (7:17–25, 28:18–22, 29:2–4, 30:13–14,17), but Yahweh will arrest its power before it can destroy the nation completely. Assyria itself exhibits pride and unbelief to a degree which demands the judgment of Yahweh, and his judgment is manifested in his defense of Jerusalem (10:5–19, 31:4–5,8–9). Now the narrative of Isaiah 36 and 37 presents Isaiah as speaking exactly in the same terms as the royal or court prophets of the ninth century. There is no rebuke of the sins of the rulers and of the people, but a simple oracle of deliverance. The verification of this oracle by the events presents a historical problem which biblical theology cannot solve;[37] but biblical theology must notice that according to the Assyrian records as well as the biblical, Jerusalem was not captured, the kingdom of Judah was not destroyed like the kingdom of Israel, but survived to remain a vassal of Assyria for the next seventy years. This is not exactly a glorious deliverance, but neither is it total destruction. The Isaiah of the narratives is not entirely consistent with the Isaiah of the collection of sayings, but neither in fact is the Isaiah of the collection entirely consistent with himself. One may reconstruct a change in his attitude which varied from an early position (6:9–13) as rigorous as the position of Amos to a recognition that the people of Yahweh could not perish and leave the world to be governed by a power which did not recognize Yahweh. It is doubtful that the Isaiah of Isaiah 36 and 37 is as historical as the Isaiah of the collection of sayings, just as the withdrawal of Sennacherib from Jerusalem has been transformed in the narrative into an unhistorical event. The event was the outstanding example of the prediction of an unexpected deliverance by a prophet which was vindicated by the issue. The "deliverance" should be qualified by a reference to Isaiah 1:6–9, which may and could describe the country after the invasion of Sennacherib, who took forty-six fortified cities,[38] and by the establishment of Assyrian overlordship over Judah. Perhaps the most distinctive and the most enduring contribution of Isaiah to the prophetic message is found in his declaration that political and military action could not preserve Judah in its most severe crisis. This established a principle which other prophets maintained and applied in different situations.

[37] Brevard S. Childs, *Isaiah and the Assyrian Crisis,* Studies in Biblical Theology, 2nd Series, 3 (London, 1967); Bright, op. cit., 282–87.
[38] ANET 288.

The chapters identified as First Isaiah contain a number of sayings which promise deliverance. Not all of these are certainly expansions. They will be treated in Chapter VI, Section 2, "The Monarchy"—Isaiah had a special interest in the dynasty of David—and in Chapter VII.

ZEPHANIAH

Zephaniah is dated in the reign of Josiah and before the cultic reforms instituted by Josiah in 621. His brief message is a threat against Judah and Jerusalem; on the threats against foreign nations see Section 7, "Yahweh and the Nations," in the following chapter. Judah and Jerusalem are rebuked for various forms of polytheistic cults and for oppressions for which religious and civic leaders are responsible. The period of Assyrian vassalage was a period of the patronage of foreign cults in Jerusalem.

Zephaniah presents the judgment as "the day of Yahweh," a theme which first appears in Amos 5:18–20 and is repeated in Isaiah 2:12–21. The theme ultimately becomes eschatological and is treated in Chapter VII. In these early prophets the theme is not eschatological, but represents the intervention of Yahweh in judgment upon Israel and Judah. Amos seems to invert its popular meaning, and it is generally thought that the original day of Yahweh was a day of victory and deliverance for Israel, perhaps a day commemorated in some regular festival. This would be a "judgment" in the sense of a vindication; the prophets turn it into a judgment in the sense of a condemnation.

In Zephaniah the judgment is not destructive but purgative. Jerusalem passed through a period of purification from which it emerges "humble and lowly" (3:12). This phrase is characteristic of the postexilic community and is a term in which that community described itself. The idea of purification is more probably a rationalization by which the postexilic community explained its survival.

NAHUM

This prophecy is entirely an "oracle against a foreign nation" and is treated in Section 7, "Yahweh and the Nations," in the following chapter.

HABAKKUK

This small book, most probably to be dated not much later than 625, presents an unusual number of critical and exegetical problems.[39] Chapter 3 is a psalm which belongs to the type of poem called "theophany," to be treated under the theology of nature. Habakkuk asks a general question concerning the failure of Yahweh to punish wickedness. There are roughly three answers. The first is the announcement of the coming of the Chaldeans as agents of judgment; since the Chaldeans were no threat to anyone before 625, this compels a date later than 625. The second answer is an encouragement to faith, summarized in the single line, "The righteous man shall live by faith" (2:4), quoted by Paul of Christian faith (Rom 1:17; Gal 3:11). "Faith" or fidelity here is the virtue by which one remains a believer in Yahweh and obedient to his law. The third is the series of five woes against the wicked. The woes are addressed to the moneylenders, the wealthy, the violent, the drunkards, and the worshipers of idols; these are much the same rebukes as we find in earlier prophets.

JEREMIAH

Jeremiah, we have noticed, is the prophet whose inner life and feelings are best known. He is also the prophet whose biography is best known.[40] The book of Jeremiah (the longest book of the

[39] Eissfeldt, op. cit., 417–20.
[40] John Bright, *Jeremiah*, Anchor Bible (Garden City, N.Y., 1965), lxxxvi–cxviii.

Old Testament) includes not only his collected sayings but also extensive anecdotes concerning his life, especially in the years during and after the collapse of the kingdom of Judah and afterwards. These chapters can be compared to the prophetic legends of Elijah and Elisha, with the important difference that the anecdotes of Jeremiah are much more reliable historically. In addition, there are some doublets in the sayings of Jeremiah; thus the temple discourse of chapter 7 is given in a more abbreviated form but with a full account of the situation and of the incidents which it provoked in chapter 26.

It is something of a commonplace to rate Jeremiah somewhat lower as a theologian and a poet than Amos, Hosea, and Isaiah. (Note, for example, Curt Kuhl: ". . . manifestly not a man of the stature of an Isaiah. His ideas are not as original as those of Hosea and theologically he has not the significance of Deutero-Isaiah."[41] The longer one studies Jeremiah, the less one is ready to share such patronizing judgments. Jeremiah was the interpreter of the most critical event in the entire history of Israel. No one believes that he failed to interpret the event in its full significance.

The career of Jeremiah began in the reign of Josiah, probably about 625, and continued past the fall of Jerusalem in 587 B.C. As for Isaiah, there is not much which can be dated certainly in his middle career, and most of the material comes from the reigns of Jehoiachim (609–598) and Zedekiah (597–587). The reader will notice that a lamentable lack of arrangement of the material makes his task no easier. In a modern edition he will also notice the mixture of prose and verse. The verse comprises prophetic sayings, most of them from Jeremiah; the prose comprises anecdotes, both biographical and autobiographical and prose summaries of discourses.

In spite of the length of the book, Jeremiah does not utter rebukes as sharp and precise as we find in Amos and Isaiah. He uses the figure of the adulterous wife, original with Hosea (Hos 2:2–20), to signify the adoption of polytheistic cults in Judah. The figure is worked out with less personal feeling than in Hosea, but with more candor. This theme is probably to be placed early

[41] *The Prophets of Israel,* 104.

in Jeremiah's career, before the cultic reform of Josiah in 622–621. He speaks of a general breakdown of honesty (5:1, 6:13) and even of that mutual confidence which is the cement of normal social relations (9:4–6). In such passages as these Jeremiah makes one ask whether the prophets at times did not overstate their case, as so many preachers have done. He does speak of the greed of the wealthy and the oppression of the poor, seen at an unusually vile level in the anecdote of the release and the repossession of the slaves of Jerusalem (34:8–22); but in one passage he fails to show the usual prophetic sympathy for the poor, finding them as wicked as the great (5:4–5). He charges the religious and civic leaders with failure in their responsibilities; and in particular he inveighs against the false prophets for their predictions of "peace" (6:14, 5:30–31), by which they deny the coming judgment of Yahweh, and against those who demand that the prophets speak what the people desire to hear. The most responsible leader is the king of Judah, and the compilers have collected a series of oracles about the kings, all but one hostile (22). Jeremiah was the first to announce the end of the dynasty of David in Judah (22:30); in treating the monarchy and the future of Israel we shall ask whether he ever revised this prophecy.

The prediction of the downfall of the dynasty of David is part of a larger pattern in which Jeremiah announces the end of all the political and social institutions of Judah: the monarchy, the temple and priesthood (7:1–15), the ark (3:16), prophecy (23: 33–40), and *torah* (31:33–34). For none of these does he announce a restoration—setting aside some critical questions concerning the monarchy. Like Amos, he predicts a total end; more than Amos, he specifies in detail the end of the most sacred and cherished institutions.

The threat of Jeremiah is the threat of a hostile invasion. The threat is vague in his early sayings, but after 605, the year in which Babylon was surely established as the major power of the Near East, the threat becomes specific.[42] Much of the collection is taken up with sayings which announce the certainty of the coming collapse. The incident of Hananiah (ch. 28) discloses that even at

---

[42] Bright, *History of Israel,* 303–6.

that late date a large number of people did not take the Babylonian threat seriously. The threat was as certain as the wickedness of Judah, which demanded judgment. Jeremiah seems to have no expectation that Judah would repent of its ingrained malice; it is the Ethiopian who cannot change his skin, the leopard which cannot change his spots (13:23). Jerusalem is the city which keeps its wickedness fresh, as a well keeps its water fresh (6:7). At one point in his career—reserving for later discussion the question of Jeremiah's view of the future of Israel—Jeremiah had no hope for his people except for the community which Nebuchadnezzar had exiled to Babylon (29:1-9). For Jerusalem and Judah and their population, nothing but ruin was announced.

In the certainty of this coming judgment, Jeremiah made a statement which ran directly counter to the political and military defense of the nation and which imperiled his life. Since the Babylonians were the agents of Yahweh's wrath, who would rise from sickbeds if necessary to take the city (37:9-10), resistance to them was resistance to Yahweh. Organized military defense only compounded the wickedness of Judah. Since the government had betrayed its subjects by resistance, Jeremiah advised the individual soldiers to desert (38:1-6). No explanation of the response of the government to this prophetic word is necessary; at the same time, no criticism of the logic of Jeremiah is possible. No clearer statement of the morality of the unjust war has ever been made so briefly; the statement is not paralleled elsewhere in the prophetic canon. It is the final inversion of the ancient image of Yahweh the warrior.

When Jeremiah's selected sayings are reviewed in summary, it may appear that he is the most radical of the prophets since Amos. He is the most radical, surely, in the practical application of the prophetic sayings; for effectively, he denied that Judah could claim either the religious or the political allegiance of its subjects. He thus raised the question of the personal relation of the individual to Yahweh, a problem which recurs for Ezekiel. Both of these prophets see no religious structure enduring in which the individual person can hope to achieve communion with Yahweh. It is for this reason principally that we shall maintain that some oracles of Jeremiah which touch this problem must be accepted as authentic. Ezekiel, as we shall see—or one of his continuators—has a detailed description of the restored structure. Jeremiah has no such detailed reconstruction. As we shall see in treating the future of Israel, he does have vision of a future. In this he goes beyond the rigor of Amos and at the same time escapes the ambiguity of Isaiah concerning the future. The man who lacks the stature of Isaiah and the originality of Hosea and the theological importance of Second Isaiah actually brought together in a single strand all the prophetic threads which were in his hands. One cannot go to Second Isaiah except through Jeremiah.

EZEKIEL

It has already been noticed that the book of Ezekiel presents complicated critical problems.[43] In this case the critical problems do obscure the theological interpretation of the prophet; it does make a difference whether Ezekiel spoke in Jerusalem or in Babylon or in both, and it makes a considerable difference whether the book is a hundred and fifty years earlier or two to three hundred years later; both extremes have been proposed. Hence our summary of Ezekiel must remain within rather general lines.

Of all the prophets whom we have reviewed, Ezekiel is easily the most general and the least specific in his accusations. There are a few occasional enumerations (e.g., 22:6–12) which resemble a list of commandments. Particular allusions are most frequently concerned with religious sins; idolatry is frequently charged, and this is somewhat remarkable when Ezekiel is compared with his contemporary Jeremiah. The most extended as well as the most interesting and difficult passage which deals with this topic is the temple vision of chapter 8. It is quite difficult to identify the rites and the apparatus mentioned in this chapter; and there is no clear answer to the question why this vision of Ezekiel should be represented as a miraculous transport from Babylon.

Unlike his predecessors, Ezekiel treats the entire history of Israel as apostasy from the beginning. This is seen in his two allegories of the unfaithful wife in chapters 16 and 23 and in the discourse

43 G. Fohrer, *Ezekiel*, HAT, 13 (Tübingen, 1955), vii–xix.

of chapter 20. In contrast to this pessimistic view, one may cite Hosea 2:15 and Jeremiah 2:2–3. In this view of total and radical depravity, it is possible that Ezekiel speaks of superstitions which did not exist at the time he spoke. Punishment is certain for ample grounds; Ezekiel has as deep a certainty of judgment as any prophet. He seems to think about Judah as one might think of a man who has committed many murders; if the man is executed for one, it does not make much difference which one it is.

Ezekiel's view of the judgment becomes what we shall have to call "theocentric" for lack of a better word, since I do not wish to imply that Yahweh is peripheral in the other prophets. By this I mean that Ezekiel interprets the events in terms of the "glory" (the manifest holiness) of Yahweh with almost no reference to the further history of Israel. Israel suffers defeat and exile in order that the righteous judgment of Yahweh may be recognized, and in Ezekiel's view of the restoration, Israel is restored not for its own sake but that it may be a witness to the saving power of Yahweh. This is the burden of the refrain so frequent in Ezekiel: ". . . that you (they) may know that I am Yahweh." This rigorous theocentrism gives Ezekiel a somewhat hard and unfeeling tone. Israel is not so much a "witness" in the sense of a person who attests as it is "evidence," an object from which one draws conclusions.

Ezekiel, like his predecessors, reserves his harshest words for those who have the obligation of leadership. He too inveighs against the prophets of "peace" (13:1–6), the same prophets with whom Jeremiah was engaged. In one poem in the form of a dirge he bewails the last kings of the dynasty of David (19:1–4). In this poem, like Jeremiah, the fall of the dynasty is seen with no prospect of a future restoration. Yet these kings are not charged with any specific crimes; they are simply the heirs of the long tradition of wickedness which dominates the thinking of Ezekiel.

Like Jeremiah, Ezekiel faced the problem which the collapse of the political and religious structures created for the individual Judahite. Two parallel versions (18:1–32 and 33:1–20) of the solution have not been favorably received by interpreters. The complaints of the injustice of collective guilt is expressed by Ezekiel's contemporaries in the proverb of the fathers and the children and the sour grapes (18:2), quoted also in Jeremiah 31:29. Ezekiel's response is a flat affirmation of a due proportion between innocence and guilt on the one side to deliverance and death on the other. This solution resembles the doctrine of the friends of Job so closely that interpreters think it evades the problem. It is unrealistic, since it denies the obvious fact that all men are to some degree involved in collective guilt; we do suffer for the sins of others. In Ezekiel's doctrine only the guilty perished in the fall of Jerusalem, and only the innocent escaped. The difference between one group and the other is not final; the righteous may turn wicked and the wicked may turn righteous, and in neither case will former righteousness or wickedness be taken into account. This further rationalization allows the prophet to explain difficult cases. Yet ultimately the effort is clumsy and must be regarded, like the doctrine of Job's friends, as a denial of the problem rather than a solution.

The solution of the problem, whether it is to be attributed to Ezekiel or to his compilers, is the vision of the future in the last portion of the book. This future, as we shall see in more detail, is simply the restoration of the earlier structures. Thus Ezekiel really has no message of personal religion for those whom he addresses, the Judahites exiled in Babylon. Apparently he thinks of the Palestinian survivors of the catastrophe as not involved. Effectively they are dead and irrelevant, even if by mere accident they have survived.

SECOND ISAIAH

Second Isaiah indicates the unknown author of Isaiah 40–55, whose sayings were uttered in Babylon about 550–545 B.C. The entire content of these chapters is best treated in Chapter VII, "The Future of Israel." This itself raises something of a problem, for the arrangement may seem to imply that Second Isaiah had no message for his own contemporaries. In fact, the message was an emphatic assurance that Israel would endure beyond them and that nothing deserved their fidelity more than the future prospects of Israel, which most of them could hardly expect to live to see.

Their warrant of fidelity, however, would be found in the unexpected restoration of the people of Yahweh, which would happen in the very near future.

HAGGAI

Haggai's sayings are dated in 520 B.C., seventeen years after Jerusalem was resettled by Jews returned from Babylon. It is easily evident that in him the character of prophecy has changed. There are no rebukes against religious, political, and moral corruption. His almost exclusive concern is the rebuilding of the temple. Since the rebuilding of the temple was included in the decree of Cyrus in 538 permitting the resettlement of Jerusalem (Ezra 1:2), there was some room for the prophet's impatience. He attributes the poverty and misfortunes of the struggling community to this failure; and the community, moved by his exhortation, finished the temple within the next five years. To those who thought the temple was an inferior restoration of Solomon's temple, Haggai responds with a prediction that this temple would receive the treasures of the nations. This prediction is akin to such passages as Isaiah 49:22–23, 60:5–6,13–17, but no literary dependence is implied; the restoration of Zion is one of the themes of Chapter VII, "The Future of Israel," and it is discussed there. The failure to rebuild the temple keeps the people unclean. The sayings conclude with a messianic restoration of the dynasty of David in Zerubbabel; this theme appears more fully in Zechariah.

ZECHARIAH 1–8

Zechariah 1–8 is dated 520–518 B.C.; Zechariah 9–14 (Deutero-Zechariah) is assigned by critics to another author notably later.[44] As in Haggai, one can discern a notable change in the character of prophecy. Most of these chapters are concerned with the eight night visions of the prophet; in these, symbolism and allegory are used as they are in no earlier prophetic work. The visions represent

---

[44] Eissfeldt, op. cit., 435–40.

the restoration of Judah and Jerusalem; and while this topic must be treated in Chapter VII, "The Future of Israel," it may be noted here that the restoration of Zechariah envisages the restoration of most of the important institutions of the past—the temple, the priesthood, and the dynasty of David in Zerubbabel. Almost all critics and historians think that the coronation scene of 6:9–14 has been altered from the original text so that the coronation now happens to the priest Joshua instead of Zerubbabel.[45] The moral exhortations of Zechariah are limited to 8:16–17; however, Zechariah's interpretation of the exile as the work of Yahweh's judgment on the wickedness of Judah is an indirect moral exhortation (1:2–6, 7:8–14). The moral purification of Judah is described in the vision of the woman Wickedness hidden in an ephah which is transported to Babylon, where it is set up as an idol (5:5–11).

MALACHI

Malachi is not the name of the prophet but the title of the book, derived from "my messenger" (3:1), perhaps meant as a title of the author. He can be dated no more closely than the period 500–450 B.C. The book falls easily into six sections or discourses: Yahweh's love of Jacob and hatred of Edom—the statement of election; the rebuke of the priests for offering unworthy and defective victims; condemnation of divorce; rebuke of those who doubt the effectiveness of the judgment of Yahweh; explanation of misfortunes as due to the failure to pay tithes; another statement of the certainty of divine judgment, distinguishing between the reward of the righteous and the punishment of evildoers. This distinction between the true and the false Israelites appears also in Third Isaiah. Like Haggai and Zechariah, the interests of Malachi are cultic rather than moral, and religious integrity is more closely identified with proper cultic observances. Malachi's brief references to the future of Israel are discussed in Chapter VII.

[45] Sigmund Mowinckel, *He That Cometh* (New York, 1954), 119–22, 160–62.

THIRD ISAIAH 56-66

Isaiah 56-66 are not the work of a single author; Third Isaiah is simply a convenient name to distinguish a collection which comes from various hands.[46] All the pieces are most probably to be dated in the period 500-450 B.C., the period which lies between the rebuilding of Jerusalem and the temple at one end and Nehemiah on the other. This period is without documentation except for the prophetic passages which are to be assigned to it.

Third Isaiah is concerned with cultic observances (56:1-2, 58:1-14); these passages may be compared to Haggai, Zechariah, and Malachi. But the poem of 58:1-12 is an attack in the style of the pre-exilic prophets on cultic observance maintained with no attention to the law of Yahweh or to the relations between man and man. Failure to maintain good human relations—for example, between rich and poor, owner and tenant, lender and borrower—is the reason why the salvation promised to the community is delayed (59:1-20). In 66:1-4 appears the most candid and unqualified attack on cultic observances as such in the entire Old Testament. One may explain this singular polemic by supposing that to this writer the priests had become simply invalid and incompetent mediators between the community and Yahweh; see Malachi 1:6-2:9.

Third Isaiah exhibits "the piety of the poor," a theological view paralleled in several of the psalms, a scheme in which "poor" and "needy" become synonymous with "righteous" and "pious." In the early phase of the postexilic community, the phrases could probably have been applied to the community as a whole as well as to its individual members. By the time of Third Isaiah the "poor" were not the entire community but a class within the community—a majority in numbers, possibly, but still a class. A smaller class of the wealthy and powerful had appeared which controlled land ownership, employment, and moneylending. The attitude of the postexilic prophets towards the priests suggests that the priestly class had acquired a considerable portion of the available wealth.

[46] McKenzie, *Second Isaiah*, xviii-xxiii.

The poor were the genuine Israelites; the rich and powerful were spurious Israelites. This distinction profoundly affected the eschatology of the writers of Third Isaiah. No future collective judgment such as that of the exile could be envisaged for the future; this would be a mere re-enactment of what had already happened. The judgment of the future, which would be apocalyptic, would sort out the good for reward and the wicked for punishment; see in particular chapters 65–66. This topic will again be discussed under the heading of "The Future of Israel." Both the eschatological judgment and the "piety of the poor" had important lasting echoes; see, for example, Matthew 5:3–6; Luke 6:20–21, in which the titles used are all synonymous with "poor."

Third Isaiah exhibits in some passages a remarkable tolerance toward foreign peoples, announcing the admission of foreigners not only to the community of Israel (56:3–7) and to worship at Zion, but even to the priesthood and the Levitical order (66:18–21). Critics generally locate this attitude of ecumenical breadth in the postexilic period; it is found also in Ruth and Jonah and is in obvious contrast to the oracles against the nations and the Deuteronomic attitude towards foreign nations; see Section 7, "Yahweh and the Nations," in the following chapter. In Third Isaiah one may easily assume that the attitude grows out of Second Isaiah's idea of the mission of Israel (see Chapter VII) and out of the distinction between the genuine and the spurious Israel. Since legitimacy of descent and position in the community no longer designate the true Israelite, the qualification of moral character and sincere worship of Yahweh make the Gentile acceptable to Yahweh rather than the Israelite who lacks both the character and the worship.

JONAH

This book does not really belong among the prophets; the name of its hero is found in 2 Kings 14:25, but the fictitious story belongs after the exile. The parable is a form proper to wisdom rather than to prophecy. It is not without interest that Jonah is the only prophetic book besides Jeremiah which contains an inner personal conflict between the prophet and his mission; but this is accessory to the story. The prophet is unwilling to offer a chance of repentance and forgiveness to the Assyrians, the ancient enemies of Israel and Judah, extinct by the time the book was written. The answer of Yahweh is that his compassion is extended even to the Assyrians—and even to their animals. The Assyrians, like the Samaritans in the New Testament (Lk 10:29-37; John 4:7-42), were the most unlikely objects of compassion which could be proposed. The story seems to run directly counter to the ancient theology of election and covenant; and in addition, the author implies rather obviously that the Assyrians might have repented had they had a prophet as Israel did; Israel refused to repent after it had heard the prophets. As we have noticed in Third Isaiah, the author has begun to evaluate men's position to Yahweh according to their response to the word of Yahweh and not according to their ethnic and religious groupings.

JOEL

This entire book is best treated with apocalyptic in Chapter VII, "The Future of Israel."

OBADIAH

This book is discussed in Section 7, "Yahweh and the Nations," in the following chapter.

DEUTERO-ZECHARIAH 9-14

This book is treated with apocalyptic in Chapter VII, "The Future of Israel."

Summary

Perhaps the most obvious feature of the prophetic message seen in summary is that the prophetic charisma in its classical form arose while the kingdoms of Israel and Judah both enjoyed national sovereignty, endured through the crises in which both kingdoms came to an end, and weakened and disappeared in the period when Judea was a province of the Persian Empire. Plainly, the prophetic message was addressed with most vigor to a people who enjoyed the power of national self-determination. The demands made by Amos, Hosea, Isaiah, and Jeremiah were important and urgent; they called for decisions on the national level, decisions which determined not only foreign and domestic policy but the very character of a people in crisis—the crisis compared by Hosea (13:13) to the crisis of birth. The earlier prophets spoke to a people which could decide what its future would be. Ezekiel and Jeremiah spoke to a people who were making that decision—for a failure to decide is itself a decision. Second Isaiah still sees a possibility of self-determination; the people can accept the mission which Second Isaiah has discovered for Israel. When one turns to Haggai, Zechariah, and Malachi one turns to prophets whose positive calls are for ritual correctness plus a few conventional moral imperatives drawn from earlier prophets, and who otherwise dream of a future which will not be determined by the people to whom they speak. Amos, Micah, and Jeremiah announced the destruction of the temples; Haggai pleads for the collection of funds to build a temple. It is enough to make one wonder whether we can speak of the same prophetic charisma in all these men. In modern times similar questions of priority have been raised; and it may be recalled that the sale of indulgences which sparked the Protestant revolt was carried on to collect funds to finish the basilica of Saint Peter. The modern Roman Church may recover from the Protestant revolt before it rids itself of the marble barn which is a monument to papal ambition and vanity. Except for Third Isaiah, the moral indignation of the earlier prophets burns at a low flame in their postexilic successors.

Within this general sequence, which may be called a sequence of deterioration, some rather clear patterns emerge in the progress of prophecy. No pre-exilic prophet offers Israel and Judah a cheap and easy way to escape the judgment. In none of them is there any doubt that the judgment is certain or that it is deserved. Within this consensus there is some variety in the responses. Amos simply expects no improvement; he has only to announce and to explain the judgment. Hosea likewise expects no improvement; his "emotional conflict" mentioned above does not revolve around the possibility of a conversion of Israel, but around the possibility, recognized as unreal, that Yahweh might let his heart run away with his head, to use an anthropomorphism no cruder than the anthropomorphisms of Hosea. Isaiah entertains, as we have seen, the possibility of an escape from judgment, or at least from this particular judgment of which the Assyrians are the agents; we have observed an unsatisfactory ambiguity in his attitude as it can be seen in his preserved words. But this ambiguity, if it is there, should be matched with his absolute assurance that the kingdom of Judah takes means to escape judgment which are not only wrong but ineffective. A nation under judgment cannot escape judgment by the skills of politics and war, and that nation compounds its guilt by its attempts to escape. It is really an easy step from the position of Isaiah to the practical recommendation of Jeremiah: if the nation obliges you to serve in a war which is an attempt to escape from a deserved judgment, it is your duty to desert. The prophets do not measure the guilt of Israel or Judah against the guilt of Assyria or Babylon, and modern readers may think that this is a massive defect in their moral analysis. They measure the guilt of Israel and Judah against the absolute standards of the law, the covenant, and the word of Yahweh. The failure of the people of Yahweh to meet the demands of Yahweh deprives them of their right to resist aggression; for the aggressors are the agents of Yahweh.

The nation can escape the judgment only by conversion; and the full meaning of the word should be noticed, since it means much more than accepting membership in a church or the renunciation of certain gross bad habits. For Jeremiah conversion was the change of the skin of the leopard or of the pigmentation of the black man and therefore altogether unlikely. It meant a moral revolution of a dimension so radically different from the dimension of experience that its fulfillment was ultimately considered as possible only in the eschatological age. But this "ultimate" view was the view of despair born of history; the prophets, we may be sure, exhorted no one to attempt the unreal. Were such a moral revolution entirely unreal, the prophetic message would make no sense. To many who think it is unreal and asks too much of feeble nature, the prophetic message makes no sense. The cost of national conversion is beyond calculation; if it could be calculated, one could be sure that conversion was not yet accomplished.

The reward of conversion is vaguely stated by the prophets. Isaiah (1:19) offers the rather modest assurance: "If you are willing and obedient, you shall eat the good of the land." The fruit of conversion is not empire or even modest military victory; it is not wealth, nor even the exotically abundant eschatological prosperity of the time when the plowman shall overtake the reaper (Amos 9:13). The fruit of conversion is simply the survival of Israel as a nation. Evidently, the mere survival would be meaningless unless Yahweh revealed a purpose for the modest remnant beyond that which Israel knew in its traditions of election and convenant. Actually, such a purpose is not stated before Second Isaiah stated it; and no other postexilic prophet produced any other statement of purpose. Israel had to have a purpose to survive; this did not make it different from other nations, which had no purpose and did not survive. Neither for Israel nor for the nations did the prophets consider that mere national existence was a primary end which needed no further explanation. Israel and Judah under their monarchies had lost any purpose and any justification for their national existence; for such meaningless nations to practice war and politics was a sin.

As a whole, the canon of prophetic literature grows in intensity of the realization of judgment. In this it follows the course of Israelite and Judahite history during the period of the classical prophets. The idea of national and religious institutions as vehicles of salvation simply disappears with the march of events. The prophets really do not give a code of behavior for politics, external or internal. Politics as understood and practiced, either in ancient Israel and Judah or in the modern world, includes a compromise with evil for which the rigorous moralism of the prophets leaves no room. Whatever the prophets had to say about a restoration of Israel, they have no idea of a restoration of that political-religious reality which perished finally in 587 B.C. We shall see what the future of Israel did mean, and we shall observe that ideas of the future of Israel took several forms, ranging from the quite realistic messianism of the cultic community of the Chronicler and the priestly code to the fancies of apocalyptic literature. Actually, the classical prophets contributed very little to the forms of the future of Israel. The type of national decision to which they spoke was not to be realized again.

4. *The Inspired Book*

In the postexilic community of Palestine, the community which was the embryo from which Judaism developed, revelation took on a new form which has had permanent effects both in Judaism and in Christianity. The Old Testament itself, as we have attempted to show in the preceding discussions, knows only the revelation of covenant law and the revelation of the word of Yahweh spoken by the prophets. In the books of the Old Testament are collected the laws and the sayings of the prophets; the writers of these books clearly thought that Yahweh had spoken to the men whose words were collected, but not to the scribes who collected the books. In addition, narratives were collected which, as we shall see in the following chapter, were intended to recount the Israelite experience of the work of Yahweh in the history of Israel. Besides these there were collected the cultic directions and cultic hymns and prayers; in these Israel responded to Yahweh. A last category was the collection of wise sayings. These also we shall discuss under a separate heading, and we shall note that the collection of wise sayings is an ancient form of literature far older than anything in the Bible.

In none of these areas is the claim made that the writing itself is "inspired"; and the theory of inspired composition is clearly an application of the prophetic experience to the work of the scribe. This application was made somewhere in the period between the restoration of the Jerusalem community and the New Testament, for it appears in the New Testament and in the rabbinical writings.[47] The rabbinical writings exhibit the belief that prophecy

[47] H. Strack and P. Billerbeck, *Kommentar zum Neuen Testament*, v. IV,

ceased with Malachi, the last of the twelve; actually, we cannot be sure that Malachi is the latest prophetic book, and the belief presupposes the collection of the prophetic canon. But the collection of the prophetic canon cannot be dated except within wide limits. The belief of the rabbis is a part of the process by which postexilic Judaism became a community of law and cult, both of them based upon a collection of books which had become sacred. A sacred book is not precisely the same thing as an inspired book, particularly since the definition of inspiration in this use can be extremely ambiguous. In its earliest (and most enduring) form, it was very probably a belief that the inspired scribe wrote what God dictated to him. This too indicates complications in the development of the belief. Moses could not be regarded as the inspired writer of the Law (identical with the five books of Moses) until these five books had been assembled into a whole and attributed to him. The books themselves represent Moses as an inspired speaker but not as an inspired writer. Once the quality of inspiration was attached to the collection of "sacred" books, it was necessary to find inspired writers, and these were found among the great men of Israelite history: Moses, Joshua, Samuel, David, Solomon, and the prophets. These were sufficient to explain the origin of the books, since no one was asking critical questions. Inspiration was not attributed to the postexilic scribes who, it must be assumed, were principally responsible for the compilation of the sacred books. It could only be attributed to the great men of the past, for the idea of the collection was involved with the belief that revelation had ended. Thus it did not occur to the grandson of Sirach that his grandfather was an inspired writer. A careful reading of the prologue of Sirach does not suggest that he thought the other books were inspired either; and there is no doubt that what he meant by "the law, the prophets and the other books" is substantially the collection of the Old Testament.

It remains impossible to discern why and how the belief in inspiration was attached to the scribes as well as to Moses and the prophets; no foreign influence can be recognized which would have

---

1 (Munich, 1965), 435–51; G. Moore, *Judaism*, v. 1 (Cambridge, Mass., 1962), 235–50.

led to the belief, and, as we have seen, the books themselves do not even imply such a claim. We may speculate, but it is mere speculation, that the Jews responded to the obvious merits of classical Greek literature with the claim that their own books were written by the dictation of God himself. This antithesis can be seen in Josephus' defense of the quality of Jewish literature;[48] Josephus does not precisely claim inspiration, but he does affirm that the credibility of the books is based on "the exact succession of the prophets."

I spoke of enduring effects of this belief in sacred and inspired books. The first we may notice is that God is not thought to speak to the living generation; all that God has to say to mankind has already been said and it is preserved in writing. This imposes the necessity of making the writing relevant to the living generation. The first step in this process is to detach the writing from its roots in history and to give it a timeless quality; for in the hypothesis that the literature is a complete and final package of revelation, it cannot be admitted that God took a deeper interest in men of past ages than he does in the living generation. The writings cannot be simply read by those to whom they are not addressed; they must be interpreted, and interpretation at once demands experts. But the experts cannot be really charismatic, for by hypothesis the power of uttering God's word is no longer communicated to man.

The word of God is proclaimed not by the prophet but by the scribe and the teacher, the student and the expositor of the inspired books. And since the charisma of the scribe and teacher is technique, then there comes with the scribe and teacher a system of tradition, school or schools in which the technique and the learning it produces are preserved, expanded and transmitted. Since there is no other channel of revelation except the sacred books, the scribes and teachers have a monopoly of revelation, although they themselves never claim to utter revelation. But they do claim to be the ultimate judges of revelation, and thus the ultimate judges of religious belief and practice.

The theology of inspiration thus does not belong to the theology

[48] *Contra Apionem* 1, 8.

of the Old Testament except as it deals with the inspiration of the prophet. It does belong to the theology of the New Testament, and there it cannot be understood unless the New Testament acceptance of inspiration is understood as a part of the Jewish heritage of the New Testament. This does not mean that Christian teaching introduced no modification into the belief in inspiration; but many treatments of the subject fail to attend to the Jewish origins of the belief. The books of Ezra and Nehemiah indicate that the construction of the temple alone was not sufficient to assure unity and stability in the struggling community of Jerusalem. Once the belief and cult of the community were based on an authoritative collection of sacred books interpreted by acknowledged experts, Judaism found the key to survival and to strength.

III

History

1. *General Remarks*

It has been said, I forget by whom, that the only historical religions are Judaism, Christianity and Islam; all other religions are mythological. Equivalently, as we shall see below, this means that all other religions are nature religions; Judaism and the two religions which have originated at least in part from Judaism experience God primarily in history rather than in nature. History is used in two senses, either as event or as record of events; we speak of the experience of God in history as the experience of God in events, but in discussing the theology of history in the Old Testament we mean the theology of the record of the events.

A consciousness of history, meaning the historical character of events, and the ability to write history, the record of events, is the exceptional rather than the usual in mankind. Only a small part of the human race has left a written record of its history, and the record is recent, beginning in the third millennium B.C. By a consciousness of history we mean the perception that a series of events form an intelligible unity. The lack of this perception led Greek philosophers to deny that history was a science; for them science dealt only with the universal, and the single person, object, or event is experienced, not understood. The Greek philosophers were not entirely wrong; for historical understanding is not the type of understanding which is usually meant by "scientific," and it always retains some of the obscurity which is a feature of our experience of the contingent and the particular.

How, then, is a series of events seen to have an intelligible unity? Not simply because of the unity of subject; many individual persons lack the perception of the unity of their own personal experience.

There is practically no history of clan and tribal societies; such societies assure their survival by not deviating from a routine which integrates them with their cultural situation, and there can be no history of an undeviating routine. Many political societies have left only sketchy historical reports; perhaps their records have perished, but perhaps also they did not have a real consciousness of history. The consciousness of history means the realization that the past lives in the present because the past has determined, antecedent to the decision of the present generation, the character of the group which makes the present decisions. The past has endowed the group with its peculiar strengths and weaknesses and at the same time has limited the options available to the group. A consciousness of history means that the group knows that it can affirm its identity only by affirming what it has been. It draws from its awareness of its past responsibility for its obligation, encouragement from what it has achieved and warnings from its failures.

Such awareness has been manifested only by those societies which we call civilized; and historical consciousness, which can be seen in early Egypt and Mesopotamia, does not imply the ability to write history in the sense that the past is described as the unified experience of a social group. In Egypt, for example, the preservation of the records of the past showed a consciousness of the unity of the Egyptian experience over a period of 2,500 years. But we have no Egyptian effort to synthesize this series of events or even a single part of it in a unified literary account. Mesopotamia, which did not have a political unity like the unity of Egypt, possessed a conscious cultural unity. Records of the past were preserved, but again we have no single synthesis of the past. In both Egypt and Mesopotamia we have the materials of history rather than history itself. In 645 B.C. Ashurbanipal reported that he had brought back from Susa, the royal city of Elam, a statue of Ishtar which the Elamites had plundered from Erech 1,635 or 1,535 years earlier.[1] Modern scholars believe his calculation is in error, but the reference shows a consciousness of history. It is quite late in Mesopotamian history, and it comes from the king who made the

[1] D. D. Luckenbill, *Ancient Records: Assyria and Babylonia* (Chicago, 1927), v. 2, 309–11.

most serious effort to collect all the literary and historical materials of Mesopotamia from earliest times. When Nineveh fell to the assault of the Median and Babylonian armies in 612 B.C., not long after the death of Ashurbanipal, the tablets of Ashurbanipal's library were deliberately smashed so badly that only a relative few have survived intact. This does not attest lack of civilization—at least for the Babylonians—as much as it attests hatred of the Assyrians, not difficult to understand. The attack was anti-historical in so far as the attackers intended to wipe out the very memory of Assyria and were nearly successful.

In the ancient Near East, Israel alone created a literary form which expressed its historical consciousness. It is possible to see the beginnings of this literary form in the reign of David; and the finished historical works which modern scholars find in the Old Testament, to be discussed in more detail below, were mostly completed in the sixth or fifth centuries. These works were thus slightly older than Herodotus and Thucydides, and independent of them. The earliest specimens of Israelite historical narrative show techniques of composition in no way inferior to the best Greek historians. Their techniques of criticism are another question; and this leads us further into the discussion of what history is and how the historical record is produced.

We have already distinguished between the materials of history, the record of events as they happen, and the consciousness of history, the perception of the unity of a series of events. This perception arises from the perception of factors which do not emerge in the chronicles of particular events. Such a factor may be a particular strength or a particular weakness which is not recognized as an enduring factor until it has been observed a sufficient number of times. Such enduring factors then become the decisive factors, but their decisive weight is not recognized by the actors in the events. It is not merely observation and experience but the analysis of experience which disclose such factors. Once the existence of these factors is recognized, they can be perceived or deduced in other events where the record does not show them.

Cicero defined history as "the remembered past,"[2] and it is

2 *Tusculanarum Disputationum,* III, 33.

nearly impossible to improve on this definition, which succeeds in incorporating both event and record. The object of historical record is rarely to present a complete and objective account of even a portion of the past; a complete account of anything besides a quite recent and very definite event is impossible; and the objective and detached historical consideration is really a myth cultivated by nineteenth-century historians about themselves and their discipline. Herodotus wrote his history to show that the Greeks defeated the Persians because they were a superior people with a superior civilization. Thucydides wrote the history of the Peloponnesian War to show that the war was rather lost by the Athenians than won by the Lacedaemonians; the collapse of civic morals made victory impossible for the Athenians. The historian who sets forth the principle of unity in a series of events must prove something which is not found explicitly and formally in the materials of history. When we deal with Old Testament history, we find that here, as in most historical writings, the account of the events is intended to prove something; history is not written simply because the past is interesting, but because the past is relevant. It lives, as we have said, in the present generation.

Another ancient adage venerated history as the *magistra vitae*, the school teacher of life. Modern historians generally disclaim this title and function, while at the same time they wish their work to be considered by those whose actions will form the material for future historians. While they are sure that history does not repeat itself, they are quick to point out patterns in situations which resemble each other. Whatever is to be said about the pedagogical purpose of history in general, there can be no doubt that Old Testament history was written with a pedagogical interest. This puts it into the classification of wisdom (see below), which was based on the firm conviction of the validity of experience. The Israelite scribes expected Israel to learn from its past experience. This does not stand in opposition to what we have said about history as the affirmation of a people's identity. Few if any national histories besides Israel's have affirmed national sin and guilt as one of the enduring factors which unified the series of events.

It is true of all histories that the consciousness of history arises too late for the early history to be very well written. We have here something similar to the personal consciousness of self; when one becomes fully conscious of the power of one's developed mature personality, one is unable to remember the formative years of infancy and childhood. We are all aware of the tendency to interpret the memories of our childhood in terms of our adult responses. No one ever remembers what it was to be a child. Nations also have an imperfect memory of their beginnings, and they fill up the gaps with their adult responses. As we shall see more fully when we treat of myth, Israel handled the problems of its origins in an unparalleled way; but like other peoples, it had imperfect memories. Other ancient peoples put a "mythological time" at the beginning, which Mircea Eliade has designated as *illud tempus*.[3] This mythological time is an eternal present, for it is the time when all reality comes into being, and it endures in enduring reality. It is the time in which the mythological events recur. As we shall see, the Israelite account of origins is mythological in its thought patterns, but it really historicizes myth.

Modern criticism asks questions about the reality of the events narrated which, as far as we can understand them, ancient scribes did not answer. Some degree of historical criticism they certainly had, for no one is totally credulous; but a technique of criticism they did not have. Speaking absolutely, they were more credulous than the modern historian, just as the modern historian is much less credulous than most of his contemporaries. Nor should it be thought that the ancient scribes should have developed techniques of criticism. The modern reader has difficulty in grasping their attitude that accuracy in detail was neither possible nor desirable. They dealt with the remembered past, and it was the remembered past that was important. The principles by which Israelite scribes interpreted their sources were quite different from the principles employed by the modern historian.

Let us first attend to the distinctive and peculiarly Israelite understanding that their history was the story of their encounter with Yahweh. No modern historian would conceive such a story as falling in any way under historical investigation. Had the ancient Israelite scribes known what historical investigation is, they would

[3] *The Sacred and the Profane* (New York, 1959), 68–113.

THEOLOGY OF THE OLD TESTAMENT

have agreed entirely with this judgment. They would more easily have understood G. Ernest Wright's description of their work: "biblical theology as recital."[4] It is not the history of Israel but the recital of the acts of God which they thought they were composing, and they must be read in terms of their own intention and purpose. Faith that they encountered God in events is not a presupposition of Israelite historical writing; it is the purpose of the historical writing to set forth the acts of God.

Israelite history was an affirmation of Israel's identity. Israel's identity was the people of Yahweh. The meaning of this somewhat ambiguous phrase was not understood univocally in each of the documents of Israel's history. It always meant that Israel had a relation with Yahweh not shared with any other people. In the later phases of Israelite belief it was seen that even this definition of the people of Yahweh was inadequate in that it failed entirely to state the relation which Yahweh, it was perceived, must have with other peoples.

The relation of Yahweh with Israel had to be purposeful. Neither was the purpose of Yahweh understood univocally throughout the course of Israelite history. One of the traditional errors of biblical interpretation was to assume the same degree of enlightened understanding in all the biblical writers, an error which was an unhappy consequence of a rather primitive theology of inspiration. The understanding of the purpose of Yahweh is less important for our considerations here than the fact that Yahweh's acts were believed to be purposeful, indeed, that the record of history showed no other purpose apart from the purpose of Yahweh.

This leads to the linear view of history as contrasted with the cyclical. The cyclical view is attributed to the Greek conception;[5] the term means what it says, that history does repeat itself, that it returns to a point of origin. It is associated with the Aristotelian view that the world is eternal and that it never changes from its present condition. Likewise, it gives events something of that universality which the Greek philosopher demanded for intelligibility. In biblical thought, history is a single Now, unique and irreversible.

4 *God Who Acts: Biblical Theology as Recital* (Chicago, 1952).
5 Ibid. 40–42.

God's action occurs only once, for he is one and he does not need to repeat his acts. The line must have a beginning and an end; and therefore the Bible has a protology and an eschatology. We shall see that the protology of the Old Testament appears in greater clarity than the eschatology. Greek history has neither in a proper sense; Greek mythology, which is much older than Greek philosophy, did have both. Both the protology and the eschatology, as we shall see, are historicized in the Old Testament.

While our consideration in this chapter emphasizes the historical books of the Old Testament, it should be understood that Old Testament history is not confined to the historical books. The prophets are "historical" in the sense that they interpret history, as we have seen; they do not record it. The wisdom books are unhistorical to a degree which will demand special consideration. On the other hand, many of the principal moments of Israelite history we have considered (the covenant) or shall consider (Israel's constitution) in themselves. We are concerned exactly with what Wright has called "theology as recital," certain themes that dominate the historical books.

Literary and historical criticism lie outside the scope of theology, as we have had occasion to remark more than once. Nevertheless, we must advert to the fact that the "historical books" of our Bible are compilations of pre-existing literary productions, some of them quite complex compilations of compilations. The historical-theological significance of any passage may have two or even three layers; the meaning which it had in its oldest form may not be the same as the meaning which it receives when it becomes part of a larger context. This can be easily illustrated from the stories of the sacrifice of Isaac and the wrestling of Jacob.[6] In such passages we can trace the growth and development of Israelite historical and theological understanding of its past. A number of scholars have in recent years attended to the phenomenon which French scholars call *relecture*—rereading and reinterpretation. This means that the scribe, reflecting on a biblical recital, finds in it new meaning applicable to his own situation. His meaning is actually derived

[6] John L. McKenzie, "The Sacrifice of Isaac (Gen 22)," *Scripture,* 9 (1957), 79–84; "Jacob at Peniel: Gen 32:24–32," CathBiblQuart, 25 (1963), 71–76.

from his own situation as much as from the text; he seeks in the text an answer to the questions of his own time. In a certain sense the entire activity of biblical theology can be described as *relecture,* but it began with that anonymous biblical author, probably one or a group of scribes in David's palace, who is designated as J.

The modern reader of the Bible is somewhat puzzled by a paradox which he sees either in biblical historiography or in modern interpretation or in both. On the one hand he hears the interpreters say that the Israelite religion is a historical religion in the sense that it is based on historical and not on mythological events. On the other hand he hears the same interpreters point out a remarkable freedom in the way in which biblical authors handle history. One can resolve the paradox, which should not be denied, by distinguishing once more between history as event and history as record. We ourselves make the distinction, at least implicitly. No one doubts the reality of the event of the invention of the wheel nor of the lasting historical influence of this event. It is no less real because there is no record of the event, but in the precise sense of the term the event is not historical; that is, it is not recorded. The Israelites believed their faith reposed upon real events. It is obvious from the character of much of the narrative that they had no record or a very fragmentary record of the events. They composed the historical accounts by deducing certain propositions from the fragmentary memories of events interpreted in the light of certain principles of faith. All historical narrative is the result of reconstruction of the materials of history.

It must be remembered that the Israelite scribes were under the limitations of their time and their culture. We have already pointed out and shall notice again that they produced an entirely new technique of historiography, and in this they broke through the limitations of their culture. We should not complain that they did not break through all the way into modern times. As we have observed, they were more credulous than modern historians, but not more credulous than modern man in general. They were quick to explain events in terms of the acts of God and less inclined to look for an explanation in nature or history. They were simply unaware of almost all of the historical and scientific learning which has been amassed since ancient times. Their horizons, while broader than the horizons of most men of the ancient world, were after all quite narrow. They were simply incapable of certain achievements in historiography. What they could write were the collected popular memories of their people arranged in such a way that the writing became the recital of the acts of God in Israel.

Did Israel have a secular history? The mention of gods in the chronicles of Egypt and Mesopotamia make it clear that no ancient nation thought of itself as having a "secular" history. Not until the Greeks did such an idea arise; and even the secular histories written by Greek agnostics were not free of moralizing. The Israelites could not have grasped the idea and could not have produced such a secular history. The modern historian who attempts it faces some real problems, especially if he shares the Jewish or the Christian faith. Both of these faiths have incorporated the Israelite belief in God's acts in Israel into their own creeds. If the historian is not a believer, he has the problem of interpreting sources which are entirely motivated in their narratives by their belief. It seems safe to say that the history of Israel, like the life of Jesus, does not yield to a quest for the historical Israel. The secular historian cannot overcome the embarrassment of the fact that no one else ever wrote this kind of history.

2. *Promise and Fulfillment*

The chapters 1–11 of the book of Genesis are usually designated primitive or primeval history and will be treated elsewhere. Genesis reaches historic times with Abraham, and it is with him that "pre-Israelite" history properly begins. Abraham, Isaac, and Jacob are the ancestors of historic Israel, and indeed Jacob receives the name Israel as a second name. The twelve sons of Jacob are the eponymous ancestors of the twelve tribes of Israel. The historian must add that the last statement has some reservations. Levi is one of the sons of Israel but not one of the twelve tribes. Joseph is likewise one of the sons of Israel but not one of the twelve tribes; his sons Ephraim and Manasseh are not sons of Israel but are two of the twelve tribes. This history has to be called "pre-Israelite" because the narrators in no way supposed that there was a tribal or national community called "Israel" in this early period.

The ancestors are described as seminomadic herdsmen, to use the modern designation.[7] From the beginnings of history down to modern times the Near East has known the distinction between the desert, inhabited by pastoral nomads, and the sown, inhabited by peasants and city dwellers. The difference between the two is not ethnic but cultural. The nomads do not till the soil or live in houses; they live in tents and move with their flocks and herds from pasture to pasture according to the seasons. Relations between the two are much like the relations between distant cousins. The nomad feels he has freedom; the peasant feels he has security. The nomad believes the peasant is a slave; the peasant thinks the nomad is a starveling bandit. The villages and cities of the ancient Near East have been populated by migration from the desert; one can trace such acculturation in the Habiru of the Mari and Nuzi tablets of the eighteenth century B.C.[8] The name is very probably related to that name which we translate "Hebrew," but it is now known to designate a status and not an ethnic group.

There is, then, nothing remarkable in the Israelite popular memory that their ancestors had been nomadic herdsmen. It is remarkable that the patriarchs are not located outside Canaan but within it. Abraham, it is true, is identified as an immigrant from Harran; according to all the probabilities this would make him an Amorite, but he is not so identified—in fact, he is never given any ethnic affiliation. There is a tradition that Jacob was an immigrant, but in the final compilation of the text, if not earlier, this immigration was represented as a return from a long sojourn in Mesopotamia. Jacob looks much like an Aramaean; his kinsmen surely do. Another tradition of immigration, which became the dominant episode of the literary tradition, was the tradition of the entrance of all Israel into Canaan under the leadership of Joshua. Let it be said at once that this last immigration, in the terms which we have used, was unhistorical as event; the problem will recur in the following section.

[7] William Foxwell Albright, *From the Stone Age to Christianity,* 164–66; R. de Vaux, *Ancient Israel,* 13–14; J. Pedersen, *Israel I–II,* 20–21.
[8] M. Greenberg, *The Hab/piru* (New Haven, 1955), 63, 69, 86.

Modern historians have little doubt that the genealogical connection of Abraham, Isaac, and Jacob is artificial.[9] Each is recognized
as a legendary ancestor of some of the groups which united themselves into the tribal league of Israel. The artificial connection was
established as a part of the literary unification of Israelite traditions; we shall see that this is best explained as a product of the
political unification of Israel under David. There is no doubt that
the patriarchs are described as resident in Canaan; but Abraham
alone, in a tradition which is found in a late literary source, is
described as owning land in Canaan. One can hardly doubt that
this is an attempt to remain faithful to the memories of Israel's
ancestors; the Israelites knew that their ancestors had not been
landlords.

One may ask at this point what genuine historical memories
the Israelites could have had of their ancestors, either in Canaan
or elsewhere; and if one assumes that the clan and tribal memories
of early Israel were as retentive as other clan and tribal memories
which have been studied, one does not easily see how they could
have surely remembered anything. The origins of Israel were much
more complex than the development of a single family stem of
a father and twelve sons, so complex that modern historians have
not yet surely reconstructed them even in vague outline. This writer
has often likened the origin of Israel to the development of the
United States from thirteen British colonies. Actually the nation
incorporates French and Spanish peoples and traditions, but the
bulk of the population are the descendants of a mass of proletarian
immigration of the nineteenth and twentieth centuries. This vast
group had no memories either of Europe or of North America.
For them the dominant tradition became the tradition of the thirteen colonies and their war of independence from England. Except
for local traditions the French and the Spanish components are
forgotten, the Negro occupies a place something like that of the
Gibeonites, and the American Indian, like the Canaanites, is exterminated where possible, treated as nonexistent where he insists on
surviving.

There can be no reason for the prominence of Abraham, Isaac,

[9] M. Noth, *History of Israel,* 124, 127.

and Jacob except that they and they alone were remembered from the early Israelite period. It is also important that they were remembered as living in Canaan, for it is this that makes it possible for the history of the patriarchs to be one pole of the themes of promise and fulfillment. Yahweh promised each of the patriarchs an innumerable progeny and the possession of the land in which they "sojourned." The Hebrew word *gēr*, "sojourner," more accurately translated "resident alien," is often used of the patriarchs in Canaan. The land is promised to them, but they neither purchase it nor take it by arms.

The promise of a numerous progeny signifies the historical memory of an ancestral group of small numbers. This is emphatic. The patriarchal groups are always a family (including more than one wife and a large number of children). The P source continues this emphasis even in the exilic or postexilic field when it counts the persons who went to Egypt with Jacob as seventy (Gen 46:8–27). Certainly the P source regarded the promise of a numerous progeny as fulfilled at the exodus, when P numbered Israel at about 600,000 adult men besides women and children—which would project to a population of about 2,000,000 (Ex 12:37). The older sources still thought of Israel as small enough to be thrown into panic by the approach of the Egyptian chariot corps (Ex 14:6–12).

It is a routine Old Testament theme that fertility, whether in men, animals, or nature is the gift of Yahweh (see below). Hence the emphasis on the promise of a numerous progeny and its fulfillment, like the promise of the land, implies some particular event or some particular belief which is not obvious on the surface. What is obvious is that the theme of promise and fulfillment is the basis of the claim of the people of Israel to the land of Israel. Yahweh had promised both the land and the people to dwell in it. The fact of Israel's dwelling in its land was the base of Yahweh's attribute of fidelity; he is a god who keeps his word, whose power and integrity are daily demonstrated in the existence of Israel in its land. The dispossession of Israel, as we shall see, evoked another chain of theological reflection.

Promise and fulfillment run through much of Israelite history. The promise of a son is given to Abraham and Sarah (Gen 17), to Manoah and his wife (Judg 13), to Elkanah and Hannah (1

Sam 1). David is promised a kingdom and an everlasting dynasty (2 Sam 7). Second Isaiah presents the restoration of Israel and Jerusalem as the fulfillment of promise (Is 41:26, 43:1–7,12, 44: 7–8, 45:21, 46:10–11, 55:10–11).

To the Israelites the unannounced event was not significant. They believed that Yahweh governed their history; they believed that he owed it to himself, to Israel, and to others to make it known when he performed a significant action. The exultation with which Second Isaiah declared that only Yahweh can promise and fulfill shows the importance which the attribute of fidelity had for him (Is 41:21–24, 42:9, 43:9–10, 44:6–8,24–28). The modern reader of the Bible may have some trouble assuring himself that the promises were actually given. We cannot, for example, find in our Bible texts which illustrate the promises to which Second Isaiah alludes. And while the existence of inspired spokesmen is not under question, the formal promises which seem to be implied in this proclamation of the fidelity of Yahweh often appear to be promises subsequent to the fulfillment.

Such an explanation of the promise-fulfillment is obvious, but it very probably credits the Israelites with more naïveté than they deserve. There is such a thing as foreshadowing, in spite of the abuse which this idea has received in theology. The Old Testament is full of allusions to the significance of names both personal and local, even where etymology has to be strained to find the significance. Recent events can be seen to resemble events from the more distant past, and the remote events are then narrated in terms which emphasize the resemblance. This is a type of the *relecture* referred to in the preceding section. Hope itself is a kind of promise when it is joined to prayer. The attribute of fidelity demands that Yahweh declare the word which is to be believed. There are many ways in which Yahweh can declare his word. Unless one believes that Yahweh is active in events and that his activity follows an ethical and rational pattern, one can hardly discern the promises implicit in events and in inspired speech.

Throughout the ancient Near East, and indeed most of the ancient world, the practice of divination flourished; and in forms more refined than liver divination, it flourishes in modern civilization. Divination is a superstitious practice based on the belief that the gods or whatever superior powers in which man believes indicate in some cryptic manner the course of future events. Occult skills are necessary to decode the symbolic indications. The Israelite belief in promise and fulfillment was not a type of divination, but it was an expression of Israelite belief that Yahweh indicated what he intended to do. The same principle was applied to the judgments of Yahweh. If man is to respond to the acts of Yahweh, man is entitled to know what to expect from him. We shall see under other headings that Israel could not stand the idea that God is capricious or irrational. Man is unable to take refuge in his ignorance of God's plans and God's acts.

3. *The Saving Acts of Yahweh*

The encounters of Israel with Yahweh revolve around two poles: salvation and judgment. Historically, the awareness of salvation is all but certainly earlier than the awareness of judgment; but in the literary tradition the awareness of judgment is placed in the wilderness experience. The meaning of salvation is best seen in the paradigmatic saving act, the exodus from Egypt. The prominence of this event in Old Testament history is clear from the numerous allusions to the exodus in all phases of the literature. There can be no doubt that it was celebrated in the cult, and, as we have noticed, it is altogether probable that cultic recitals were the earliest forms of the narrative of the exodus.

The "standard" form of the narrative is found in Exodus 7:8 through 15:21, compiled from JEP. The allusions to the exodus are numerous in the prophetic books (Is 10:26; Jer 2:6, 31:32; Ezek 20:5,10; Hos 11:1; Mic 6:4) and in the Psalms (78:12–13, 105:26–42, 106:8–12, 114:1–4, 135:8–9, 136:10–15). The Song of Miriam (Ex 15), clearly a cultic composition, is regarded by several recent scholars as older than the J and E sources of the Pentateuch.[10] None of the allusions to the event outside of the book of Exodus show any significant variations in the character of the event. The content of the narratives must have been settled

[10] F. M. Cross and D. N. Freedman, "The Song of Miriam," *Journal of Near Eastern Studies*, 14 (1955), 237–50.

rather early. One can, however, see how the P source has heightened the marvelous character of the event. Thus in each of the plagues of which P has a version, the wonder exceeds the wonder in J and E. In the older sources the Nile is turned to blood, in P all the water in the land of Egypt is turned to blood. The plague of flies becomes dust turned into mosquitoes, and the cattle plague becomes a plague of boils on men and beasts. The waters of the sea stand like a wall to the right and left of the Israelites. Such a transfiguration of the wonder is not surprising; but the process was ended with the P version of the exodus.

The paradigmatic character of the exodus can be thus summarized: the need is desperate, and the candidate for salvation is helpless. The power of Yahweh is interposed in such a way that the persons saved need do nothing. The threat is formidable; Egypt was one of the great powers of the ancient world, and Israel faced the power of Egypt in the very land of Egypt. The intention to save is declared not once but several times (Ex 3:16–22, 4:21–23, 7:4–5); as we noticed in the preceding section, the act of God is not meaningful unless it is recognized as the act of God. The powers of nature are turned from their normal courses by the will of Yahweh to produce marvelous and paradoxical effects harmful to the enemies, salutary to the Israelites. The confrontation issues in the total defeat of the Egyptians, the complete deliverance of the Israelites.

Kurt Galling pointed out years ago that in a number of passages the wonder of the exodus is defined as the event which brings Israel as the people of Yahweh into being.[11] A review of some of these passages is worthwhile because of the importance of the theme: the first act of salvation is the creation of a people with whom Yahweh shall dwell in covenant. In the exodus Judah became the sanctuary of Yahweh, and Israel his dominion (Ps 114:1–2). Yahweh brought Israel out of Egypt through the wilderness to possess the land of the Amorite (Amos 2:10), and in the exodus Yahweh "knew" Israel alone of all peoples (Amos 3:1–2); that is, he recognized Israel as his own. Yahweh loved Israel as a child and called his son out of Egypt (Hos 11:1); this identifies the exodus with

[11] "Die Erwählungstraditionen Israels," BeihZATWiss 48 (1928), 5–37.

an act of adoption. Yahweh is Israel's God from the land of Egypt (Hos 12:9, 13:4), and he "knew" (see above) Israel in the desert (Hos 13:5). In Micah 6:4 the exodus and redemption from the house of bondage are Yahweh's first acts for Israel. The exodus is also the first saving act in Jeremiah 2:6–7; in the same context the prophet calls the time of the exodus the time of Israel's youth and espousals to Yahweh (Jer 2:2). In Psalm 81:1–10 a feast (very probably the New Year; see Chapter I, Section 1) is attributed to a "statute, ordinance and decree" established at the exodus. This includes a profession that Yahweh alone is God (Ps 81:9, a close paraphrase of the first commandment). The feast recalls the saving act of the exodus and makes the saving act of the past an assurance of the saving power and will of Yahweh in the present.[12] The day of the exodus was the day when Yahweh "chose" Israel and made himself known to Israel (Ezek 20:5).

In Second Isaiah the creation of a people in the exodus is the paradigm of the new wonder which Yahweh creates in the time of the prophet when he restores Israel. There was no hope in history for a people which had perished in the conquests of Babylon and survived only to see the power of Babylon seized by an even greater and better organized empire. Second Isaiah regarded the second act of salvation as more wonderful and paradoxical than the first. It was Yahweh the creator of Israel and its king who brought Israel through the water and the desert; now he does a new thing (Is 43:16–21), restoring the people whom he had formed for himself. The mythology of creation (see below) is used to describe the saving act of the exodus and the new creation of Israel (Is 51:9–10). In the exodus narrative (Ex 19:3–6, mostly if not entirely E), Yahweh declares that Israel, which he has delivered from Egypt, will become his own people if they obey his voice and keep his covenant. The same theme and possibly the same passage are echoed in Jer 7:22–23.

These texts represent a wide selection of Old Testament literature both in dates and in literary types. They indicate that Israel understood that it came into being as the result of the saving act of Yahweh. This is of more than slight interest when we recall

---

[12] A. Weiser, *The Psalms* (Philadelphia, 1962), 553–55.

that other peoples of the ancient Near East had not even a mythological account of their origins; they had no memory of a time
when Egypt or Babylon did not exist. Strictly speaking, the Israelite
belief that Israel came into being as the people of Yahweh in the
saving act of the exodus is mythological rather than historical; the
origins of Israel are surely much more complicated than this, and
it is all but certain that "all Israel" did not exist at the period
of the exodus. The paradigmatic experience of salvation which happened to a small group at most became the experience of "all
Israel" and the event in which "all Israel" was born. What genuine
historical memory lies behind the belief must be a memory of the
rise of a special relation between Yahweh and a group to which
we can give no certain name. We have adverted in the Introduction
to the problem created when biblical theology touches upon uncertain historical areas. No historical area is more uncertain than the
period of Israelite origins. Israel never resolved the historical uncertainty, and the written traditions of Israel have not yet been
sufficient for modern scholars to resolve the uncertainty. The firm
belief that Yahweh's first saving act for Israel was to bring Israel
into being cannot be radicated in sure history. But when Israelite
scribes prepared accounts of Israelite origins, they made faith in
the creative and saving act of Yahweh the key to the reconstruction
of the past which they produced.

The compilation of historical traditions into the historical books
of the Old Testament include a number of other saving acts, all
except one inferior in magnitude of the saving act by which Israel
is created. No one can fail to notice that Joshua is presented in
many respects as a lesser Moses; Joshua led Israel across a river
instead of a sea and promulgated a covenant (Jos 24) instead
of a code of laws, as Moses did in Exodus-Leviticus-Numbers-
Deuteronomy. The gift of the land, as we have touched it and
shall discuss again below, was the saving act which completed the
exodus. The book of Judges is a recital of the saving intervention
of Yahweh on behalf of Israel through charismatic heroes.

The dangers of the period of the Judges were ended by another
great saving act, the election and installation of the dynasty of
David. The full theological significance of the dynasty of David
must be discussed under a separate heading; but that saving act

which made David a messianic king and Jerusalem the seat of Yahweh's presence in the temple has had wide and lasting effects both in Judaism and Christianity. One may add Islam, which held the sacred site of the temple from the ninth century A.D. until 1967, longer than it was held from the reign of Solomon to the campaign of Titus. Yet we must realize here that our Old Testament writings in this respect represent Judahite rather than Israelite traditions, for most of Israel seceded from allegiance to the dynasty of David. We have no explicit literary attestation, but it must have been a belief of most Israelites that the saving act of Yahweh freed them from the secular tyranny of Solomon and his son. Surely some must have likened this event to a new exodus from the house of bondage; for forced labor, which the Israelites called slavery in Egypt, was imposed by Solomon on his subjects and became the occasion of the rebellion of the kingdom of Israel (1 Kings 12:1–19).

That one act which was even greater than the exodus was the restoration of Israel after the exile, which Second Isaiah described as the new exodus (see the passages cited above). There seems to be no doubt that Second Isaiah described the coming event in terms somewhat too magnificent for his contemporaries and for those who lived to experience the restoration. The glory of the new Jerusalem hardly reached the glory of the first, and Jerusalem did not become a world center at which all nations recognized the supremacy of Yahweh (Is 45:9–25). The mission which Second Isaiah saw for restored Israel (to be discussed in Chapter VII, "The Future of Israel") did not come to a realization in the period of the exile. Some poems of Third Isaiah, such as chapters 58–62, are responses to the disappointment felt when the promises of Second Isaiah did not seem to be fulfilled. We shall see below how the postexilic period had to be somewhat carefully interpreted as the result of a saving act.

In the prayers of the Psalms the petitioner, whether he speaks for himself or for the community of Israel, petitions for the saving act in the hope, based on the historic experience of Israel, that the saving act will be performed. The petition on behalf of the people does often recall the great deeds of Yahweh in the past. But the motivations invoked for the saving act are many and varied.

Yahweh can be asked to save simply because he would rather save than not save; it is in his character to be a saving God. Or he may be asked to save because he is a generous and forgiving God who will not allow the memory of the faults of the petitioner to keep him from acting in the manner which most becomes him. Or he may be asked to save to protect his own reputation; the heathen may scoff that he is unfaithful to his promises or unable to keep them. These various motivations cannot be rationally synthesized. Whenever man invokes the deity for assistance, he invokes with the assurance that the deity is able and willing to help. If the deity is able and willing, one need not look too hard for the right motive; if the deity is unable or unwilling, no motive will move the deity to help. In Israelite petitions for help, the only thing which might keep Yahweh from helping the petitioner is the sinfulness of the petitioner; but if Yahweh does not recognize repentance and grant aid in spite of sinfulness, he would not be manifested as a forgiving God.

The character of Yahweh as a saving God is not fully revealed in particular saving acts, whether they are done on behalf of the people or on behalf of individuals. The belief in Yahweh's power and will to save leads to a formation of a saving act which is terminal and delivers in such a way that no further saving act is necessary. This belief finds expression in the eschatological saving act, which we treat in Chapter VII, "The Future of Israel."

Belief in the power and will to save, taken by itself, leaves an unbalanced theological perspective. Like the belief in election, it makes Israel the object and the focus of Yahweh's saving will. Hence the belief can easily become a vehicle for religious and ethnic self-centeredness and can turn the God of the Bible, as unbelievers have said more than once, from the God of mankind to the God of a particular people or a particular sect. It would be foolish as well as dishonest to pretend that the expressions of Yahweh's saving power and will in the Old Testament always rise above religious and ethnic narrowness; one may as well admit the obvious fact that many ancient Israelites and some of their scribes believed that the saving power and will of Yahweh were directed exclusively to the people of Israel. Belief in salvation needs other themes as counterweights, and the heaviest counterweight to this particular theme is the theme which we shall discuss in Section 5, below, "Judgment."

4. *The Land of Israel*

We return here to a theme introduced in Section 2 of this chapter, "Promise and Fulfillment." The promise, we noticed, had two elements: a numerous progeny and possession of the land. Unless the progeny were numerous, the possession of the land could not be guaranteed. Even in the earliest Israelite literature it is evident that the importance of the land for the lasting identity of the people was recognized. It is a fact, although one can hardly credit the Israelite scribes with this insight, that nomadic tribes do not make history. It is not only that their instability works against their lasting importance; it is also that nomadic tribes can preserve the memory of their deeds only by oral tradition. They do not build lasting monuments. Furthermore, tribal societies all over the world assure their survival by close fidelity to an established and traditional routine of life. In the deserts, the jungles, and the arctic wastes of the globe, to trifle with the routine of survival is to flirt with death. Tribal societies do not make history because they refuse adventure. The necessity of adventure, such as a migration, is a crisis in tribal life which is recognized as the danger of extinction. This does not imply the literal death of the members of the tribe; it has often meant the loss of identity either by merger with another tribe or by absorption into civilized communities. Tribal societies may and do outlive civilizations just because they adhere to proved routines and do not take the demonic risks of civilized man; but in direct confrontation, the tribal society is no match for the civilized community.

The traditions of the patriarchs and the exodus witness that the Israelites knew that their permanent identity was assured only when the land bore the name of the people. It is a common thesis of Deuteronomy that the land is the gift of Yahweh. The phrase "the land which Yahweh gives you" is a cliché in the book. The Israelites will take possession of cities which they did not build, houses full of good things which they did not fill, cisterns which they did not hew, vineyards and olive trees which they did not plant (Deut 6:10–12). The orator does allow himself a bit of poetic fancy. Both the archaeology of thirteenth-century sites and the biblical accounts of conquests indicate that cities, houses, and cultivation were totally destroyed. Although the peoples of the land are more numerous and more powerful than the Israelites, Yahweh will destroy them at a conveniently gradual pace (Deut 7:17–24). The donation is not made because of the righteousness of Israel, for Israel has a history of unrighteousness from the desert (Deut 9:4–29). The gift of the land of Israel excludes the lands of Edom (Deut 2:5), Moab (Deut 2:9), and Ammon (Deut 2:19), which Yahweh has assigned to these peoples as he assigns the land of Israel. The writer pays no attention to the theological implications of this statement for the relations of Yahweh with these peoples; his interest is in affirming that Yahweh and no other god assigns lands to peoples.[13] The same belief is stated in the Song of Moses (Deut 32:8–9).

The gift of the land is also seen in the narratives of the conquest in Joshua 2 to 11. There are serious reasons for questioning the historical character of this narrative not only in details but also in general, and for taking the passage as a reconstruction based on incomplete dim memories of past events.[14] It is of theological interest that in the battles of Jericho, Ai, Gibeon, and Hazor the enemy are scattered by a panic induced by Yahweh and the Israelites are left with nothing but what is called in modern warfare "mopping up." The narrators did not intend to describe wars and battles in the conventional sense of the term, for they did not think of the gift of the land as coming to Israel through conquest in the conventional sense of the term.

Gerhard von Rad in an important monograph outlined the theopolitical Israelite scheme of the "holy war."[15] Von Rad deduces the elements of the Holy War both from the laws of war in Deuter-

[13] J. L. McKenzie, "Historical Prologue to Deuteronomy," *Acts of the Fourth Jewish Congress* (1967), 95–101.

[14] Noth, op. cit., 53–97; J. L. McKenzie, *The World of the Judges* (Englewood Cliffs, N.J., 1966), 76–120.

[15] *Studies in Deuteronomy*, tr. by D. M. Stalker, Studies in Biblical Theology 9 (London, 1953), 45–59.

onomy 20–21 and 23–25 and from some of the narratives of Joshua and Judges. The main elements are the consultation of the oracle, the solemn declaration by religious authority, the charismatic leader, the consecration of the warriors (probably by continence and abstinence from wine and spirits), the battle cry of the Holy War, and the law of the "ban," the rather horrible practice of complete extermination of the defeated people and the destruction of their property. Von Rad suggests that while the laws and the narratives are much later than the premonarchic period and therefore to a large extent theoretical, they preserve memories of the early practices.

I am in entire accord with this theory, and I would add only the suggestion that the Holy War was undertaken to acquire the promised land or to defend it; any other war was secular. I suggest also that the Holy War was the only war to which "all Israel," whatever "all Israel" may have meant in the premonarchic period, could be summoned. The provision of the relation of the war to the land helps to explain the "ban," I believe. Ancient war, like modern war, was candidly a plundering expedition. It may seem rather subtle to see an elevation of the morality of war in the killing of captives rather than their enslavement, and I would not wish to use the term "elevation." But if the Holy War is understood as a war for the land which was the gift of Yahweh, then the war was simply an extension of the gift. A war for booty, and in particular for slaves, the most prized type of booty, was not commissioned by Yahweh, nor could men be consecrated for such a war, nor would Yahweh grant victory without combat. The practice of the Holy War, according to Von Rad, did not endure beyond the reign of David; and in fact, I find nothing in the narratives of Saul and David except the Amalekite campaign of Saul (1 Sam 15) which suggests the Holy War. The wars of the monarchies of Israel and Judah were often wars in defense of the land, but nothing indicates that the theology of the Holy War was ever invoked.

The same Deuteronomic theology which insists that the land is the gift of Yahweh also insists that the retention of the gift is conditioned on the fidelity of Israel to the revealed law of Yahweh. This view of the land certainly reflects the prophets of the eighth and seventh centuries, but it is not necessary to suppose that the condition of fidelity was created by these prophets. We have already noticed that covenant and covenant law are now regarded by scholars as the earliest elements of a properly "Israelite" religion and polity. The earliest treaty forms contain stipulations, and there is no reason to doubt that Deuteronomy reflects the earliest understanding of the way in which Israel possessed its land.

The permanent influence of the gift of the land should be noticed, and the influence has been more than theological. The legend of the "wandering Jew" reflected the conviction shared by both Christians and Jews during all of the Christian centuries that the Jew is always an exile. It was implicit in the long refusal both of Jews to accept citizenship in European countries and of countries to accept them as citizens. There was a vague but firm feeling that the allegiance of the Jew belonged to a country from which he was temporarily excluded. When the Zionist movement was initiated, millions of Jews regarded it as a return to their own country, even though most of these millions had no intention of actually returning. The establishment of the modern state of Israel is understood by Jews as a return and a repossession; by Arabs it is understood as an invasion. The Israeli claim to sovereignty is at least as theological a claim as the claim which the books of the Old Testament establish for the land; but in the modern world, as in the ancient world, there is no room in international treaties and conventions for a theological claim to territory. None of the contestants have yet appealed to a theological disputation as a way of settling the dispute. Until they do, the ancient claim of Israel to its land can precipitate a major and quite unholy war.

5. *Judgment*

While we placed the judgments of Yahweh in antithesis to his saving acts, a frequent use of the word and probably the oldest use makes "judgment" synonymous with "salvation." In petitions such as the opening lines of Psalm 43:1, the psalmist cannot be understood as asking that he be submitted to a judgment in the forensic sense. Hence, modern translations use another word than "judge" (RSV "vindicate"). The judge is often seen in the Old Testament as the defender of the weak and the helpless. To appeal for judgment is to appeal for defense; it is not conceivable that the weak and helpless could be guilty of anything. Hence the "righteous" judge is considered—somewhat naïvely—as a judge who gives verdict in my favor, for "my" cause can be nothing but righteous. The word "righteous" then can come to mean "victorious," and the "righteousness" of Yahweh can be translated in some contexts exactly as "saving act." For the victor in a contest is proved righteous by the fact of victory.

It is evident that there is some lack of refinement in this view, and the beginning of refinement is usually seen in Amos 3:2: because Yahweh has known no people except Israel, his judgment upon Israel will be severe (the word "judgment" is not used, but punishment implies judgment). The act of judgment must include a vindication of the righteous and a punishment of the guilty. We shall see below that a tradition of Israel's guilt seems to be included in the earliest traditions. In spite of this, and in spite of the theme of covenant stipulations, Israel does not seem to have been very quick to accept the fact, clearly stated several times by Amos (see also 9:7-8), that moral obliquity is just as odious to Yahweh in Israel as it is in any other people.

It has been observed above that the covenant in its earliest forms must have included stipulations which conditioned the continued good will of the overlord. Failure to meet these stipulations entitled the overlord to withdraw his support or to punish according to the gravity of the offense. The covenant form leaves no room for a period in which Israel thought of itself as absolutely and without condition assured of the good pleasure of Yahweh. Several of the prophets attest that this attitude could be found in Israel and Judah under the monarchy (Is 5:18-19, 28:14-15; Jer 7:4-10). But it is scarcely possible to assert that the covenant of Yahweh with Israel was not morally conditioned from the beginnings. Hence by the terms of the covenant Israel was exposed to judgment.

This does not mean, as indicated above, that these conditions were always clearly perceived, and hence Amos and Isaiah could indeed have proposed judgment to their hearers as something new

and unexpected. Jeremiah was threatened with death for announcing judgment on the temple, and he was saved in part because
the precedent of Micah 3:12, in which destruction was predicted
for the temple, was invoked. It is somewhat surprising to find that
in the later years of Isaiah and in the years of Jeremiah and
Ezekiel this false security not only endured but seemed to grow
in strength. Yet the kingdom of Judah had barely escaped extinction while the larger and more powerful kingdom of Israel was
annihilated by the Assyrians. One can perhaps understand why
the Judahites thought that this unexpected escape was due to the
purpose of Yahweh to maintain the people of his covenant, his
king, and his temple.

Amos in fact did not address the kingdom of Judah; scholars
agree that the allusions to Judah in the book come from the glosses
of Judahite scribes.[16] Quite probably he spoke to the kingdom
of Israel precisely because it was larger and more powerful and
because it set the tone in the politically divided Israelite-Judahite
community. His message was entirely an announcement of judgment; notes of encouragement are again the work of glossators,
who expanded the text after the survival of some remnant of Israel
had become a fact of history.[17] The moral collapse of Israel, which
Amos describes as nearly total, had removed any title to the protection of Yahweh; Israel stands in no position before Yahweh different from the position of other nations (Amos 9:7–8a). But Amos
does not imply that the other nations which fell before Assyrian
power were in the same way under judgment for sin. The other
nations were not in a covenant relation with Yahweh; just as fidelity
entitled Israel to special protection, so infidelity merited special
punishment (Amos 3:1–2). The judgment of Yahweh on the nations is a particular problem to be discussed under its own heading.

Hosea also spoke only to Israel, but he was, unlike Amos, an
Israelite. The judgment which Hosea predicts is ultimately as total
as the judgment predicted by Amos; but we have seen that his
anthropomorphism represents the judgment as a decision which
Yahweh reaches after an emotional conflict. Like Amos, Hosea
describes by allusion a nearly total moral collapse; and since he

16 Otto Eissfeldt, *The Old Testament: An Introduction,* 400.
17 Ibid., 400–1.

wrote some years after Amos, he also alludes to the political chaos of the kingdom of Israel after the death of Jeroboam II (746 B.C.) (Hos 8:4,10, 10:3, 13:10–11). This political instability should have meant that Hosea's predictions of judgment should not have been so incredulously received as the predictions of Amos. As far as we can tell, Amos announced extinction in the near future at a time when Israel enjoyed the most prolonged peace and prosperity it had known since the reign of Solomon, nearly two hundred years earlier. Thirty years after Amos had spoken the kingdom of Israel had ceased to exist. Yet the Israelites who heard Hosea seemed no more ready to listen to his threats. Both prophets, like their successors, found it extremely difficult to convince the Israelites and Judahites that the moral will of Yahweh was serious and that those who knew it and refused to submit to it had to be removed from the human scene. This, I take it, may be an instance of what has often been called rigorous Old Testament morality. But the message of judgment is that no one sins and gets away with it.

Isaiah and Micah spoke to Judah not long after Amos and Hosea. While Micah may have been as uncompromising as Amos, Isaiah nowhere clearly announces that the kingdom of Judah will perish as Israel perished. In fact it did not perish until a hundred years later, and we shall have to point out that when this happened the prophetic theology of this event had been constructed. Again, it was not to be conceived that Israel or Judah were the victims of history like the Moabites or the Ammonites, for instance. At the same time, Isaiah had no theological explanation of the destruction of Judah; as he knew Judah, this would leave Yahweh without a people and a covenant. The annihilation would be the annihilation of Yahweh too; some biblical writers allude to those who scoff at Yahweh because he was unable to save his people from destruction (Jer 18:16, 19:8; Lam 2:15). Even with the words of Amos and Hosea presupposed (which Isaiah may never have heard), the fall of Judah and Jerusalem could be understood only as a defeat of Yahweh, both by the Assyrians (Is 36:13–20, 37:10–13) and by the Judahites (Is 37:17–20).

With this important reservation, Isaiah's statements of the necessity of judgment are as uncompromising as the statements of Amos and Hosea. Biblical theology owes to Isaiah the idea of a remnant which survives judgment, an idea which exhibits a remarkable ambiguity in its various uses in different writers. One can find the idea without the word in Amos 3:12; and since the line occurs in Amos, no one doubts that the animal of which only two legs or an ear is preserved is surely dead. There is no reason to think that Isaiah's remnant of Judah, which Yahweh preserves, was meant to signify more than that minimum which was required for life to continue (Is 1:9, 6:13, 7:3, 10:20–22). For Isaiah judgment meant the reduction of Judah to a people which would be politically impotent; nowhere does he imply that political power or action will save Judah from judgment. His demands for dependence on faith alone and on inaction ("rest and quiet") were as incredible to the politicians of his time as they would be to the politicians (including ecclesiastical politicians) of our times (Is 7:4–9, 30:15–16). The scope of Isaiah's judgment was not as far behind the scope of Amos's judgment as many of his readers have thought, and the theme of the inviolability of Zion, if indeed it was a theme of Isaiah, signified very little for the political pomp and power of Judah.

Later uses of the theme of the remnant by continuators of the Isaiah tradition and by other writers have focused less on the remnant as a threat and more on the remnant as a promise (Is 11:11,16, 37:32; Mic 2:12, 5:7–8; Zeph 2:7,9, 3:13; Zech 8:12). It does make a difference whether one says, "Only a remnant will survive," or, "Indeed a remnant will survive." We have mentioned before and will have occasion to mention again the fact that the survival of Judaism in any form was unexpected and paradoxical; and it seems quite probable that the "only a remnant" of the preexilic prophets became "indeed a remnant" of the postexilic prophets. This theme will be treated again when we speak of survival as a particular form of the saving act. The original threat became a messianic promise.

The exhortations of Isaiah to faith and inaction develop into something more explicit in Jeremiah, who saw the threat to Judah reach its consummation in the fall of the kingdom. Isaiah predicted judgment; he commanded repentance but promoted no steps to avert the judgment. If it was the purpose of Yahweh to moderate the judgment so that the destruction was less than total, no action to alter the course of events could be effective. In the great discourse of 28:9–29 Isaiah spoke with harshness to those who would attempt to protect themselves by politics; such plans he called a covenant with death and a league with Sheol, which will surely fail of its purpose.

Jeremiah, on the other hand, had no promise that even a remnant would survive; his message was that Judah would disappear as Israel had disappeared. It is difficult for us to enter into the minds of the leaders of Judah and find the base of their strange, foolish confidence that the supreme disaster somehow would not happen. It may not even have been a religious misunderstanding; it is possible that the leaders of Judah in its last years were men to whom religion had become largely meaningless. In any case, they were determined to resist the advances of the Babylonians with all the strength of their own resources and all the foreign assistance which they could obtain.

The response of Jeremiah to these measures of defense was to counsel the common soldiers to abandon the service and desert to the Babylonians (Jer 21:8–10, 38:1–3). This counsel was treated as treasonable by the officers of Judah, and only the confused politics of the last days of Judah permitted Jeremiah to escape alive (Jer 38:4–28). There were men high in the councils of Judah who believed, although not necessarily for the religious reason proffered by Jeremiah, that resistance to a large and powerful army was the kind of folly which would not only destroy the kingdom but cause many needless deaths. No doubt Jeremiah would have agreed with these considerations, but it is necessary to understand that his proclamations, which no nation at war could treat as anything but treasonable, had a theological and not a political base. He affirmed that the kingdom of Judah had lost that moral sovereignty which enables a nation to conduct war. The cause of Judah was proved totally unrighteous because of its infidelity to the law of Yahweh; it had lost any right to assert itself or to defend itself. In the process of judgment, it was now the Babylonians who waged a holy war against the wicked. Yahweh was on their side, and they would defeat Judah even if their army were defeated (Jer 37:9–10). The nation which wars against judgment cannot win, no matter what the political odds may appear to be.

It seems to have been the prophetic theme of judgment rather than the historic experience of Israel which led the Deuteronomic historians to conceive the history of Israel as proceeding through cycles of sin and judgment. This view is seen most easily in the book of Judges; here the stories of the judges have been set in a framework of sin, affliction, repentance and prayer, deliverance, and repose, after which the cycle is repeated. However accurate this view may be theologically, it does not reflect the experience of Israel as history knows it. It does reflect the conviction mentioned above that no one sins and gets away with it; but the writers of the Old Testament books had to arrive at a more sophisticated expression of this conviction. We shall return to the problem when we treat wisdom.

The same theme of judgment runs through the primitive history of Genesis 2–11, most of which comes from J. Judgment is invoked upon the first human couple for disobedience to a command of Yahweh. While this judgment does not in the J narrative quite reach the scope of the later Christian doctrine of original sin, it is intended by the writer to be an etiology of at least some features of the human condition; and the basic sin is most probably represented as idolatry, a form of the fertility cult. A synthetic view of Genesis 2–11 shows that the chapters contain a whole series of "falls," each of which is an instance of sin and judgment extending far beyond the persons immediately guilty of sin. Thus the narrative contains the story of the first murder, the invention of the blood feud—the customary way of punishing murder—the deluge as a collective judgment on all mankind, and the story of the erection of the Tower of Babel (a second account of the building of the first city) and the dispersion of mankind. The author-redactor has not made a notable effort to reduce the items of the collection to a unified narrative, but the theme of judgment does emerge as dominant. When Yahweh reveals himself to Abraham, this comes as a saving act which breaks the sequence of judgment.

One element of this collection raises some questions of its own. Interspersed in these stories of judgment are stories of the inventions of the skills and crafts of civilization. Whether Jabal, Jubal, and Tubal-cain, the inventors of cattle herding, music, and metal-lurgy, were in the original form of the story the descendants of the murderer, they are in the final scheme; and Tubal-cain is very probably a *Doppelgänger* for his nearly homonymous ancestor, Cain (smith). The first murderer builds the first city; the original form of the story of the Tower of Babel very probably made Babel the first city, but the consequence of the erection of Babel was not unity but dispersion. Noah, the hero of the deluge, is also the in-ventor of viniculture; the original story may have been attached to another hero, but the effect of the invention is intoxication which becomes the occasion of a family disgrace.

When these are viewed at one glance, one is moved to ask whether the author-redactor did not intend to present the develop-ment of civilization as moving parallel to the growth of human wickedness. The view would not be entirely simplistic if that were what the author intended; other observers besides J have noticed that the growth of civilization multiplies both the scope of tempta-tion and the scope of human malice. Certainly the view that man might reform himself morally by abandoning civilization and re-turning to a more primitive manner of life seems overly simple; the basic vices are possible and have been practiced in primitive conditions. But one remembers a witticism current at the time the first nuclear bomb was exploded. A scientist, asked what the weapons of the next war would be, answered that he did not know, but that the war after the next one would be fought with sticks and stones. The implication is that man's murderous malice towards his own kind would neutralize itself and return man to conditions in which the killing of large numbers of people is impossible. Hosea saw the repentance of Israel beginning with a return to the desert; in the concrete, this meant the abandonment of civilization and a return to nomadism. Does J mean that man comes under judgment simply by developing the skills of civilization? If he meant this, he was careful not to say it, unless so subtly that we cannot be sure of his meaning. He seems to have been quite well aware of the moral risk involved in civilization and of the moral price man has paid for his civilization. Only by the introduction of this im-plication was J able to arrange the anecdotes of prehistory in such a way that they become stories of judgment.

6. *Survival*

More than once we have taken notice of the fact that the survival of an "Israel" after the Babylonian conquest is in itself an exceptional historical fact, apart from any theological significance which is attached to survival. We place "Israel" in quotation marks simply because the historian of the ancient Near East may very well question the continuity between the monarchy of Judah and the community which is most accurately designated "Judaism." The continuity in fact is enough to justify the claim of Judaism to be the religious heir of Israel and Judah; Judaism preserves the worship of the deity called Yahweh in Israel and Judah, it collected and preserved the literature of Israel and Judah which is called the Old Testament, and it preserved many of the religious institutions of Israel and Judah. Political continuity it did not have, and the ethnic community is not as pure as the Jews of the fifth century B.C. wished to make it (Ezra 10; Neh 13:23–27). But no other small tribe or state which fell under the Assyrian and Babylonian conquests survived with anything which approached the continuity of Palestinian Judaism with Israel and Judah of the monarchical period.

The exegete and the theologian are not embarrassed in their search for a theological interpretation of the survival of Israel; they are embarrassed because the Old Testament presents too many theological explanations of the survival to allow a theological synthesis. Most of these theological explanations must be treated in Chapter VII under the general topic of "The Future of Israel"; these studies will disclose that the postexilic community had a more difficult time explaining its historical existence than Israel, whether premonarchic or monarchic, had.

A political community or a tribal society has no problem in explaining its existence. It is the frame of life within which its members live. Not only in the ancient world but in much of the more recent world another frame of life is regarded by the members of tribes and political communities as no better than death; in our own times many have said, "Better dead than red," and it could be dangerous to question their sincerity. As long as Israel and Judah could preserve an Israelite-Judahite way of life for the subjects of the kings, they needed no justification. They were the political realities in which the covenant of Yahweh with his people was realized; but even if they had not been the realization of the covenant, they furnished that identity and that security which any nation must furnish its citizens if they are to support it. It did not occur even to Elisha and his followers to exchange the Israelite monarchy for a non-Israelite monarchy or to overthrow the monarchy and return to the tribal confederacy.

The postexilic community furnished no political identity and no political security. Identity and security were sustained by the Persian Empire, and it did a better job in both respects than the monarchy of the last years of Judah. It is not by accident that the Jews of the period seized upon every remark of Cyrus or any Persian king which could be taken as a confession of the divinity of Yahweh. In fact, the Persian kings were worshipers of all the gods of the peoples of the empire,[18] and they did not, like the Assyrian general of Sennacherib (2 Kings 18:28-35), patronize or mock these gods. That Cyrus might speak of the divinity of Yahweh and prescribe the establishment of his cult with Persian subsidies did not make Cyrus a Yahwist in the proper biblical and Israelite sense (Ezra 6:2-5). But it was all the postexilic community could appeal to in an empire where peace and security were no longer obviously in the hands of Yahweh. The postexilic community had to justify itself as a religious community; and we who have so long taken "churches" for granted do not realize that this was the first community known to history which had to justify itself as religious.

We have mentioned above that the restoration of Judah was a saving act which demanded a separate classification. One did not inquire into the motives of Yahweh (Is 45:11). But while his purpose in establishing a people led by Moses which could have a glorious destiny might be mysterious, his purpose in restoring a remnant approached the incomprehensible. There must have been Judahites—they have left nothing in the Old Testament—who did not believe this event was a saving act; it was merely an accident

[18] A. Scharff and A. Moortgat, *Ägypten und Vorderasien im Altertum* (Munich, 1962), 466-69.

of history. If Yahweh was still concerned with his people, he owed it to them to show more clearly his concern and his purpose. One did not need to explain why life was granted to a human being in the first place, but when dead bones were restored to life (Ezek 37), some other purpose than another death had to be manifested.

Thus until what is generally called a "messianic idea" of restored Israel became clear, the existence of the postexilic community remained not only mysterious but irrational. It should not be there, and it was hard to see what good it served by being there. These considerations may help to explain the unbelief which is reflected in much of Second and Third Isaiah and in other postexilic prophetic writers. Their contemporaries had ample reason to think that the hand of Yahweh was shortened (Is 59:1). To recall the saving acts of the past must have seemed to them scarcely more than a mockery. It could not be expected that such saving acts could be repeated.

Where the Israelites and Judahites of the monarchy felt that they were the heirs of promises, the postexilic Judahites felt that they were the heirs of guilt. The statement that the fathers ate sour grapes and the children's teeth were set on edge (Jer 31:29–30; Ezek 18:1–3) is such a natural response to experience that we must believe it was very frequently repeated. How could the little community of the restoration ever hope to rid itself of the burden of the guilt of several centuries? The idea of collective guilt is a reflection of a mysterious element of reality, and we shall have to return to it under several headings. Many of the writings of the postexilic period show that collective guilt can hang like a millstone, discouraging enterprise and ambition. Collective guilt was the obvious and easy explanation of the postexilic community, and some of the sayings of the Old Testament could suggest that Yahweh had left this remnant as a monument to his righteous anger (Deut 29:22–28). Had the beliefs of the postexilic community rested here, there would be little to say about the theology of the Old Testament for any period.

7. *Yahweh and the Nations*

The Hebrew language has two words which can be translated "man" in the sense of mankind, and standard Hebrew lexica list several passages in which these words are used in the abstract sense. It seems to be a safe generalization that the interest of the biblical authors is rarely centered on mankind in general and on the human condition seen abstractly; such interest can be seen in the wisdom literature and in Genesis 1–11. The story of the Tower of Babel is a mythological explanation of the division of mankind into nations, in spite of the fact that the "Table of Nations" (Gen 10) precedes the story in the compilation of these chapters. Man is usually seen by the biblical writers as identified with some people or nation; and it is difficult to show in the Old Testament any idea of a relation between Yahweh and man, meaning mankind. Yahweh stands in a peculiar relation to the Israelites, a relation which is shared by no other group and no other individual. If Yahweh is not related to a people by covenant, the Old Testament in most of its books is unaware of any relation.

The primitive history of Genesis 1–11 in both J and P recognizes that Yahweh is the maker of man; we shall touch this idea more fully when we treat of creation. But the rest of the story is, as we have already indicated, the story of man under judgment. The collection is the preliminary to the story of the revelation of Yahweh to Abraham, which initiates the peculiar relationship of promise and fulfillment, already reviewed. The fulfillment is reached in the covenant of Yahweh with Israel. Other peoples are ignored in this development. If they are akin to Israel or were thought to be akin, they are recognized as the descendants of brothers and cousins; so, for instance, the people of Moab, Ammon, and Edom, neighbors of the Israelites and ethnically related, were given remote common ancestors. Even older than these common ancestors was the curse on the eponymous ancestor of the Canaanites (Gen 9:25–27); yet ethnically, culturally and linguistically the Israelites were a part of the Canaanite group.

The Old Testament has no explanation of the religious difference between the Israelites and other people except that Yahweh had revealed himself to the Israelites and not to others. Their own ancestors, when they lived across the River (the Euphrates), had served other gods (Jos 24:3). David could call exile from Israel a compulsion to serve other gods (1 Sam 26:19). It was altogether natural and expected that other peoples worshiped their own gods; and in the course of the development of Israelite belief and literature, the other gods came to be identified with idols and the religion of the nations with simple idolatry. But neither in the primitive history nor in the later history does the origin of idolatry ever appear as a "fall," with the possible exception of Genesis 3.[19] One cannot doubt that in the Old Testament generally idolatry is the basic sin, the radical vice from which all other vices flow. There is some ambiguity in treating idolatry both as the radical human vice and as the normal human condition; and some etiology of idolatry ought to be sought. If this etiology is not found in Genesis 3—and if it is found there, it is extremely subtle—one must conclude that the biblical writers generally had no interest in the religion of the nations nor in how the nations arrived at the gross superstition in which they were sunk. Since the Israelites themselves, according to the testimony of the Old Testament, often adopted beliefs and practices of other religions, it does not seem likely that the religions of the nations were widely misunderstood or unknown.[20]

In most of the narrative books of the Old Testament, the nations are viewed simply in their relations to Israel—in Genesis, in their relations to the patriarchs. An outstanding exception to this may be mentioned at once; the exception is the Cities of the Plain, which are destroyed by a judgment of Yahweh in chapters 18 and 19 of Genesis. The literary relation between these cities and Abra-

[19] In an earlier article I proposed an interpretation of chapters 2 and 3 of Genesis as an etiology of the fertility cults ("The Literary Characteristics of Genesis 2-3," *Theological Studies*, 15 [1954], 541-72). Most of my colleagues found this interpretation too subtle for their taste.

[20] I have elsewhere expressed my doubts about the thesis of Yehezkel Kaufmann that the Old Testament shows absolutely no apprehension of the real character of mythological religion. See "The Hebrew Attitude Toward Mythological Polytheism," CathBiblQuart, 14 (1952), 323-35.

ham is universally regarded as editorial; the story, it is thought, must be older than the stories of the patriarchs. The story therefore illustrates not the usual view of the nations found in the narrative books, but rather the prophetic view, which we treat below. Outside of this episode, the nations are viewed neutrally. In the stories of the patriarch's wife in the harem (repeated three times in Genesis, in chapters 12, 20 and 26), the foreign ruler is threatened with punishment; but the punishment is never inflicted, since the ruler acted in ignorance. Once he heeds the warning, he is not held guilty. These stories, like the other stories of the patriarchs, are set in a monotheistic world; the worship of any other gods is not mentioned. The Egyptians are treated in a very favorable light, since they accept the sons of Israel as guests in their country.

The tone of the narrative changes sharply in Exodus. Here the Pharaoh and the Egyptians set themselves in direct opposition to the will of Yahweh revealed through Moses. For this opposition, and not for any general or particular moral corruption or for the worship of other gods, the Egyptians become the object of the great typological saving act of the Old Testament. They are not totally destroyed as Sodom and Gomorrah were, in spite of the obduracy of Pharaoh (in which it is assumed that his people support him). Yahweh does not demand that the Egyptians worship him but that they let his people go. When this demand is attested with sufficient clarity, then Yahweh delivers his people at great cost to those who refuse to hearken to his voice.

It is a component of the theme of the exodus that Yahweh saves his people and overcomes those who threaten them. We have noticed when we discussed this theme that in its earliest form the will of Yahweh to save Israel can sometimes appear to show little moral discrimination. This is one of the areas in which the Old Testament approaches not only narrowness but religious and ethnic prejudice. This is not easily said of the exodus traditions; here Yahweh appears as the liberator of the oppressed and the helpless. A clear invitation is extended to the oppressors to cease from oppression, and the invitation is repeated after a number of punishments, which grow in intensity as the Pharaoh becomes more hardened in his obduracy. At the same time, the background is set for the belief that Yahweh is the savior of his people who destroys its enemies. This belief is much refined in the prophetic writings. But until the prophetic interpretation appears, the nations are treated with benevolence by Yahweh if they are friendly with Israel, and the enemies of Israel are his enemies. It was Yahweh who gave David and Solomon rest from their enemies round about (2 Sam 7:1; 1 Kings 5:1), although the wars of David, briefly reported as they are, seem to be clearly wars of aggression and conquest. It is in passages such as this that Israelite chauvinism appears most transparently. The nations have no place in Yahweh's world scheme, no origins and no destiny. They are judged purely in relation to the people of Yahweh; to threaten this people is to risk destruction, and to be friendly with this people is the only way to make some of their blessing rub off on others.

Both the course of history and the course of prophetic insight combined to change this primitive attitude towards the nations into something more sophisticated, if not immediately more humane. The change begins with the opening chapter of Amos, judged quite surely by critics to belong to the original words of Amos. Amos utters threats against six peoples well known in the Old Testament as Israel's neighbors, sometimes friends and sometimes enemies. All are threatened with total or nearly total destruction; the motivation of the threats is of peculiar interest because the offenses of these people are not clearly acts of hostility towards Israel. Commentators have generally noticed that they can all be grouped as crimes of inhumanity—extraordinary cruelty in war, the slave trade, and profanation of corpses. These six charges (the threat against Judah is universally regarded by critics as secondary) lead to a climactic seventh charge, against Israel itself; for inhumanity Israel can expect no more merciful treatment than the nations deserve. From the beginning, the collection proceeds to its penultimate saying (Amos 9:7): The Israelites are not different before Yahweh from the Ethiopians, the Philistines and the Aramaeans. Yahweh brought all of them from abroad into their present homelands; he now looks upon the sinful kingdom of Israel to destroy it from the earth. With these words the original collection of the words of Amos closes; and with these words is heard the first Israelite speaker who denied the privileged position of the people of Yahweh. There is no difference between Yahweh's moral judgment of Israel and his moral judgment of the nations.

The saying is revolutionary in more ways than one. Just as Amos denies that the judgment of Israel is different, so also he affirms that the nations are subject to the moral judgment of Yahweh whether their actions affect Israel or not. Amos affirms a moral standard which is valid both for Israel and for the nations, and the sanction of Yahweh is behind this standard both for Israel and for the nations. The nations are brought into the world which Yahweh judges. Amos does not discuss the plea of ignorance which might be entered. The kind of crime which he has chosen to cite is not a crime for which ignorance is easily pleaded. We do wrong to the men of the ancient world when we think that they could not recognize barbarism as barbarism, although standards of what is and is not barbarism vary from one period and one culture to another. Amos was not the only man of his time to regard the cruelties of war and the slave trade as inhuman; neither in his time nor in other times was the number of such men very large.

We spoke of both prophetic insight and history as affecting the Old Testament attitude towards the nations. The arrogant indifference of the Israelites toward the nations arose in a period when Israel encountered no people which was its superior in numbers and strength. The memories of the exodus preserved not even dim recollections of the majesty of the eighteenth and nineteenth dynasties of Egypt; the Egypt of the exodus stories was closer to the enfeebled Egypt of the eleventh century and later. History during the premonarchic period and during the monarchy up to the rise of Assyria in the eighth century actually favored the theological rationalization of Israelite victory as the saving act of Yahweh and Israelite defeat as a punishment for a temporary defection. But Assyria was a power of dimensions which very few people in the eighth century were able to recognize quickly. When they did recognize it, they had already been defeated by the Assyrians. One of the few who did recognize it was Isaiah; and the recognition opened to him an insight into the relation of the nations with Yahweh.

In two poems—or two collections of sayings (Is 10:5–11,13–19)—Isaiah calls Assyria the rod of the anger of Yahweh. Instead of the object of judgment, Assyria becomes the instrument of judgment. Assyria is sent against a godless nation, the people at whom Yahweh is angry (10:6); the people meant is certainly Israel, but Isaiah does not clearly mean that Assyria is the rod of Yahweh's anger against other peoples such as Calno, Carchemish, Hamath, Arpad, Samaria, and Damascus (10:9). It is not clear that Yahweh has a judgment against these peoples such as he has against Judah. Yet the text as we have it includes Samaria with no particular emphasis; and it is clear that Isaiah thought of Samaria as a peculiar object of the judgment of Yahweh. It may be excessive subtlety to see in the inclusion of Samaria in this line an expression of the ignorance and indifference of the Assyrians to the purposes of Yahweh. Samaria and Judah are indeed the objects of judgment against which Yahweh sends the Assyrians, but to the Assyrians they are simply two more in the list of conquered peoples. Hence Isaiah cannot call Assyria the rod of judgment without adding a threat against Assyria for its pride; the threat is uttered in the second of the two poems. But Isaiah, a historical realist, could not utter a threat for the immediate future.

To explain Assyria as the rod of Yahweh's anger did indeed explain the power of Assyria over Judah; it was not a sufficient theological explanation of the phenomenon of Assyria, and it was expressed entirely in terms of the relation of Assyria to Judah. In a way, this is a repetition of the old narrowness of view. In Jeremiah one reaches a fuller explanation of the imperial powers, which again arises both from prophetic insight and from history. Jeremiah, a hundred years after Isaiah, lived in a nation which had experienced conquering imperial power as Isaiah had not experienced it. Jeremiah retained the theme of the instrument of judgment and indeed expanded it, as we have seen; the war of Babylon against Judah was a holy war, and it was a sin for Judah as a nation and for Judahites as individuals to resist the instrument of judgment. But Jeremiah also considered the relation of the conquering empire to other peoples.

Jeremiah, in chapter 25, utters an oracle which not only predicts the destruction of Judah by the Babylonians but also the world reign of Babylon for seventy years. The number seventy here may have some of the indefiniteness which is often associated with seven and its multiples;[21] but it may also signify the ideal span of life, and thus the saying means that no one living at the time would survive to see the fall of Babylon.[22] Jeremiah then enumerates nearly all the peoples of the ancient Near East, perhaps even extending his view into Asia Minor ("the kings of the north," 25:26) and extends to them the cup of wrath which Yahweh compels them to drink. Babylon is the rod of Yahweh's anger not only for Judah but for all the nations which Babylon conquers. The idea of judgment upon these nations is not as emphatic and nuanced as the idea of the judgment upon Israel and Judah, nor does Jeremiah imitate Amos in charging them with specific crimes. The prophet simply applies the prophetic principle of righteous judgment to the events of world history. Yahweh is the lord of history for the whole world, not merely for Israel and Judah. That event which is a judgment when it happens to Israel and Judah is not senseless and meaningless when it happens to other peoples. The nation which is conquered by an imperial power has experienced the judgment of Yahweh, and his judgments are righteous. Thus the Deuteronomic theology of history becomes the theology of world history as well as of Israelite history. And in this, one returns to the overthrow of Sodom and Gomorrah and to the theology of the deluge: since the judgments of Yahweh are righteous, there can be no explanation of such massive catastrophes except the wickedness of those who suffer them. We shall see when we treat the wisdom literature that this simplistic theology had to be submitted to more searching discussion.

In the Septuagint of Jeremiah, the oracles against the nations are inserted at 25:13 of the Hebrew (and English). The compiler of the Septuagint thus identified the oracles with the delivery of the cup of wrath, an identification which can only doubtfully be attributed to Jeremiah himself; for there is considerable critical doubt whether the oracles against the nations are the words of the prophet. These oracles are a particular and well-defined literary

[21] So, for example, in the seven fat and the seven lean years of Egypt, the seven times and the seventy times seven times as the model of forgiveness.
[22] From the fourth year of Jehoiakim to the conquest of Babylon by the Persians is a period of sixty-six years, 605 to 539 B.C.

species which are found in a number of the prophetic books. The first chapter of Amos is the earliest example of passages which can be called "oracles against the nations," but other passages so much resemble each other and in content and form and are so different from the sayings of Amos that it is better to classify Amos by himself. The type of oracle which is found in Amos 1 had no echo in later prophetic literature.

In the order in which the prophetic books appear in the Bible, the oracles against the nations are found in Isaiah 13–23;[23] Jeremiah 46–51; Ezekiel 25–32; Obadiah (the entire book); Nahum (the entire book); Zephaniah 2.[24] This collection of poems comes from unknown authors who wrote at uncertain dates. It has been suggested that the oracle against Moab, found in variant recensions in Isaiah 15 and 16 and Jeremiah 48, may be of non-Israelite origin. Things like this add to the difficulties of their interpretation; the exegete cannot always be sure whether the poet is referring to actual events or whether he is presenting his visions of the future. If the poet is referring to actual events, it is often impossible to relate his poems to known history. At times the compilers were misled; it is not certain that the topic of Isaiah 14 is the king of Babylon, as we read in 14:4. Through most of the oracles runs a highly emotional tone, almost dithyrambic. The imagery is abundant and often so rich as to be obscure or contrived. It is difficult to say that they are poems of hatred, although this can be affirmed of Nahum and of the poems against Edom. In most of the other poems there is a tone of compassion rather than of hatred, at times almost haunting; this tone has led some to believe that the poem of Moab mentioned above may be of Moabite origin. The tone of the poem is strangely similar to the poems of Lamentations. In comparison with the oracles of the prophets against Israel and Judah, as we have observed, the oracles against the nations lack the clear moral charges which justify the ways of Yahweh with Israel and Judah. It seems that when the Israelite prophets and poets contemplated the scene of world history, they found it too

[23] The compilers of Isaiah, misled by the title in 22:1, included here two poems which deal with Jerusalem and one of the officers of Hezekiah.

[24] Ezekiel 38 and 39 and several passages of Deutero-Zechariah belong to apocalyptic literature.

much for them, even with such themes as the prophetic judgment and the Deuteronomic history. Yahweh was not in covenant with the nations, nor had he revealed covenant law to them; ultimately his purpose in the history of the nations was impossible at this phase of biblical theology to discern. The rise and fall of nations in the "oracles" is in the last analysis as meaningless as the rise and fall of animals.

This is scarcely a very satisfying theology of history, and the theological development of the Old Testament does not stop in this blind alley. We shall pursue its further development under the heading of "The Future of Israel," for it was only when the future of Israel was seen with some clarity that the purpose of Yahweh in the history of the nations could be discerned. The oracles against the nations, when closely examined, may appear as the first genuine expressions of fellow feeling towards the nations which we have in the books of the Old Testament. This fellow feeling was achieved by the awareness that mankind is one great community when it faces the judgment of Yahweh. No people and no person is free of this judgment, and for each one it is equally righteous. Awareness of the fellowship of mankind in judgment did not of itself bring with it an idea of fellowship in salvation; and one concludes this discussion recognizing that it was difficult for the Israelites to develop an awareness of human fellowship under any aspect.

IV

Nature

1. *Mythology*

Philosophical thinking as it is known in western civilization began
with the Greeks, and the first philosophical thinking concerned
itself with the *kosmos*—that is, with the natural world. Only with
Socrates did philosophers turn their consideration to man, and
this meant, in the first instance, to ethics. With Plato the consideration of man turned to psychology. Thus there appeared the
categories of thought which still dominate the thinking of educated
western man. At the risk of overstating the difference between
Greek and Israelite thought, it can be said that none of the categories mentioned in the preceding sentences appears in the Old
Testament. We have already observed that the priorities of the
Israelite experience direct us to study the Israelite experience of
God first in history; the Israelites also experienced God in nature,
and in this experience they were much more affected by the beliefs
of other peoples than they were in their experience of God in
history.

Another dangerous generalization is to say that the religions of
the ancient Near East were nature religions. One of the Greek
ideas which made philosophy possible in Greece was the idea
expressed by the word *kosmos*.[1] The word has the basic meaning
of "order"; in philosophy it means the world as ordered, and
finally the world itself. The world precisely as ordered is an object
of intelligence; the question of Greek philosophers was not
"Whence?" or "Who made the world?" but "Of what is the world
made?" Philosophically, this appears to be a question which can

[1] H. Sasse, "Kosmos," Kittel ThW: 868–78.

be answered from observation of the world and thought about it. The world as *kosmos* is rational, not mysterious. Furthermore, to the Greek philosophers the *kosmos* was a primary datum; it was not explained, but it was that in terms of which all reality was explained. Greek philosophy did not know the idea of creation; philosophers who spoke of a demiurge thought of an agent who introduced order into reality.[2] Aristotle affirmed that the world and its prime mover were equally eternal, for an eternal mover demands an eternal moved.[3]

Greek philosophy suppressed, except as literary ornaments, the early Greek mythology of creation, which can be compared in many details to the mythology of the ancient Near East, much of which is echoed in the Old Testament. In fact, as we shall see, "mythological" is the best word to designate the biblical apprehension of creation both as process and as object; in order to validate this assertion, it is necessary to premise some general observations on mythology and mythological thought.

In popular speech, "myth" is often used as synonymous with "falsehood." Myth is often false, but so is science or philosophy. None of the three are falsehood by definition; they are false when they misapprehend reality or misinterpret reality. There is no reason to look for a special weakness in any one of the three approaches to reality; there are many things which operate in such a way as to give man the occasion to deceive himself, and there is no peculiar "mythological" way to error, just as there is no peculiar "philosophical" or "scientific" way. In an earlier article on the subject, I followed the explanation of Ernst Cassirer; nothing since I wrote the article has modified my own understanding of myth, and I summarize the article here.[4]

Cassirer's major contribution, I believe, was to classify myth with art, language and science as one of four symbolic forms of expression.[5] I call this "major" not so much because myth is

[2] Ibid. 874.

[3] *Metaphysics,* XII: 7, 1072a: 18–25.

[4] "Myth and the Old Testament," CathBiblQuart, 21, 3 (July 1959), 265–82; *Myths and Realities* (Milwaukee, 1963), 182–200.

[5] E. Cassirer, *Language and Myth* (New York, 1946), 8, noted in my *Myths and Realities,* 183.

identified as a symbolic form as because science is identified with a symbolic form; and science can here be taken to include philosophy and in fact all forms of learned speech which are abstract and discursive. To choose a rather obvious example, the model of Botticelli's "Birth of Venus" was symbolically portrayed by the artist. To define the model in terms of height, weight, mathematical proportions, pigmentation and enumeration of physical origins would be no more "real" than the symbolic expression of art. A description in language would have to be poetry; many poetic descriptions of the beautiful woman have been written in practically all languages, and no one questions that they are symbolic. The "Venus" whom the model represented was one of many mythical expressions of the beautiful woman; such mythical expressions resemble each other not because beautiful women all look alike, but because the response of the male to the beautiful woman comes close to being typological. Yet the beautiful woman is not an object which transcends experience. She is symbolically expressed in all the symbolic forms because of the belief that no one form gives perfect expression to the experience. She does not transcend experience, but she transcends expression, or is thought to transcend it.

It is not of the nature of symbolic forms that their objects transcend experience or expression; but the understanding of reality which the form is intended to communicate is not directly experienced nor completely and perfectly expressed. Thus in science the purpose of the symbolic form is to give expression to the order which the mind finds in the objects of observation or which the mind imposes upon the objects for the purposes of clarity of discourse. In art and language the symbolic form attempts to translate the total psychic experience of the object as the writer or artist conceives the experience. Great art is recognized as great because the artist or the poet understands man well enough for him to translate an experience which is universal rather than purely personal. Such experience, like the order of philosophy and the sciences, is directly attained by no one, and in this sense the form deals with the transcendent. Certainly transcendence of this type is not the same type of transcendence as we attribute to the atom, which has never been directly observed or experienced by any one. Like the beautiful woman, its best expression is symbolic. It hardly needs to be added that the total psychic experience in the two examples differs about as much as any two psychic experiences one might mention.

Both the definition of symbolic form and the definition of transcendental are eternally imprecise both because of the development of the range of experience and because of the development of symbolic forms. Only in recent times has man been able to employ the symbolic form of science to express his experience of nature and his understanding of nature. In our generation, man has walked on the moon; nothing could more effectively demythologize the moon, although a total of twelve men have had the direct experience. In fact their experience demythologizes the whole solar system, indeed, the whole celestial universe. A Soviet cosmonaut was quoted as saying he did not observe God "out there"; but no one ever claimed that he had observed God "out there." At least one of our own astronauts confessed to a deeper awareness of God "out there"; and a comparison of the two suggests that it is one's previous awareness or nonawareness of God which shows him God's presence or absence in an entirely new situation.

The earliest process of demythologizing known to history occurred in Greece when philosophy replaced mythology. In spite of the skill of Greek poets, Greek cosmic mythology in its early periods lacked none of the crudeness which is characteristic of so much mythology. A god who castrates and devours his father has to be called crude in any mythology. As an explanation of the phenomena, mythology was so obviously inferior to philosophy that no intelligent person in Greece could take it seriously. It has to be noticed that since Greek religion was essentially mythological, philosophical criticism also destroyed Greek religion. The basic error in the Greek philosophical system was to take mythology as an explanation of the phenomena. To anticipate a point which the following exposition is meant to support, mythology did not intend to explain the phenomena but simply to make it possible for man to face the phenomena and live with them.

If myth has a proper object, it must be defined as that which lies outside experience, not necessarily that which transcends experience. Myth, which is almost without exception classified by both scholars and amateurs in the same way, deals with the relations between the divine and the human and with origins and ends—protology and eschatology. The relations between the divine and the human do indeed transcend experience; such things as beginnings and ends can be discovered through scientific investigation in ways unsuspected by earlier peoples who could discuss beginnings and ends only in mythological language. The relations of the divine with the human admit different conceptions in different cultures and different historical periods. Modern man not only does not attribute bad weather to the anger of the deity; modern man literally cannot make this attribution. He cannot make the attribution not because man understands God better but because man understands the weather better. Modern man can recognize that the very qualification of weather as "good" or "bad" is mythological; the weather is neutral and cannot be judged purely in terms of human likes and dislikes. If Southern California had the rainfall of the Middle West, it would cease to be the paradise which so many people find it to be; other people find that a desert falls short of their idea of paradise.

Where myth deals with objects that can with new techniques and skills be submitted to direct experience, it suffers demythologizing from philosophy and science. Yet if we return to an earlier statement that myth does not explain the phenomena but enables man to live with them, we observe large areas which seem to lie permanently outside experience; that is, they transcend experience in the proper sense of the word "transcend." The divine is the most obvious example of the transcendent, but one need not appeal to this exclusively. As a phenomenon, death seems to lie under the analysis of science and philosophy; to tolerate mortality most men must still appeal to some mythical form. The problem of evil, whether in general or in detail, admits no scientific or philosophical analysis; man faces the problem of evil by mythicizing the problem. Science has not yet analyzed the origin of life, even subhuman life; this particular beginning is still seen in a mythical form. Myth formulates in an acceptable way that unknown which man recognizes but cannot define. In some way this unknown can all be summed up in the divine. In Mesopotamian mythology the origin of kingship was explained mythologically;

kingship came down from heaven.[6] The political forms in which the peoples of Mesopotamia lived were patterned after heavenly forms. This had not unimportant political consequences; for the order of politics, like the order of nature, was the earthly counterpart of the celestial prototype. Such a theopolity obviously made for stability. In Egypt, Pharaoh was the incarnate Horus son of Re. One wonders how Egypt could exhibit the degree of instability which it did, but historians recognize that the political system of Egypt had a stability which has never been paralleled elsewhere. One doubts that this should be attributed entirely to the climate. Modern man does not think of politics as a point where he has relations with the divine; again, he not only does not think this but cannot. Yet it is only a few hundred years since the divine right of kings was seriously defended and exercised in European nations. The divine right of kings was a modern political myth. Because this myth has been abandoned, it does not follow that the contemporary world has no political myth. The political myth of the ancient world was an effort to counter the native instability of political forms and to shore up stability with a theological motif.

The symbolism of myth is achieved by turning the pattern or the institution into an event. The event is the pattern or the archetype which endures or recurs in the historical or natural pattern or institution. Kingship was legitimate and it endured because it was instituted by the gods, who in their own community exhibit this form. In Israel kingship was instituted by Yahweh, but there is no celestial pattern of kingship because Yahweh is alone. The collapse of such an institution causes severe theological problems which in the ancient world could be met only by a new myth; in Israel, the collapse of the monarchy was explained in two ways. One was the myth of the judgment of Yahweh; the other was the myth of the restoration of kingship. In calling the theme of judgment "mythological," it is not my intention to say that this was a false interpretation of event; in the treatment of judgment presented above, it was our purpose to suggest that no other interpretation of history is reasonable. But the proper name for this type of thinking is "mythological"; myth, like philosophy, theology and

[6] ANET 265.

science, can be a symbolic way of expressing the truth. In judgment the Israelite saw the recurrence of the archetypal event; when Yahweh was first known to mankind he was recognized as a judge. The archetypal event will be seen with most clarity when we treat of creation. All myths are stories; when an event is given the dimension which we call recurrence or endurance, the event is conceived mythologically.

It is characteristic of mythological thought not only that it describes reality in terms of the archetypal event but also that it understands phenomena in terms of personal realities. This may with probability be defined as the essential characteristic of myth. Myth is entirely anthropomorphic. Man can deal with persons because persons act from motives which can be comprehended, even if they are not known. At the same time he recognizes that persons are unpredictable and that the full potential of the person is never known even to the person himself. Before the Greek *kosmos,* nature was seen by man not as order but as disorder, strife and confusion. The peoples of the ancient Near East saw in nature the same qualities which they saw in human society; man must live in human society, but it is often dangerous and frequently fatal. In the epic of Gilgamesh the hero Enkidu is created to live with beasts; he is seduced by a harlot and finds that the beasts will not accept him any longer, and he is compelled to dwell with his own kind in the city.[7] Thorkild Jacobsen described the Mesopotamian world view as the vision of "a multitude of powerful individual wills, potentially diverging, potentially conflicting, fraught with a possibility of anarchy."[8] It is significant that in Egypt, which has a much more regular climatic cycle than Mesopotamia, this theme of the theomachy is almost entirely missing from mythology. Myth enables man to face the phenomena, and Egypt had a different set of phenomena. One cannot explain why Egypt had such a well-developed mythology of death and the afterlife and why Mesopotamian mythology collapses before the phenomenon of death.

If the processes of nature are seen as things, man can face the phenomena only by understanding the processes. Knowing what a

[7] Ibid. 74–75.
[8] T. Jacobsen, "Mesopotamia," in H. Frankfort et al., *Before Philosophy* (Baltimore, 1949), 139.

hurricane is does not arrest it, although predicting it may help one to find shelter; but knowledge about it frees man from the haunting terror that a supernaturally powerful person is angry at him for unknown reasons. Mythological man, on the contrary, believes that a personal being can be reached by a personal approach. His anger can be appeased or turned away, his benevolence can be cultivated. In any case, he has personal desires and habits which can be learned, and while man is unable to meet or to avert his terrible power, he can integrate himself with the known desires and habits of the personal reality on whom he depends and whom he fears. The mythological response to this integration is in the first place cult, in the second respect for a revealed moral code. Thus the myth discloses both the character of the personal beings who govern the world and the way in which their good will can be sought and obtained.

Myth can ultimately be no more than an intuition of the reality which lies outside experience and is subject to neither philosophical nor scientific analysis. The intuition can be formulated as an unproved conviction that the ultimate explanation of reality must be personal. Implied is the assertion that man himself is of the same character—to find the exact word here is difficult—as the personal beings whom he recognizes. John Wilson called this principle "consubstantiality."[9] If man could not deal with them as persons, despair would be the only reasonable response. Mythology did not exclude despair, as we shall have occasion to notice again when we deal with ancient wisdom. To see the gods as personal beings, and particularly to see them as potentially diverging and conflicting (Jacobsen), left open the possibility of a personal failure in the gods like the personal failures man could see in himself and in his society, a *Götterdämmerung*. If the cosmic order (including the political order) failed because the gods could not maintain peace in their own household, man could feel himself the innocent victim not of divine malice but of divine incompetence. Perhaps this was the ultimate consolation mythology could give those who knew no other approach to transcendent reality. Naturally, we recognize this as a failure of mythology, not of di-

[9] J. Wilson, "Egypt," in H. Frankfort et al., *Before Philosophy* (Baltimore, 1949), 71–79.

vinity. In the Israelite mythological world, no personal failure in God was conceivable; only man failed. This too was a mythological pattern, but it does not become a pattern of despair. The ultimate anchor of dependence and assurance for the Israelite was not reason nor cosmic order, but those personal qualities which they defined as *hesed we'emet,* "kinship love and fidelity." Where the Mesopotamian mythology saw the root of ultimate insecurity, Israelite mythology saw the ultimate security—in the power of a personal will.

Myth is not an inferior substitute for science, philosophy, and theology. It is a distinct symbolic form, and it is the only approach to transcendental reality when science, philosophy, and theology are unable to apprehend and to interpret transcendental reality. Yet in the discussion presented above it may appear that myth has been assigned a position and a function which is very similar to the position and the function of theology. In the introductory chapter of this work the nature and methods of theology in general and of biblical theology in particular have been treated rather extensively; and the point was made that theology in the proper sense is not found in biblical literature. The questions which modern man discusses theologically were handled by Israelites in mythological thought and language; in this respect the Israelites talked like other peoples of the ancient world. Myth is not a theology nor a substitute for theology, but it deals with problems which we treat theologically. A biblical theology begins with biblical material, which is habitually exhibited in mythical patterns. To convert these patterns simply into abstract rational discourse is to destroy them, and with them the peculiar biblical insights which biblical theology seeks most intensely.

In my own article "Myth and the Old Testament," cited above, I quoted a number of examples of biblical mythological thought and language mentioned by Hermann Gunkel.[10] The enumeration deserves to be repeated here: the treatment of natural phenomena as the action or the experience of personal beings (Ps 19:6; Is 14:12–14); the rainbow (Gen 9:12–17); the description of the eschatological period as a return to the conditions of the primitive

[10] "Mythus und Mythologie," *Die Religion in Geschichte und Gegenwart,* v. 4 (Tübingen, 1930), 382–83, 387–88.

period of creation; etiological stories such as the creation of woman from the rib (Gen 2:21–24); the origin of human toil and the pains of childbirth (Gen 3:16–19); the union of the sons of God and the daughters of men (Gen 6:4); the world catastrophe conceived as a reversal of creation and a return to chaos (Is 17:12–13, 24:19–20); the sword and judgment of Yahweh upon the nations (Is 34:5); the golden age (Is 11:6–9). The list could be expanded, and other examples will appear in subsequent discussion, as some have already appeared; the list shows us that we encounter mythical thought and language frequently and in a number of very important themes.

In dealing with biblical history, we had occasion to refer to the historicization of myth and its companion technique, the mythicization of history. The mythical event, we have noticed, is turned into a contingent event by the narrative form; the reality which is symbolized by the event is a recurrent or an enduring reality. Myth is historicized when the mythical event is seriously given a once-and-for-all character, the particularity of the contingent historical event. History is mythicized when the particular contingent event is given an enduring or a recurring dimension; and this dimension is not the same as the enduring effects of a contingent historical event. The mythical event endures in itself, not only in its effects. Examples of the historicization of myth can be seen in the biblical creation account, particularly in the insistence of the P writer of Genesis 1:2–2:4a that Yahweh "rested" (ceased) from his work on the seventh day. He could hardly have stated more clearly in his own language and speech patterns that creation was not annually renewed; we shall see the significance of this when we discuss creation. The mythicization of history is more difficult to illustrate from the Old Testament; yet we are familiar with the common idiom in which a person or an event is said to become a myth or a mythological figure or event. In fact, the common idiom is sometimes inexact, if we are to define the mythological dimension as enduring or recurring; the word is sometimes used to mean no more than "unhistorical" in the sense that the record is no longer faithful to the event. The most obvious example of the mythicized event is the saving death and resurrection of Jesus Christ in Christian belief; yet most Christians would think that the historical reality of the event would be denied if the event were said to have a mythological dimension. Yet it is that religious event in all world religious history to which is attached the dimension of duration; and this is what mythological means. Were it not an enduring event, Christians could not conceive of it as a saving event.

Perhaps the exodus in the Old Testament (which we have discussed above) has a mythological dimension. We have referred to a certain mythical dimension of events which are celebrated in religious feasts; the recital and the re-enactment are declarations of the recurrence or the endurance of the event. The dynasty of David appears to be mythologized when it is promised an eternal duration; the promise is made to the founder but lasts with the dynasty. With less doubt, the mythological dimension is affirmed of the covenant, which outlasts even the catastrophe of national existence.

Certainly when we speak of mythicization and historicization we make a distinction which the biblical scribes did not make and would not have understood. Yet when we apply these terms to their speech in order to interpret it, we are not distorting their speech or their thought. They could and did distinguish between the merely particular and contingent event and the event of larger than historical dimensions. The modern historian would prefer to speak of the enduring effects of events or of endurance and recurrence in processes and institutions; but then he has no way of distinguishing between the enduring effects of Caesar's crossing of the Rubicon and the enduring effects of the saving death and resurrection of Jesus Christ. If he is a Christian, he will find that his fellow Christians insist on a distinction; they will speak not of enduring effects but of enduring reality.

2. *Creation*

In general, the idea of an absolute beginning has been difficult for the human mind to grasp. Aristotle thought he had proved that the prime moved, like the prime mover, had to be eternal;[11]

---

[11] *Metaphysics* XII: 7, 1072ª:18–25.

and Thomas Aquinas asserted that man would not think of an absolute beginning without the teaching of revelation.[12] The myths of creation more clearly speak of the beginning of the world of experience than they speak of an absolute beginning from nothing; and behind most of them one can discern the belief that creation is part of a cyclic process. It is not an obvious or easy philosophical or theological piece of reasoning to deduce how anything can come into existence in the hypothesis that once nothing existed.

The major problem in the history of religions and philosophy may not be so much the problem of creation as the problem of dualism. Supposing that a divine being exists of sufficient power and wisdom to create the world from nothing, how can one explain the numerous and obvious defects in the product? A deity with a power so defective could not be imagined as powerful enough to create even defectively. Hence the answer recommends itself that the power is opposed by another contradictory power and that creation is somehow the result of a conflict between the two powers which is never resolved. As we have observed, mythological thought is impressed more with the disorder of nature than with its order. The same nature which sustains man's existence threatens man's existence. To reduce these two movements to a single purpose has been too much for man through most of his history.

The two powers can be designated as light and darkness, life and death, good and evil, or order and chaos; and such designations reveal why the idea of an absolute beginning is not only difficult but can appear even repugnant. For this dualism, by these or other terms, is a fact of experience in the universe in which man lives. Both powers are alive and active, and both are competing on equal terms. If it is this way now, nothing suggests that it was ever different. In a totally good world, how could evil emerge? In a totally evil world, what would bring forth good? Hence the two powers must be conceived as the basic cosmic data, so to speak; there is no way either by philosophy or by mythology to go behind them. There can never have been a time

12 *Summa Theologiae* 1, 46:2.

when they were not, and hence there can be no absolute beginning.

This is not the explicit reasoning of the men who produced the creation myths of the ancient world, but it seems that some such reasoning is a faithful interpretation of their thinking in abstract rational discourse. Of particular interest, of course, are the creation myths of Mesopotamia and Canaan, the latter being less well known than the former. These myths have been known only since the latter half of the nineteenth century, the Canaanite myths in their original form only since 1930; that the Israelite beliefs and ideas about creation are related to them is now beyond dispute. The Israelite beliefs differ sharply, but the Israelite literature moves in the same world of thought and language.

The study of the mythological literature of Mesopotamia and Canaan, composed for cultic recital, makes it clear that creation was a cyclical event: annual in Mesopotamia and very probably, although less clearly, annual in Canaan also. The struggle between the two poles is seen in the annual cycle of life and death in vegetation. Life in animals and in men also exhibits the cycle of life and death; both are constant features in the world, and neither ever prevails over the other. The myths show no hope of a world from which death has been expelled nor any real fear of a world in which life ceases entirely. They deal, we have said, with the two ultimate principles, without beginning and without end, and irreducible as far as the men of the ancient world could perceive. Creation is the defeat of the forces of death and chaos and the production of new life. The cycle of life is the earthly counterpart of the events in the celestial world of the gods. The ritual integrates man with the celestial forces. It may be cruder than the thinking of the ancient world actually was to think of the myth and ritual as assuring the recurrence of the cycle of life; it may have been rather the celebration of the event. But behind the myth and the ritual was the awareness that the monster of chaos would again have its turn. Life was to be enjoyed and death accepted. Man could sustain death because the myth taught him that the gods gave him only a portion of life and the capacity of enjoying it. We shall see that this simple doctrine broke down under catastrophe; but these peoples were neither the first nor the last to find a simple mythological faith sufficient in most contingencies of the normal

life. Those who had to face catastrophic breakdowns of nature
or society have rarely been able to leave a record of their religious
sentiments.

Sex as a principle of life was prominent in the myth and ritual
of creation. This is certain, although some of the most notable
lacunae in the Mesopotamian and the Canaanite texts occur just
where this element should be prominent. But the sacred marriage
of god and goddess, re-enacted by king (or priest) and priestess,
was a part of the New Year ritual as far back as Sumerian times.[13]
The Canaanite Aleyan Baal is slain by demonic adversaries; after
he rises and vanquishes them, the cycle of life is restored by his
sexual commerce with the goddess.[14] The allusions to temple or
sacred prostitutes suggest that the worshipers entered into communion with the gods in the renewal of the life cycle by intercourse
with a priestess who represented the goddess.

In the Mesopotamian creation epic, there is no doubt that the
material from which the creator god fashions the universe is the
carcass of the monster of chaos which he has just slain.[15] This
is indeed imposing order upon chaos. Allusions to the death of
the fertility god in Mesopotamia are too obscure and ambiguous
to permit the reconstruction of the myth. But it is clear that Tiamat,
the monster of chaos, is ultimately the mother of all life, gods
included. Somehow these men of the ancient world could not escape the vision of a primal chaos best symbolized in the limitless
waters of the ocean. Man did indeed live on the fringe of chaos,
and nature smote him often enough to keep him reminded that
the victory of the creator over chaos was cyclical at best. Perhaps
the myth masked a fear that chaos would be the ultimate victor,
as it had been the original source. Genesis too begins with *tohu
wabohu,* "desolation and waste," a formless and limitless watery
abyss. Life springs from it only after the creator god has spoken
with authority.

In the book of Genesis, chapters 1:1 through 2:4a have become the standard biblical account of creation, and in much Christian theology it has become the standard theological pattern, from

[13] H. Saggs, *The Greatness That Was Babylon,* 381–89.
[14] ANET 139–42.
[15] Ibid. 67.

which one deviates at the peril of heresy. In fact it is only one of the Old Testament versions of creation; it has become a pattern because it is complete, and also because it stands where a creation account ought to stand, at the beginning of the Old Testament. This does not mean that it is an early document. Modern critics assign the passage to P, the most recent source of the Pentateuch, mostly postexilic. Some recent critics are inclined to believe that it is an earlier recital preserved in P. If one compares it to the creation myths of Mesopotamia and Canaan, it is probable that the passage was a cultic recital. If it was, there is no situation for it except in the pre-exilic New Year festival discussed above.

The narrative of Genesis 2:4b–25 is not another creation account. The creation of the world is treated in the barest allusions. This passage is an account of the origin of man, and in particular of the origin of the sexes; we have discussed this earlier. Hence before we begin to discuss the creation narratives, it is in place to ask why, as critics unanimously agree, there is no clear doctrine of creation in pre-exilic literature. The first biblical source in which the theme is prominent is Second Isaiah, whom we consider below.

The existence of the creation myths cited shows that there were beliefs to which the Israelites had occasion to respond; it is a problem why the response came so late. As we have indicated, we probably misunderstand ancient mythology if we treat the creation myths as an explanation of beginnings. The myth does not intend to describe a beginning which explains the present situation, but to mythologize the present situation in a recurring event. If this were the question, the early Israelites simply ignored the problem. For them, as we shall see, the universe was not explained as the product of tension between two equal forces. The problem of the absolute beginning was not raised by them, nor had it been raised by any one. They were familiar with the creation myth; the books of the Old Testament are full of allusions to the adoption of Canaanite fertility cults in Israel. The fertility cults were the recital and the re-enactment of the cyclical renewal of fertility, the annual creation. Orthodox believers in Yahweh could not discuss creation in terms of strife and sex in the world of the gods; having no other terms in which to discuss the world, and very probably not interested in its origins, they simply rejected the myths of creation in their totality. When they had to meet the problem, they met it by writing another myth of creation.

To call this new production a "myth" is to strain the word somewhat. We have already cited creation as an example of the historicization of myth. In chapter 1 of Genesis, creation has clearly become an event once and for all after which Yahweh rests; he ceases from his work which he has finished (Gen 2:1-3). But the intellectual and linguistic frameworks are mythological. This does not refer merely to the view of the cosmic structure in Genesis 1, the view which is found throughout the Old Testament and other ancient Near Eastern literature. The universe is seen from the viewpoint of earthbound man. Man stands on a disk floating in an abyss of water which has no limits—the lower abyss. Above him there is another watery abyss from which rain descends. The disk is covered by an inverted bowl, called in Genesis by a name which designates a plate of beaten metal. In this bowl are fixed sun, moon and stars. Elsewhere the earth is said to stand upon pillars; we do not ask what supports the pillars (Ps 82:5; Prov 8:29; Is 40:21). A poet also speaks of storehouses of snow and hail (Job 38:22-23). The stars march across the sky in due order when Yahweh calls them by name (Is 40:26). There are a few other features to be mentioned below which reflect more clearly the cosmogenic myths of Mesopotamia and Canaan. But as far as the picture of the universe given here is concerned, it is not mythological but expressly antimythological. The sun, moon and stars have no relation to gods and goddesses. They are not astrological signs but simply means of measuring time. Like the watery abyss, they have been depersonalized and depotentiated. The works are done in the order which is logical in a universe thus conceived except for the creation of light before anything else. This must reflect the ancient belief, found both within and outside the Old Testament, that light is the sign of the presence of the victorious saving god.[16] The division of light from darkness is an echo of the ancient dualism; the darkness of night is not the cosmic darkness of chaos, although it is often likened to chaos in biblical imagery. Once God has made light, that chaotic darkness is ex-

[16] G. van der Leeuw, *Phänomenologie der Religion*, 57.

pelled permanently from the universe. It is very likely that the repeated affirmation that the work is good, said of individual works and of the whole, is a denial that the evil principle of dualism is a constitutive element of creation.

The first chapter of Genesis exhibits in itself a certain ambiguity towards the work of creation, an ambiguity which has led some critics to wonder whether the passage is not compiled from two different sources. God is said to create both by word and by work; what is meant by working is not specified, but one may illustrate from Genesis 2:7,19 in which Yahweh is said to "form" man and the animals. The verb is used of the work of the potter and is actually illustrated by an Egyptian representation of the god Khnum forming a king and his *ka*.[17] The word "build," used of the creation of woman (Gen 2:22), probably does not signify a different image. Obviously, creation by work is more anthropomorphic than creation by word, which indicates the fullness of power. The power of Marduk is tested in the creation epic *Enuma Elish* when he is required to make a garment vanish and reappear by the simple word of command.[18] Since we find the creation in word in a document which on other counts appears to be a counterstatement to known myths of creation, it is very likely that the repeated use of this phrase is deliberate and purposeful. A strange parallel to creation by word is found in an Egyptian text, written in its present form about 700 B.C. but composed about 2700 B.C. In this text Ptah creates by thinking of the reality and then pronouncing its name.[19] There can scarcely be a mutual influence, but the text of Memphis is explicit in an unparalleled manner, even more explicit than the Old Testament. It is in sharp contrast to the almost unparalleled coarseness of some other Egyptian creation myths.[20]

Not all Old Testament allusions to creation historicize the myth; but there is no other version as complete and as well organized as the recital of Genesis 1. A description based on allusions found in the text of the Old Testament does not produce a synthesis of even the loose organization which is tolerated in myth. Yahweh

[17] ANEP 569.
[18] ANET 66.
[19] Ibid. 4–5.
[20] Ibid. 5–6.

divided the sea, broke the heads of the dragons, crushed the heads of Leviathan (Ps 74:13–14).[21] Yahweh rules the raging of the sea, stills its waves, crushed Rahab, made the heavens, the earth, and the world (Ps 89:9–11). He punishes Leviathan the fleeing serpent and Leviathan the twisting serpent with his great, hard, and strong sword and slays the dragon in the midst of the sea (Is 27:1).[22] Yahweh cut Rahab in pieces, pierced the dragon, dried up the sea, the waters of the great deep (Is 51:9–10). The helpers of Rahab bowed beneath God (Job 9:13). God stilled the sea and smote Rahab. By his wind the heavens were made fair (an allusion to the storm) and his hand smote the fleeing serpent (Job 26:12–13). He shut in the sea with doors, clothed it with clouds and darkness, set bounds, bars, and doors for it, and addressed it forbidding it to go any farther (Job 38:8–11).

These allusions reflect a combat between Yahweh and adversaries who can be identified from the Canaanite myths of Ugarit. Leviathan the fleeing serpent and Leviathan the twisting serpent occur in these myths. The serpents or dragons are associated with the sea, as they are in Ugarit, where Prince Sea and Judge River (perhaps two titles of the same individual) are enumerated among the adversaries of Baal. Rahab as a serpent or a dragon is otherwise unknown. The sea is not slain but stilled, imprisoned, or restrained. Since the prevailing winds on the Palestinian coast are westerly and the coast itself is generally rocky, the almost ceaseless dashing of the waves against the coast rather easily permit the image of a chaotic monster under restraint. Did not the creative deity hold it under his hand, it would rise to destroy the land.

These allusions do not tell us whether there was an Israelite version of the creative combat or whether the Israelite poets simply made Yahweh the hero of a mythological story whose original hero was Baal. The Israelites, we know from allusions in the historical and prophetic books, were often open to the practice of the Baal cult. Some allusions suggest that the Baal cult was transferred to Yahweh. In either case, the rite must have included the recital of the mythical narrative. It seems unlikely that orthodox

[21] Leviathan is now recognized as the dragon Lotan of Canaanite mythology (ANET 137, 138).
[22] Cf. ANET 137, 138.

Yahwist scribes would easily have incorporated mythical allusions which they could recognize as allusions to an idea of the deity completely out of harmony with Yahwism. Evidently these allusions were not seen as completely out of harmony, and at least the writers saw nothing suspicious in the mythological idea of victory of Yahweh the creator over chaotic and demonic monsters. It seems more probable that there was an Israelite recital of this combat, and it is best located, as we have seen, in the pre-exilic New Year festival. Hence, if Genesis 1 is a myth which is really antimyth, it may have been directed as much or even more against Israelite mythology than it was against Mesopotamian or Canaanite mythology. This does not imply that the Israelite myth of the combat actually included those features of the cosmic myths of Mesopotamia and Canaan which were openly repugnant to Yahwism; it is far more probable that the myth, if it was used in the New Year feast, simply narrated a victory over the monsters of chaos without any allusions to chaos as the primal source of being or to the function of sex in the cycle of life and death.

The ambiguity of the creation myth prevented us from including creation, either in the terms of Genesis 1 or in terms of the cosmic combat, among the saving acts of Yahweh (see above). Even if we speak of historicizing the myth, creation either as word and work or as the victory of Yahweh over the monster that threatens life and order has not the historical character which the Israelites attributed to the exodus. Yet when one reads several of the enthronement psalms (Ps 93, 95–100; see treatment of the enthronement festival, above), the hymnic language indeed suggests the celebration of a saving act. Yet even in these psalms the work of creation is employed as a motif in which the exodus and the creation of Israel as a people are described. I have therefore not classified creation as a saving act of history in the same sense in which other acts have been so classified; I understand the belief in creation, even though it historicizes the mythical, as remaining basically mythical.

We have noticed an opposition between the myth of creation and the "once and for all" creation of Genesis 1. The same opposition appears between Genesis 1 and the mythical allusions of the Old Testament. Indeed, the idea of creation as an act completed once and for all is not satisfying, either theologically or philosophically or scientifically; it resembles the antiquated view of the universe as a clock which has been wound up and now runs until the spring is relaxed. The Israelites were keenly aware of the acts of Yahweh in nature, as we shall see in the discussion in the following section of other aspects; the mythical allusions afforded room for the idea of creation as a continuing activity of Yahweh. It is a part of the mythological pattern of personal rather than impersonal forces manifested in phenomena. Modern civilized urban man spends almost all his time in an artificially controlled climate. He is less aware of what the poets call the "moods" of nature, less afraid of its power. He has even less sensitivity than the modern farmer or outdoor man, who also normally protects himself from nature in the capsule of civilization. Civilized urban man, with all his education and technology, is not equipped for survival in the desert, the jungle, or the arctic zone as those whom we call savages are equipped. If he is taken out of his capsule, his prospects for survival are extremely poor. Normally, he does not experience God in nature; in fact, civilized man seems to be making a serious effort to remove the nature in which he might experience God. Modern man approaches most nearly to the realization of the mythical monster of chaos.

The regularity which nature does exhibit is seen in the Old Testament not as the product of an organized system of natural powers nor as the uneasy equilibrium of many personal wills. It is a result of that attitude of Yahweh which is translated "fidelity"; it is the achievement of one powerful personal will which is free both of weakness and caprice. We shall see in the biblical deluge myth that the order of nature rests upon a decision of Yahweh. This particular decision is not echoed elsewhere in the Old Testament; but the processes of nature are often attributed to the direct operations of Yahweh. He brings forth the hosts of heaven, counts them and calls them by name (Is 40:26, 45:12, 48:13). He makes dawn and darkness; he turns dense darkness into dawn, and darkens day into night (Amos 4:13, 5:8). He gives breath to the people upon the earth and spirit to those who walk in it (Is 42:5). He brings forth fountains in the valleys, provides food in season for animals and men; when he removes his breath from animals they die, and when he sends forth his breath he renews the face of the earth with life (Ps 104:10,14–15,28–30). This creative activity in nature can be distinguished from what we shall discuss as the moral function of nature in history. As we have stated, ancient man lived on the fringe of chaos. Israelite belief manifests a kind of security which we do not find in the Mesopotamian and Canaanite creation myths; at the same time, this security could not be retained without the assurance that Yahweh's creative power was constantly active to prevent nature from relapsing into chaos.

The generally accepted critical view of the books of the Old Testament makes Second Isaiah the first Old Testament writer to consider creation extensively. This once suggested to some interpreters that Second Isaiah was the originator of the belief. This opinion is no longer tenable; but Second Isaiah is the first to appeal to creation as a motive of faith in the promises of Yahweh, and most scholars have felt that some explanation is required why this development comes so late. We can now be sure, as we have noticed, of the antiquity of the creation myths. I have accepted the suggestion that pre-exilic cult employed the theme of creation in the New Year festival; but it must be admitted that the literary evidence of the pre-exilic belief is not abundant.

It was not Israel's first encounter with the myths that stimulated Second Isaiah, nor was it Israel's first encounter with world powers which worshiped other gods. Second Isaiah himself uses mythological imagery (Is 51:9–10). He obviously felt the need of a statement of the belief of creation in a form which had not yet been produced. I have suggested elsewhere[23] that the mythical account of creation did not show with the desired clarity the absolute supremacy of Yahweh. Very probably the antimythology of both Second Isaiah and Genesis 1 were formed in response to the same situation and to a need which we can call pastoral. As the thought of Second Isaiah develops, it becomes clear that the restoration of Israel will be a more incredibly marvelous work than the creation of Israel. Cyrus must conquer the world in order to be able to restore Israel. History had to be viewed with a cosmic

[23] John L. McKenzie, *Second Isaiah*, lix–lx.

scope which was new in Israelite belief and Israelite literature. For the restoration of Israel, as we shall see in Chapter VII, "The Future of Israel," was accomplished in order that Israel might bear witness to Yahweh before the whole world. This was a more marvelous work than the conquest of Edom. The restoration of Israel is a new exodus; but Second Isaiah makes of the exodus a new creation by employing the imagery of the mythical combat (Is 51:9–10). In this passage he invokes the arm of Yahweh to show again its creative power. It is not without interest that Second Isaiah has very little of the imagery of creation; unlike the author of Genesis 1 and of the mythological poems, he does not attempt to draw a picture of the process. In an author with such rare gifts of imagination and language this is surprising; and his restraint may be connected with his antimythological intentions. Like the author of Genesis 1, Second Isaiah has historicized the mythical event. Yet he keeps some of the mythical dimension by making both the exodus and the restoration of Israel re-enactments of creation.

There is a striking difference between the Old Testament belief in creation and the Mesopotamian and Canaanite myths. In the Canaanite myth (not completely preserved), man does not appear at all. In *Enuma Elish,* man is created nearly as an afterthought.[24] The myth is indeed a creation myth in the sense that it deals with creation; but its primary purpose is less the meaning of creation than the structure of the world of the gods, the celestial reality of which the earth is the counterpart. Even in the more properly mythical forms of creation in the Old Testament, the victory of Yahweh over chaos makes the world habitable for man; in the words of Second Isaiah, Yahweh did not make the world a *tohu* (the word which describes the abyss of Genesis 1:2), rather he made it to be inhabited (Is 45:18). J's creation account in Genesis 2:4b–25 is, as we have seen, an account of the creation of man and woman; he has no account of the creation of the world. In the P account of Genesis 1, man, far from afterthought, is the climactic work of creation, described with a peculiar solemnity and at greater length than any other work. The anthropocentrism of biblical creation is

[24] ANET 68.

an important component of Old Testament optimism; because man is the chief of the works of Yahweh, man can be assured of Yahweh's concern for him, even though that concern may manifest itself in judgment. The author of Psalm 8 was not frightened by the magnitude of heaven and earth; for Yahweh had given man dominion over all the works of Yahweh's hands. Biblical anthropocentrism has suffered extensive damage since the death of the Ptolemaic system and particularly in very recent times when the extent of the visible universe has been recognized for the first time in the history of man. Men have asked whether a god who could create and rule the petty universe of the Bible has the wisdom and the power to create and rule the universe we know. This implies that the dimensions of the biblical God are determined by the dimensions of the universe. This was certainly not the mind of the biblical writers, particularly of Second Isaiah. For him the magnitude of the universe, had he known it, would have been even more ample evidence of the power and will of Yahweh to save. It is somewhat remarkable that the progress of modern science has rendered so many of our contemporaries sympathetic, even though they do not know it, to the pessimism of Mesopotamian mythology. Because the people of Mesopotamia viewed the world as a struggle of conflicting wills, each of which and all together were capable of lapsing into irrationality, they faced the universe with an attitude of fear and despair of which they could never rid themselves; this is an effect of dualism. Our contemporaries face the expanded universe with the fear that there exists no power which can maintain order in this limitless reality. It seems to be not Yahweh but Leviathan whom man should fear and worship. The biblical doctrine of creation is simply irrelevant to most people, even professed believers. No one, they think, who knew so little of the world as the biblical writers could know very much about God.

3. The Moral Function of Nature

Mythological polytheism, we have seen, explains the disorder and the diversity of nature as manifestations of different and divergent personal wills. Thus there is no idea of nature and no word for nature either in Akkadian or in the Old Testament. Gods and goddesses are associated with different natural forces and phenomena precisely because these forces and phenomena frequently are in opposition to each other. The Israelites escaped from mythological polytheism, although not from the problem created by apparent disorder and clash in natural phenomena. The prohibition of images, we have observed, made it impossible to represent Yahweh under any visible symbol. He stands above and outside all natural forces and phenomena, governing all and identified with none.

The prohibition of images was not transferred to poetry; it would have taken philosophical thinking to have uttered such a prohibition. Plato was thinking precisely if not formally of this when he expelled the poets from his republic. It would be possible to paint a portrait of Yahweh from the images used in biblical poetry, indeed, more than one portrait. The most striking of these would probably be the portrait based on the theophanies, and it would bear a strong resemblance to some images of deities of the ancient Near East.[25] These are images of the storm god in various ancient religions. In spite of the variety of religions, the storm god has a common typology: he is a warrior armed with a missile which represents or symbolizes the lightning. He often stands on the back of a lion or a bull; this very probably symbolizes not only strength but mobility. In Egypt, where rain almost never falls, there was no storm god.

I once collected the allusions to Yahweh in the storm apart from those passages called theophanies, which are discussed immediately below:[26] "The thunder is the voice of Yahweh . . ." (Ps 29:3–9). It is in a storm that Yahweh rescues his people from Egypt (Ps 77:16–20). He speaks and raises the storm wind; he stills the storm to a whisper (Ps 107:25–29). He comes from afar in blazing anger, amid heavily rising banks of clouds; he makes his glorious voice heard and the descent of his arm seen, "in furious anger, and flame of devouring fire," amid cloudburst, and rainstorm, and hail (Is 30:27,30). In the storm and tempest is his way, "and the clouds are the dust of his feet" (Nahum 1:3).

25 ANEP 486, 490, 500, 501, 531, 532.
26 McKenzie, *Myths and Realities* (Milwaukee, 1963), 102.

He is also lord of the earthquake . . . "The mountains quake before him, and the hills melt" (Nahum 1:5). He stretches out his hand, and the mountains quake (Is 5:25). He makes the cedars of Lebanon "skip like a calf," Lebanon and Hermon like a wild ox (Ps 29:6). He cleaves a channel for the torrent, "and a way for the thunderbolt"; he sends forth the lightning, and tilts the clouds (Job 38:25,35,37). The clouds are his chariots, the winds his messengers, and the lightning his minister (Ps 104:4). He is called "the Rider of the Clouds" (Ps 68:4), an epithet which is also applied to Aleyan Baal in the Ugaritic poems, which are much older than most of the Old Testament.[27]

The theophany is a poetic form of which several examples are found: Judges 4:4–5; Psalms 18:8–16, 68:7–9; Habakkuk 3:3–15. These range from brief couplets to a dozen verses. The longer poems enable us to fill out the brief allusions to Yahweh and the storm in the passages cited above. Perhaps the fullest description is Psalm 18:8–16. The elements of the theophany are earthquake, clouds, lightning, darkness and clouds, thunder and thunderbolts. It is a manifestation of Yahweh in wrath. The clouds are his chariot (or the winged genii, the cherubim, upon which he rides). I must admit that the full impact of the psalm had never hit me until I watched a desert winter thunderstorm approach and strike at Palmyra. The thunderstorm is far more fearful in the desert, where it is infrequent, than it is in pluvial climates. In fact, the desert traveler is in greater danger from lightning than the person who encounters a storm in a landscape containing other objects than himself.

The student of ancient religions is tempted to wonder whether the Yahweh of the theophany has not been modeled after Adad. The possibility is there, but the student then must face the problem of why Israelite imagery exhibits no other equally clear borrowing. The Old Testament literature was written with a great deal of painstaking effort to distinguish Yahweh from natural forces and phenomena; if the writers knew what they were doing, we cannot understand how they could fail to distinguish Yahweh from the storm. Nor did they fail; where we encounter storm gods in the

27 ANET 130.

ancient Near East, they exhibit traits which are not characteristic
of Yahweh. Like the storm, they are not benevolent. It is hard to
imagine an ancient Mesopotamian poet writing of Enlil or Adad
that his loving kindness is above all his works. Yahweh could indeed exhibit the form and figure of Enlil and Adad; the difference,
and it was great, lay in the motivation of Yahweh's storm theophany. The theophany is clearly a revelation of power but not of
blind power.

Yahweh in the storm comes as a warrior; this is obvious. He
comes in terror to attack the wicked or the enemies of Israel; here
we may find some of that narrowness of view which we have already touched upon when treating of the biblical attitude towards
foreign nations. The display of power is always motivated, and the
motivation is comprehensible. It is important to recognize that it
had to be comprehensible, and this we shall attempt to explain.

For modern man the weather is morally neutral, in the last analysis. We have no difficulty with the saying of Jesus that the heavenly
father lets the sun shine upon both good and bad and rains im-
partially upon righteous and wicked (Mt 5:46). One really needs
the evangelical revelation of the heavenly father to appreciate this.
In the ancient world where nature was the product of quarreling
wills, not of an impersonal process or of one single benevolent
deity, there was a feeling that the sun and the rain ought to be ap-
portioned according to righteousness and unrighteousness. Otherwise the gods would not seem to care much about the difference
between the two. But since the weather was and is morally neutral, men who thought in mythological terms could analyze nature
as the acts of beings who were capricious and possibly, in the last
analysis, irrational. Men were like this, and nature offered no assurance that the gods were any better.

For the Israelites to say that nature or the weather is morally
neutral was to say that Yahweh is morally neutral; this would be
blasphemy. There could be no ambiguity or uncertainty in the phenomena of nature when these phenomena were governed entirely
by Yahweh alone, whose attributes were righteousness and judgment. As we shall see, creation in the large sense is the outstanding
work of the wisdom of Yahweh. It would be neither righteous nor
wise to permit nature to respond in the same way to righteousness

and to wickedness. Yahweh in the theophany is not the storm god but the righteous judge, whose wisdom and power are not inhibited by any competitor in the heavens, on the earth, or under the earth.

To affirm with such a stout faith that nature is integrated into the moral order of Yahweh's government of mankind required some dialectic; and a completely satisfactory solution was not reached in the Old Testament. It has not been reached outside the Old Testament either. A belief that God is effectively righteous is not the fruit of observation, but rather an explication of what is affirmed if one affirms that God is a moral power at all. The problem will arise again when we come to treat of Old Testament wisdom. Manifestly, Yahweh employed nature to execute his judgments upon Israel. He grants rain or withholds it, smites with blight and mildew, and sends locusts (Amos 7–8). He gives rain in due season and sends harvest at the appointed time; but the crimes of Israel disturb this order and repel the blessing (Jer 5:24–25). Hosea prays that Yahweh will give Israel a miscarrying womb and dry breasts (9:14). The harvests of Israel will be blasted (Hos 8:7). The affirmations were made without doubt, and nothing in the course of history cast doubt upon them during the period of the monarchy. But the principle is open to criticism; we can illustrate from two passages of the Pentateuch, one of which is certainly mythological in origin and the other very probably so.

The publication of the Gilgamesh epic in 1900 removed any doubt that the biblical narrative of the deluge depends on a Mesopotamian original. The text first published came from the library of Ashurbanipal of Assyria (668–626 B.C.), but other copies have been found which are much older, and the Sumerian original from the third millennium B.C. has been found.[28] The book of Genesis has the deluge in two versions, J and P. They differ notably in that the enormous flood of J has become in P a return of the world to the watery chaos of Genesis 1:1–2. But each version, like the Mesopotamian originals, describes a catastrophe which wipes out the entire human race except the family in the ark. This disaster in the Mesopotamian myth is the work of the wrathful Enlil, and no

[28] Ibid. 42–44, 93–95.

reason is assigned for his wrath. Even the mythological mind boggled at the thought of a motive for a disaster like this; reality does break through, and man realizes that he cannot ask the storm why it is angry. Whatever the reason may have been, Ea speaks less for the gods than for man: the guilt should be laid on the sinner, not on the entire race. If Enlil's wrath demanded full satisfaction, it would have been more reasonable to release a wild beast, a famine or a pestilence.

There is no reason to think that the myth reflects an actual catastrophe of cosmic dimensions, although history knows enough of such sudden natural cataclysms which have killed thousands of people within a few minutes. To think of these as the wrath of God upsets most theologies. But the Mesopotamian myth faces the possibility and declares that such an act of God is inexplicable. Human nature is such that an angry god might send a lesser destruction, but a total destruction is irrational. And in this affirmation the Mesopotamian mythographers declare their despair of any real moral order in the divine government of the world.

We do not know why the Israelite scribes felt the necessity of rewriting this myth when they left so many others alone. To some one, this despair of the moral order demanded correction. The myth was corrected not by theological or philosophical criticism but by rewriting the myth. Like the men of Mesopotamia, the Israelites had no acquaintance with a catastrophe of such dimensions; they may have taken the Mesopotamian myth for history. Such a deluge could not be the work of nonexistent gods; only Yahweh, the lord of nature, could do this. If he did, then the fact alone demonstrates that all mankind except Noah and his family were wicked. The Israelite mythographers no doubt felt that such an example of judgment was much to the point. If Yahweh could annihilate mankind for its wickedness, he would hesitate less to annihilate Israel; and if he desired, he could preserve a single family from whom a new progeny, numerous as the sand of the seashore like the progeny of Abraham, could be generated. The myth goes from a belief in Yahweh to the affirmation of a fact, which is backward reasoning and not unknown to other theologies.

The other example is the destruction of Sodom and Gomorrah (Gen 18:20–19:29). I called this very probably mythological; others would be more precise and call it etiological. The Dead Sea and the region of the Ghor in which it lies are so hostile to life of all forms, even vegetable life, that it has long been the very symbol of a land accursed by God. In fact, the globe has other regions equally inhospitable, but none of them have had world-wide publicity in the Bible. The story of the Cities of the Plain must be a pre-Israelite story, although this cannot be proved. It is clear that the catastrophe could not have happened in the historic period (later than 3000 B.C.) and many scholars doubt its historical character entirely. Efforts to explain the phenomenon in terms of the natural character of the region have not been convincing.

Like the deluge, the catastrophe is described as total, although not universal, and the same problem of motivation occurs. The author is at pains to make it clear that the inhabitants of the cities were depraved, in particular given to that vice which has drawn its name from Sodom and which the sturdy masculine morality of the Israelites found especially revolting. The story gives a demonstration of the depravity of Sodom, and the sentence is executed. The only innocents, Lot and his family, are removed before the disaster strikes.

The story introduces a refinement not found in the deluge myth. Abraham engages in an intercessory dialogue with Yahweh. Would it not be possible to withhold the total catastrophe for the sake of those who might be found righteous in the city? How many? Fifty? Forty-five? Forty? Thirty? Twenty? Ten? The dialogue is so arranged that in each step Yahweh, if he were to refuse the request, is destroying the city not because it is entirely wicked but because of five wicked men—the difference between fifty and forty-five. But he cannot slay the righteous with the wicked so that the two fare alike; the judge of the earth must do judgment (Gen 18:25).

Obviously "judgment" here permits the judge to withhold punishment from the wicked if he cannot punish them without involving the just; and since nature is the instrument of execution, the Israelites saw no way of doing this. The wild beast, the famine, the pestilence—the examples of the poet of Gilgamesh—the storm, the earthquake, the volcanic eruption do not sort out the wicked from the righteous. If nature is used, then the objects must be wicked enough to deserve it.

It seems better not to introduce at this point the problem of collective and individual guilt. I do not myself see that this problem is involved in these passages; it is involved in some other passages and will be dealt with under the institutions of Israel (VI. 1). Neither in the deluge myth nor the Sodom myth is collective guilt adduced as a reason for not seeking out the innocent; these two stories, it seems, move precisely against collective guilt.

Nor do I think that the few righteous are viewed as silent intercessors for the wicked nor are the righteous esteemed of greater value by Yahweh. The stories are set simply in the framework of nature as men experience it, nature which strikes without discrimination. Where discrimination is required, the judge of all the earth must do judgment by some other means. The presence of even a few righteous in a community protects that community against the kind of punishment illustrated by the deluge and the overthrow of Sodom; and we may add that interpreters are still uncertain what kind of phenomenon the writer had in mind for Sodom. It does not save the wicked from more selective types of punishment, which the Israelites believed Yahweh had available. If small boys mock a prophet, the prophet can invoke bears to consume forty-two of them (2 Kings 2:23–24). Annoying as the urchins of the Near East can be, even the modern tourist is appalled at the bad temper shown by Elisha, or more probably by the scribe. This is the simplistic view which J in Genesis 18 found offensive.

Ultimately, of course, the myths do not solve the problem; we have said that mythology is not intended to solve problems but to enable men to live with them. Even modern man, who has known incidents of violence both in nature and in history which the Israelites never knew, is still sensitive enough to be somewhat appalled at the instant death of thousands of people, especially if they include the poor and children. The theology of the deluge and of Sodom does not satisfy the mind in such junctures. It did not finally satisfy the Israelite mind either, as we shall see when we turn to wisdom.

V

Wisdom

1. Conventional Wisdom

Wisdom literature is one of the oldest literary forms known. Examples of wisdom literature in Pritchard's collection of texts go back to the third millennium B.C. in Egypt[1] and to the second millennium B.C. in Mesopotamia.[2] Wisdom literature is also one of the most secular forms of ancient literature; references to the gods and to religion are rare. I have chosen the designation "conventional" for wisdom literature because its content and characteristics are remarkably similar in all the examples from the third millennium to the first millennium B.C. whether Egyptian, Mesopotamian, or Israelite. This uniformity is not purely coincidental, in the judgment of scholars; they believe that wisdom was an international phenomenon.

The seat of wisdom and of wisdom literature is recognized as the scribal offices of temples and palaces. Civilization could not arise and advance without the invention of writing. The simple alphabetic script which in modern civilized countries is taught to all children was developed perhaps two thousand years later than the earliest forms of writing in both Egypt and Mesopotamia.[3] Both the Egyptian and the Mesopotamian systems were cumbersome, employing hundreds of symbols, many of them polyvalent. The ability to read and write was a skill limited to a professional class of scribes, employed by the religious and political establish-

[1] ANET 412.

[2] Ibid. 425; *See also* H. W. F. Saggs, *The Greatness That Was Babylon,* 429–44; John A. Wilson, *The Burden of Egypt* (Chicago, 1951), 91–95, 261–64, 301–5.

[3] I. J. Gelb, *A Study of Writing* (Chicago, 1952).

ments and by the wealthy. This class formed the first administrative and bureaucratic class known to history. Since government, commerce, and cult depended upon written records and established procedures, the scribes were very close to the ruling class. As we shall see below, they were careful to keep the distinction between themselves and the rulers clear. Nevertheless, those who collect and store information are indispensable to the men who make decisions, particularly when, as in Egypt and Mesopotamia, the rulers were themselves unable to read and write. Those who furnish information are very close to becoming an advisory group.

Like many guilds, the scribes were largely a hereditary group. Yet the profession seems to have had an openness unusual in guilds in any period of history. The ability to become a scribe obviously demanded talents not found in an equal degree in all boys—such things as quick learning and retentive memory. The scribes were the only elite of talent known to us from the ancient world, and the scribal profession was the only way in which the sons of the poor and the common people might hope to rise to wealth and position.[4] The wisdom literature contains warnings to the sons of commoners to remember their humble origin when they are closely associated with kings and rich landlords and merchants.[5]

Wisdom literature is a collection of maxims which tell the young scribe how to live in such a way as to assure his success and happiness. Those who edit and publish Egyptian and Mesopotamian texts have assured us that many of the texts of this material come to us in schoolboy copies. It seems reasonable to assume that the young scribe, like the nineteenth-century schoolboy, absorbed wisdom while he learned his letters. In Hebrew "wise" and "wisdom" can designate the mastery of any technique, such as pottery or carpentry; wisdom without qualification is skill in living, in being human. The scribes were not alone in believing that this skill can be taught; and in saying that the scribal schools were the seat of wisdom literature, I do not imply that they were the seat of wisdom simply. Many wisdom texts are addressed to others than scribes. How realistic the texts addressed to young kings may have

4 Wilson, op. cit., 89–90, 261–63.
5 ANET 412–14.

been we do not know; the ideal of rule expressed in them is applicable to administrators, who were often if not usually drawn from the scribal class. There is a folk wisdom as old as humanity which expresses itself in proverbs. It is concerned with skill in living, which includes morality but also includes prudence. That any of the folk wisdom survives from the ancient Near East is due to the scribes who collected it; the biblical book of Proverbs is such a collection, better known to the general public than the Egyptian wisdom of Ptah-hotep,[6] with which the book of Proverbs has much in common.

Both folk wisdom and scribal wisdom affirm without criticism the absolute value of experience, and they believe that all the experience of the past is collected in the present elder generation. The young man begins life as a fool, and he will become wise only with experience; but a part of his experience is the assimilation of the experience of the past. If he learns this, then he will be able to contribute his own wisdom to the sum of experience. Wisdom begins with listening to one's elders; the wise men took a dim view of the new and the experimental in living. Folk wisdom does not easily anticipate the possibility of new problems and new situations for which experience has no answer; it has no prescription for crisis. In the comparatively stable societies of Egypt and Mesopotamia, wisdom would carry a man through most situations most of the time; but even in these societies there are literary remains which attest the breakdown of wisdom with breakdown of the stable social structure. But in the normal course of events, the wise man goes with experience; the assumption is not that the elders always know best, but that one cannot make a wise decision in a new situation or even recognize that it is a new situation unless one has mastered the wisdom of collective experience.

The skill in living will infallibly produce success and happiness, barring catastrophe, for which, as we noticed, conventional wisdom has no answers. One is not surprised that conventional wisdom insists on competence and diligence in one's profession. One is slightly surprised that wisdom recognized that personal relations are the major obstacle to success and happiness. The obstacles

[6] Ibid. 412–14.

may come from those of higher rank, those of equal rank, those of lower rank, from one's family and from one's friends. Where difference in rank is concerned, the wise man measures others by their present or future or possible capacity to do harm. The wheel of fortune may place one's inferiors above one; and the general rule, stated in many variations, is to make no enemies. The young Egyptian scribe is often warned against the danger which Joseph encountered in the house of Potiphar (Gen 39:6–20).[7] Wife and children can make or mar success and happiness. It is sometimes rather crudely assumed that food and clothing make a good wife;[8] and it is never doubted that the rod makes good children. The most important person in the life of the scribe is his superior, who is to be treated with unfailing tact and deference. A man of high rank is entitled to his moods; his inferior is not entitled to any. Much as this type of recommendation may seem to favor oleaginous hypocrisy, the code of wisdom should have produced men of tact and courtesy. The cardinal sin, even for a scribe who had reached high rank, was to throw his weight about. Wisdom was a discipline.

In some contexts, wisdom has implications which are distressing. Solomon was the traditional and model wise man of Israel. He was the model of success and happiness, surely achieved by a man who made gold as common as silver and whose harem included a thousand lovelies. He had the wisdom proper to a king, and he showed it in judging such difficult cases as the case of the two prostitutes who disputed over the same child (1 Kings 3:16–28). The modern historian may suspect that behind the image of the wise Solomon of the book of Kings there may be discerned the historical reality of a pompous fool, but that is not our interest at the moment. Our interest is the use of the word "wise" in David's last commission to Solomon to discharge some of David's outstanding obligations by seeing that certain persons did not go down in peace to Sheol—that is, die naturally (1 Kings 2:5–9). Solomon will find ways to accomplish this because he is wise; this means the cunning by which he can manufacture occa-

---

[7] See also ANET 413, 420.
[8] Ibid. 413.

sions for the execution of Joab and Shimei. It is the same wisdom which Solomon exhibited in his own personal interest towards his brother Adonijah (1 Kings 2:13–25). It must be recognized that the wisdom of the ruler took forms which it did not take in others; and one of the basic functions of wisdom in the ancient ruler was to retain power. Like Yahweh, the wise king showed himself loyal to the loyal, blameless to the blameless, savage to the savage, and tortuous to the perverse (Psalm 18:25–26). I said that this type of wisdom is distressing; and it illustrates that wisdom and what we understand by morality are not coterminous. It should be added that wisdom and morality are not coterminous in modern politics and that the wisdom of the ruler takes forms which would get the critizen arrested. The wisdom of the ancients is not morally neutral; it is rather that certain fine distinctions are not made.

Folk wisdom is not specialized to any profession; but its recommendations of diligence, prudent human relations, and family management are much the same. It shows little or none of the moral neutrality which we detect in the wisdom of the king; honesty, veracity, and fidelity to one's word are the virtues praised most frequently. The wise men do not, with Polonius, include drabbing as one of the enterprises which young men are expected to engage in. The wise men of Proverbs direct their longest and their most horrendous warnings against prostitutes; frankly, it is not clear that the warnings are morally based, but they are uttered (Prov 2:16–19, 5:1–14, 6:23–35, 7:1–27, 9:13–18). These warnings are in rather sharp contrast to the casual treatment of prostitution in the story of Judah and Tamar (Gen 38). It is remarkable that the entire Old Testament never manages a clear and unambiguous moral condemnation of prostitution. On the other hand, it never quite reaches the moral neutrality toward prostitution exhibited in Mesopotamian law; in the cities of Mesopotamia the prostitute furnished as useful and acceptable a service as the smith and the potter. Folk wisdom was not addressed to kings and magnates and their staffs, but to small merchants and landlords; and these had no real ambitions for high place, which was open to the wise and diligent scribe. Wisdom should give the small merchant and landlord a peaceful home and keep him out of debt and quarrels. All

in all, this objective has often been too much for the small merchant and landlord to attain.

The discussion so far has centered upon those features which
justify the description of wisdom as "secular," a term with which
the discussion was opened. If wisdom was secular, one may ask
how it is referred to God-talk, which was proposed in the Introduction as the formal object of our attention. In fact, both folk
wisdom and scribal wisdom, if we limited our attention to the
maxims which are concerned with success and happiness, should
be omitted from a theological discussion. In their original form,
which appears most clearly in Egyptian wisdom, they are divorced
from religious and theological consideration. The Israelites did
give wisdom a theological cast, or attempted to do it.

A second factor to be considered is that scribal wisdom was not
limited to maxims concerning success and happiness. A scribal
satire from the New Kingdom of Egypt shows us that the wisdom
of the scribe included what is more properly called learning.[9] The
writer criticizes another scribe for not knowing how to reckon the
number of bricks needed to build a ramp of known dimensions.
Neither can he calculate the number of men necessary to drag an
obelisk of known dimensions from the quarry to the place of erection. He is likewise unable (although the text is unintelligible for
much of this) to calculate how much sand is to be poured into the
foundation excavation of a monument and then gradually removed
when the monument is set in place. Neither could he calculate the
provisions necessary for the march of 5,000 men; this seems to
allude to an actual event. In the days before maps, it is clear from
the text that the scribes were expected to know the location of the
cities of Palestine and Syria, the distances between them, the roads,
the mountain passes, the fauna and flora and the streams. Oddly,
the language is not mentioned. We deal here with learning turned
to practical purposes, but the scribe had to know more than his
letters.

The literature produced by the scribes included religious texts.
All that ancient men knew or thought they knew about the gods
was contained in the mythological texts; this was priestly learning.

---

[9] This text is available to me only in the translation of Adolf Erman,
Literatur der Aegypter (Leipzig: Hinrich, 1923), 270–94.

In Mesopotamia a vast amount of magic and divination literature has survived. This pseudo learning is a doleful testimonial to the gross superstition of a people who must have been unusually endowed with intelligence; but it was a technique for dealing both with the gods and with the world of experience, and it was seriously and extensively studied. The satire quoted above refers to the knowledge of arithmetic; both Egyptians and Mesopotamians did remarkably well at building and irrigation with primitive mathematical techniques. The scribes also wrote and preserved the records from which modern scholars write the history of these civilizations. The Egyptian scribe taunts his adversary for quoting a book which he has not read—surely a taunt familiar enough to modern scholars. Such materials do not make wisdom any less secular, but they broaden its scope.

While it is anachronistic to speak of speculation or science in the ancient Near East, mythology, as we have seen, was an attempt to speak to certain problems which we call speculative. This will appear more clearly in Israelite wisdom than in Egyptian or Mesopotamian wisdom. When myth is used to discuss these problems, the religious factor necessarily enters. The mythological response to speculative problems is to place the answer in the mind of the gods, where it cannot be tracked down unless the gods choose to reveal it. It has already been noticed that some Egyptian and Mesopotamian wisdom is thinly veiled criticism of the mythological world of the gods; see Chapter IV, Section 3, above.

The Israelite wise men accepted without criticism or modification the content of conventional wisdom—substantially, it seems, from Egypt; there is evidence that the scribal profession of Israel was Egyptian in origin and style through the importation of scribes from Egypt to handle the palace business of David and Solomon.[10] But the Israelite scribes introduced, at a date which cannot be stated precisely, an important addition: they affirmed that Yahweh himself was the original and primary wise one, from whom all wisdom was derived and imitated. This differs more than a little from both the Egyptian and the Mesopotamian relation of wisdom to the gods; wisdom in both regions was the attribute of a

[10] Roland de Vaux, RB 48(1939), 394–405.

specialized god or gods of wisdom, who were the patrons of the scribes—Ea and Nabu in Mesopotamia, Thoth in Egypt. Yahweh never appears as the patron of the scribes; in fact, Yahweh as the only god appears as the patron of no one unless it be the poor and the oppressed.

The wisdom of Yahweh is most manifest in creation, which is seen as a work of skill and ingenuity, both of which are implied in wisdom. This is almost the wisdom of the craftsman rather than the wisdom of skill in living; but how could it be thought that Yahweh needed skill in living? This type of wisdom is seen in the production of paradoxes which no one but the wisest—that is, the most ingenious—could devise. As we shall see, conventional wisdom was not so ready to affirm that the wisdom of Yahweh was manifest in his management of history. The poet of Job 28 affirms that wisdom is found only with Yahweh; if it is found elsewhere, it must have been given by Yahweh. The poem concludes with a statement found several times, that wisdom begins with the knowledge and fear of Yahweh. This statement, especially in the form in which it appears in Job 28:28, removes the ethical ambiguity of conventional wisdom.

The Israelite religious view of wisdom is in direct opposition to the secular wisdom of both Mesopotamia and Egypt; and since the Israelites made no change in the content of wisdom, there is something of a strain between their religiosity and the maxims which they preserve from other traditions. The effort to remove the moral neutrality of wisdom was not notably successful. Translating the effort into more modern terms, one could call it the attempt of the Israelite sages to affirm that sound morality needs a religious principle for its base. But sound morality is not the same thing as success and happiness; when we consider the anti-wisdom of Job and Koheleth, we shall see how important the failure to maintain this distinction became. The gods did not give wisdom in Egypt and Mesopotamia because they were not needed to give it; one learned wisdom from the wise, from one's elders. The Israelite sages accepted this principle and repeated it; and they left no room for Yahweh to give wisdom.

Yet they affirmed that fear of Yahweh is the "beginning" of wisdom (Ps 111:10; Prov 9:10). The second quotation is easily

translated "beginning"; the first may mean "best part" or something similar, and one is tempted to paraphrase that the essence
of wisdom is the fear of Yahweh. This, however, is a mere affirmation—important, but mere; traditional wisdom was not irreligious,
but it imposed no more on the wise than conventional religious
observances. The Israelite wise men wished to say more, but they
could not find the words. They by implication identified success
and happiness with the fear of Yahweh and thus produced un-
tenable God-talk which opened the way for the God-talk of Job
and Koheleth.

The Law, the five books of Moses, was produced by the scribes
of the priestly school; it became normative in the Jerusalem community by the time of Ezra, probably the beginning of the fourth
century B.C. The Law included the Deuteronomic theology of history (see Chapter III, Section 5, above) which explained the fall
of the kingdoms of Israel and Judah as a judgment upon the kingdoms because of their failure to observe the law of Yahweh. The
restored community first built the temple in which to worship Yahweh, and some time elapsed before the scribes produced the book
by which the community should live. As far as possible, the scribes
desired no ambiguity in the revealed will of Yahweh, and the text
became the object of study and interpretation. Ben Sira, writing
about 180 B.C., identified the Law with wisdom (Sirach 24:1–34).
The identification was natural in the wisdom tradition. Here was
the skill of living, set forth in directions produced by the highest
authority, whose decisions governed the lives and fortunes of men.
The Law could be studied, indeed, it could be mastered; the ambiguity of older wisdom had been removed. Ben Sira may have
been influenced, probably was influenced by the personification of
wisdom in Proverbs 8:22–34. The wisdom of Yahweh, we noticed, was seen especially in creation; in this poem wisdom appears as a companion of Yahweh while he creates. In Proverbs 9
wisdom again appears as personified, a female figure set in contrast to Dame Folly, who has the attributes of the "strange woman"
whose lips drip honey. The wisdom of Ben Sira is also a female
figure; she exists before creation, and she seeks a place to dwell on
earth. The creator commands her to pitch her tent in Israel, and
she settles there in the book of the Law. And the full identity of

the scribe and wise man is restored in the Jewish scribe who devotes himself to studying the Law of the Most High (Sirach 39:1), whose delight is the law of the Lord, his meditation night and day (Ps 1:1–2). But the idea of wisdom as a divine revelation is foreign not only to the wisdom traditions of Egypt and Mesopotamia but also to the early wisdom of Israel. When Solomon's prayer for wisdom was answered, it was not answered with a literary corpus but with a wise and understanding heart (1 Kings 3:12).

The scribes who collected the Law also collected what we call the historical books and the prophets; they did not give these books the same normative value, nor indeed did they ever state explicitly what value they did attach to these writings. The Deuteronomic history certainly should have had the value of collective experience, and it must have been for this value that it was assembled. The prophetic interpretation of the experience of Israel had been vindicated by events, and it was the part of wisdom to recognize this. The Israelite wise man, whose model was Solomon, counted erudition among the ornaments of his profession as his Egyptian colleague did (1 Kings 4:29–34). But the wisdom which consisted in the skill of living based on collective experience yielded place to the explicit instructions of Yahweh on how to live. The prophets, both early and latter, and the wise men were interpreted according to the Law. It followed as a matter of course that the Gentiles were utterly without wisdom and that the Jews had nothing to learn from them.

Although the key word "wise" occurs only twice (Gen 41:33,39) in the Joseph story, the story is really a wisdom story; it narrates the success of a young man who begins with frightful disadvantages and rises to the highest office in Egypt under Pharaoh. Yet there are certain features of the wisdom of Joseph which makes one wonder whether the story has not been borrowed from some non-Israelite source.[11] Joseph does indeed act wisely when he is seduced by the wife of Potiphar; and this apparent misfortune becomes the occasion of his success. Virtue is rewarded, even if the reward is delayed. But the wisdom of Joseph turns out to be the skill of dream interpretation, which is not a component of Is-

[11] H. Gunkel, *Genesis* (Göttingen, 1964), 399–400.

raelite wisdom before the book of Daniel. He appears as a diviner
who works from a cup (Gen 44:1–17). The skill of interpretation
enables him to suggest the storage of surplus grain from the years
of plenty; and his administration of the surplus shows his practical
wisdom as an administrator, for he makes Pharaoh the sole land-
owner of Egypt. It appears that the Israelite scribe has superim-
posed upon a story of wisdom based upon the art of divination
the Israelite belief that success comes from the blessing of Yahweh
(39:2–5,21–23). The skill of interpretation is attributed to *elohim*
not only by Joseph (40:8; 41:16) but even by Pharaoh (41:
38–39). We very probably have here another instance of the effort of the Israelite sages to add a religious value to what was
originally a purely secular wisdom.

2. *Critical Wisdom*

We have observed above that conventional wisdom had nothing to say to catastrophe. The wise men did not realize how much
their wisdom depended on a stable social and political order; had
they attended to the stability of their world, they might have said
that the stability was the product of wisdom. This would have
been said more quickly by Egyptian sages than by Mesopotamian
sages, for Mesopotamian mythology attests Mesopotamian awareness of instability in nature and in society. A few literary remains
come from some periods of instability in both Egypt and Mesopotamia; and it is interesting that in these pieces of wisdom, more
properly called "anti-wisdom," the discourse of the wise becomes
God-talk. In Israelite wisdom likewise, the literature becomes
God-talk when it turns to anti-wisdom. The Egyptian and Mesopotamian responses to catastrophe should be briefly reviewed as
a background for Israelite anti-wisdom; for while conventional
wisdom was international, Israelite anti-wisdom is peculiarly
Israelite.

Two Egyptian texts are dated in the First Intermediate Period,
at the end of the third millennium B.C., when the centralized monarchy of Egypt had broken down and anarchy prevailed.[12] Wil-

[12] J. A. Wilson, *The Burden of Egypt,* 104–24.

son has shown that the Egyptian response was diversified: but the anti-wisdom of the two texts is clear. The first is a dialogue of a man with his soul about his decision to commit suicide.[13] The man argues in favor of suicide because it is impossible to maintain a good name in the world. This is clarified by his next argument, which describes the breakdown of law and order and even of mutual confidence. Death is praised as a release and as entrance to the world of the gods. The poet knows no skill in living which will enable him to tolerate life in his condition. And while the arguments presented by the soul are not preserved, there is no indication that the soul advances any of the prescriptions of conventional wisdom. Maxims of instruction on how to deal with magnates, colleagues, and the wives of superior officers tell the man nothing about how to deal with collapse. A theoretical discussion of suicide in any period always manifests a breakdown of character under stress and an indication of the failure of conventional discipline to equip the individual to sustain more than conventional stress. The discipline which fails in the dialogue of the man with his soul is the wisdom of the scribes.

The Song of the Harper[14] is dated roughly in the same period of disorder in Egypt. The song is a much more explicit repudiation of conventional wisdom than the dialogue; the writer mentions Imhotep and Horbehdet,[15] once praised but now forgotten. Actually the Song of the Harper is directed less at the wisdom of the sages than at the Egyptian belief in life after the tomb; the writer deduces from unbelief the doctrine of unqualified hedonism. He sees no prospect of success and happiness as the fruit of diligence and discretion; sacrifice of present pleasure for future pleasure is folly. To appreciate these two pieces it will help to remember that Egyptian thought and literature were as stable as Egyptian society and politics. The complete reversal of the conventional wisdom is more appalling than similar outbursts are in less rigid modern thought and literature. Wisdom did not adapt itself to the new situation; it simply fell silent until the traditional order and stability were restored.

[13] ANET 405–7.
[14] Ibid. 467.
[15] Ibid. 419.

Mesopotamian literature has similar anti-wisdom compositions; they are not so easily related to periods of political instability. The poem *Ludlul bel nemeqi* (I will praise the lord of wisdom) is not dated by its editor;[16] it is placed in the Kassite period, roughly the middle of the second millennium B.C., by H. W. F. Saggs.[17] The poem does not itself suggest an unsettled period as clearly as the Egyptian dialogue of a man with his soul. The Mesopotamian sufferer, like Job, is nearly the typical or even the total sufferer; he has diseases and pains which go beyond any affliction known to medicine. In addition, he suffers from enmity; this no doubt reflects the Mesopotamian belief that illness and misfortune could be the effect of black magic. The sufferer experiences a nearly miraculous deliverance through the power of Marduk, and the cure is preceded by several mystical visions. One doubts that this poem relates a historical experience either in the misfortunes or in the deliverance; and one may look for the real mind of the poet in the doubts expressed by the sufferer at the nadir of his misfortunes before deliverance comes.[18] The sufferer does not know whether the gods and men agree on what is good and what is evil; perhaps men have the whole thing backwards. The sufferer affirms that he has been deeply religious; this means faithful to cultic obligations, but this was thought to be a meaningful obligation which, fulfilled, assured the gods' good pleasure. The sufferer could have expected no worse treatment if he had been an unbeliever; how, then, can man know what the gods regard as good? The sufferer generalizes beyond his own condition to the uncertainties of the human condition. His problem is resolved by his own deliverance. One can hardly believe that the writer meant this as a genuine answer to the question; he seems aware that the solution of naïve belief is contradicted by experience. He does not, like the Harper, simply deny the meaning and value of religion and wisdom; he has his doubts, and the happy ending of his story is a tribute to conventional religion. But the doubt has been expressed, and the implication is that it cannot be removed without visions and miracles. One may

[16] ANES 160–64; see also Thorkild Jacobsen in H. Frankfort, *Before Philosophy,* 227–31.
[17] *The Greatness That Was Babylon,* 438.
[18] ANES 161.

observe that doubt is not strictly "anti-wisdom," as I have called it, but it is rather a doubt that there is any stable order in which a man may place confidence. Personal enmities and illness do not involve the collapse of political and social order; the Mesopotamian poet considers not the group but the individual person, whose private world can collapse even while the world at large remains stable. If such a personal disaster does not imply the wrath of the gods, then it and the life in which it happens become meaningless.

The Dialogue of Pessimism[19] is dated by Thorkild Jacobsen in the first millennium B.C.[20] This piece is satire, and it is not without subtlety. A master makes a series of proposals to his slave, some obviously good, some bad, and some indifferent: to drive to the palace, to dine, to drive to the country, to establish a household and have children, to do something dishonest, to make love to a woman, to offer sacrifice, to make loans, to do a good deed for the country. Each proposal is followed by a proposal to do the opposite; the master is presented as a capricious person. Each proposal is immediately supported by the slave with sententious arguments. One does not know whether the satirist is aiming at the caprice of the master or the obsequiousness of the slave, but interpreters generally think he goes beyond such obvious points. For Jacobsen it is a question of whether any action has any meaning or value over its opposite and therefore whether life itself has any meaning or value. The work may be "anti-wisdom" in the sense that maxims can be adduced for any action and just as easily for its opposite. Certainly, the final proposal hints broadly at the meaninglessness of it all: the slave, himself questioned about what is good, suggests death for both; the world is too much for man. The master qualifies; he will kill the slave, but the slave retorts that the master will not outlive him three days.

Most readers, I think, will recognize a modern element in this statement of meaninglessness. Like modern statements of meaninglessness, it is difficult to radicate the statement in any definite historical conditions. The master seems to be one of the "beautiful people," and he is entirely without purpose. He is one of those we call privileged, but he is entirely self-centered and irrespon-

19 Ibid. 164–65.
20 Frankfort, op. cit., 231–33.

sible. It is hard to believe that the writer did not recognize what he was describing. But what has happened to the ancient wisdom? It may have been selfish in an enlightened way, but it produced public servants. Now it does not speak to the master at all, and the slave has a wise saying for any contingency; he is nearly a sophist. Clearly there is more in this satire than we understand; but it appears that the writer, if he thinks of conventional wisdom at all, is describing a world in which conventional wisdom has no voice.

The Babylonian theodicy[21] is placed by Saggs in the second half of the second millennium B.C.[22] This work is a dialogue between a sufferer and his friend; the language is extremely courteous, almost ridiculously so, but one is reminded of the dialogue between Job and his friends. The text of the poem is poorly preserved, and a number of lines are wholly or partly missing just where they are needed to sustain the sequence of thought. In spite of these gaps, it is clear that the sufferer is impressed by the absence of correlation between virtue and prosperity. In a few passages which are unusually corrupt, he seems to be tempted to abandon moral integrity and turn scoundrel, for it is the scoundrel who succeeds. If the scoundrel does not have the blessing of the gods, he certainly is spared their curse, which would be manifested in his failure and downfall. The friend maintains the thesis that the gods do protect and reward the virtuous; the reader can only hope that the missing portions of the text contained material which strengthened his argument, for it marches mostly by repetition. The conclusion of the dialogue seems to represent an agreement between the two, with the sufferer bowing to the wisdom of his friend.

This work may not appear to be anti-wisdom, but rather a defense of conventional wisdom. It seems most unlikely that the writer was unconscious of the irony with which the weakness of the conventional wisdom is exposed. The sufferer affirms reality, and the friend affirms unreality. He defends the ways of the gods by denying experience. At the risk once more of reading into the work a subtlety which the author may not have intended, we notice that the final agreement includes an admission by the sage

21 ANES 165–68.
22 Saggs, op. cit., 439–40.

that wickedness prevails in mankind; men judge each other purely by wealth and poverty and attribute virtue and vice to each other according to possessions. The implication is that the world does not proceed according to the will of the gods. The sufferer, on the other hand, is brought to believe that the gods hear the prayer of the distressed, even if it is rare that one can observe this. The wickedness of man is too much for the gods to cope with. It is impossible to decide whether the author meant this as a resolution of the problem or as a final statement of the problem. He seems to leave the recognition of the human condition as the highest insight of wisdom, and in the human condition neither wisdom nor religion guarantees success.

A review of these works show that Israelite anti-wisdom need not be of more recent origin. It is not a question of literary dependence, even though literary dependence can be persuasively argued for much of Israelite conventional wisdom. It is simply a matter of recognizing that Egyptian and Mesopotamian wise men had reached enough sophistication to raise these questions long before there was an Israelite literature, and there is nothing in the little we know about the development of Israelite thought to prevent Israelite anti-wisdom from raising these questions long before there was an Israelite literature. If Job and Koheleth, and in particular Koheleth, are located in the later periods of biblical literature, the argument reposes on purely literary grounds.[23] There is a tendency among recent critics to place Job in the monarchy rather than in the exilic or postexilic period, a date that was generally accepted without question for several generations.[24] We have noticed in other contexts that theology cannot entirely ignore literary criticism, which is a tool for investigating the history of thought. For the book of Job, assured precise dating is not within reach.

The book of Job suits our description of our topic as "God-talk" better than any other Old Testament book. The five speakers and finally God himself discuss God and his acts and nothing else throughout the book. No one disputes that Job is the supreme

[23] M. Pope, *Job* (New York, 1973), XXXII–XL; R. B. Y. Scott, *Proverbs: Ecclesiastes* (New York, 1965), 200–1.
[24] Pope, op. cit., XXX–XXXVII.

product of the Israelite literary genius; it matches profundity of thought with richness of language dedicated to a topic of perennial importance and perennial difficulty. The date, as we have mentioned, cannot be determined exactly; modern scholars are convinced that both the period of the patriarchs suggested by some early rabbis and the Greek period suggested by some modern critics are both far out of line. Job does presuppose conventional wisdom, which Job attacks and his friends defend. For reasons difficult to set forth and not essential to the theological discussion of the book, I am inclined to place the book in the exilic or early postexilic period.

It is generally believed that the book of Job was expanded from a popular story of Job, which is preserved in chapters 1–2 and 42. This story falls within the category of wisdom, and its account of man who withstands severe testing is like *Ludlul bel nemeqi* in its happy ending. The story is very probably, as many interpreters have said, a naïve statement of belief that undeserved suffering is a test of virtue imposed by the deity; passage of the test is rewarded with a bonus of double one's previous possessions (including the years of one's life), for it would certainly be unfair to inflict permanent damage on a man for maintaining virtue through unusual tests. The popular story need not reflect upon experience; perhaps no man has ever been known to sustain such a test, but if such a man did appear, this would be the treatment given to him. Wisdom, like the myths of the deluge and Sodom and Gomorrah, could always explain disaster as merited. If wisdom was to maintain any idea of divine justice, it had to explain unmerited disaster in this way.

The author of the dialogue gives this naïve popular story an extremely sophisticated treatment. Neither Job nor his friends know anything of a test of virtue. The author has accepted the innocent Job of the popular story; unless Job is innocent, there is no problem. The friends of Job cannot accept his plea of innocence; his miserable condition itself is a clear proof of his guilt, for to say that he is punished without guilt is to accuse God of injustice. Wise men both in ancient and in modern times have often explained the suffering of the innocent by denying the innocence. George Bernard Shaw in a flash of wit distinguished between the deserving poor and the undeserving poor. In the last analysis, many modern wise men recognize only the deserving poor, of whom there are almost none.

This is the thesis of Job's friends, repeated through three cycles of speeches in the dialogue. Since the author was a poet of genius, one must say that conventional wisdom has never been so skillfully set forth. The speeches are repetitious, and they have to be; conventional wisdom has no great mass of evidence to support its thesis. Job's friends repeat in varied and imaginative discourses that God always punishes the wicked and delivers the righteous; if—a concession to Job—punishment or deliverance seems to be delayed, they are no less sure, and the delay means that both punishment and deliverance will come with unusual fullness when they come. These principles permit no conclusion except that Job has sinned; from gentle hints of this, the discourses come to vicious accusations of particular crimes.

The speeches of Elihu, which in the judgment of almost all critics have been added by a continuator, add nothing to the doctrine of Job's friends. Elihu expands on the theory that the suffering of the righteous has a disciplinary value; the righteous man is admonished for faults which are less than grave and in fact by punishment may be deterred from faults which he has not yet committed (33:14–30). Such a theory of admonition is meaningless when it is referred to such calamitous suffering as the suffering of Job. Nevertheless, one is inclined to think that the continuator took his theory seriously, that he was unhappy with the failure of the discourses of Job's friends to meet the difficulties raised by Job, and that he thought that he had solved the problem. Interpreters do not share his assurance.

Job himself is the paradigmatic sufferer. Efforts to identify the symptoms of his disease are predestined to failure; Job is intended to represent the summit of physical disintegration. He is a very walking encyclopedia of all the ills that flesh is heir to. In addition, he is totally impoverished. He also knows human enmity, both in some of the blows which deprive him of his fortune and in the contempt which his suffering elicits. As we have noticed, it is vital to the discussion that he is a man of integrity; the sages indeed might deny that there can be a problem of the innocent sufferer, but the poet means to affirm that the problem is real. I have long suspected that the poet is artful in distinguishing, even though slightly, the character traits of Job's friends and in thus presenting individual variations on what ultimately is the same argument. Many interpreters think this is an excessively subtle interpretation; but they do not doubt the subtlety with which the author makes Job examine his problem now from one angle, now from another. There are eight speeches of Job clearly discernible; two others in the third cycle of speeches have been partly lost and partly disarranged. It will be worth while to trace the phases of the development; yet we must bear in mind that an abstract summary fails to reproduce the impact of the speeches, which are written in poetry with insight, feeling, and imagination.

Job's introductory discourse (3) sets forth the reality of his sufferings and proceeds at once to the basic question: why is life granted to one to whom all the goods of life are denied? Job's first reply to Eliphaz (6–7) makes the point—not pure poetry—that the burden of great suffering is often too great for man's moral strength to sustain; and Job toys with the idea that God might cherish enmity against him as he cherishes enmity against the monster of chaos. Man is too small to deserve the close attention of God; it is a common human theme that the acts of the individual person are ultimately of not much importance. Job's first reply to Bildad (9–10) raises the question of God's power and asks whether God might be pure power, irrational and irresponsible; this would be the god of nature, unrefined by any nobility. Job sees no morality in the acts of God in history. Possibly, he muses, God is vindictive in a petty way as men are vindictive, perhaps God is even a sadist who enjoys inflicting pain. Job believes his doubts could be resolved if he could confront God before an impartial judge; but one cannot enter into discussion with pure power. Job's first reply to Zophar (12–14) reaffirms the power of God in history; no one else is responsible for the rise and fall of men. He arrives, however, at a more encouraging insight. Job's friends have defended God by laying false charges against Job. God neither needs nor likes such defenses. Hence, although all of conventional wisdom denies it, Job will take the risk of affirming his innocence. With the affirmation, he utters an impossible wish, the

wish that death may not be final; even a tree cut down may have
enough life in the stump to grow again. If God would "hide him
in Sheol," Job would not care how long he might have to wait. But
there is no hope.

Job's second reply to Eliphaz (16–17) falls back to a level of
depression from which he had attempted to rise in the preceding
speech. He employs figures, but the figures clearly describe God
attacking a defenseless man; God is his enemy, and thus attests
to his wickedness. As in the opening discourse, Job looks to death
as a release and Sheol as repose. Yet in one of the most obscure
lines of the poem, Job appeals to "a witness in heaven, a guar-
antor on high" (16:19).[25] A personal mediator hardly seems possible; we must create too much out of the unknown to insert such
an idea here. More probably the witness is Job's innocence, known
to God but to no one else. Job's second reply to Bildad (19) contains one of the most celebrated and most obscure passages of the
entire Old Testament (19:25–29). Job desires that his plea of
innocence be engraved for all time; but what he desires in the
concluding lines simply is unknown.[26] The Vulgate translation
of Jerome rendered the lines as a profession of belief in the resurrection of the body. This cannot be the meaning of the Hebrew.
Furthermore, the poet nowhere in the book appeals to the belief
in resurrection and the future life as relevant to his problem, and
relevant it certainly is. In such passages as 9:18–22, 13:10–12,
and 17:13–16, the prospect of survival is flatly denied. The poet
either was unacquainted with belief in a future life or chose to omit
it from the discussion. The second possibility can hardly be supported; and a belief in the resurrection of the body cannot be
clearly attested in the Old Testament before the second century
B.C. The Israelite wise men, like the Mesopotamian wise men,
faced the problem of evil without eschatology. The Egyptian Song
of the Harper shows that the Egyptian belief in the afterlife broke
down under catastrophe.[27] Job's second reply to Zophar (21)
moves to the attack. He had already denied any moral discrimination in God's acts in history; now he affirms that the wicked prosper

25 Pope, op. cit., 125–26.
26 Ibid. 146–47.
27 ANET 467.

while the innocent perish. Job's third reply to Eliphaz (23–24) asks once more for a confrontation with God. The discourse then goes on to a touching description of the destitute; such descriptions are rare in ancient literature, even in the Old Testament. The destitute are contrasted with the criminal. The end of this discourse and the replies of Job to Bildad and Zophar have been confused beyond repair.[28]

Job's final speech (29–31) contrasts the serenity of the man of wealth and position with the destitution of the poor; once again he affirms the enmity of God and describes the contempt with which men treat the sufferer. Job affirms of himself the virtues proper to the man of wealth and position, and they can be summed up as gentleness. Not only does he give to any in need, but he delivers them from oppression. Job describes his own attitude toward the poor in terms like those in which the prophets describe Yahweh as the defender of the poor. Similarly, in a series of imprecations he denies that he has yielded to the temptations peculiar to men of wealth and power. He challenges God to produce a written indictment; if it were produced, Job would wear it as a badge of honor.

The speeches of Yahweh (38–41) are regarded by many critics as the work of a continuator. They urge, not unreasonably, that a recital of the wonders of God in nature does not speak to the problem of the book. I believe one may more easily admit that the descriptions of Behemoth and Leviathan (40:15–41:34) are secondary both on grounds of style and on grounds of context. But the first speech of Yahweh does speak to the problem. In response to Job's urging that God's acts in history are opaque, God answers that the world is full of things which God made which are also opaque. Job neither created the world nor does he manage it; and he cannot understand it or explain it. This evidently does not answer Job's question, but it does speak to the question. The wisdom of God, we noticed, is attested in creation, and it is seen most clearly in those paradoxes which defy explanation. If Job believes that God is wise, he will have to accept God's wisdom even when it goes beyond his understanding. I do not imply that

28 Pope, op. cit., 187–96.

the poet means to say that the problem of evil is the same kind of paradox as the ostrich (39:13–18); but he does mean to say that if God is really wise, he will do things that are past understanding.

The wealth of poetry is not an empty background for a scholarly thesis. Job's friends, among other things, are insensitive to human suffering. When they observe it, they say that it could not happen to more deserving people. They do not know how suffering breaks down virtue and character. How are such men to learn without experiencing the burden of pain which humanity bears? The poet appeals to his resources of language in the hope that he can communicate understanding. He would not have the fortunate think that God is as insensitive to pain as they are; and he makes Job raise this charge only to drop it. Job's first move is not to God but to his friends; and what he asks of them is not "understanding," not even in the wisdom sense of the word, but compassion for the suffering, compassion before rationalization. This is what Job affirms in his final defense that he has always shown. At the risk of being too subtle, we may suggest that for the poet a large component of the problem of evil is the refusal of the smug and prosperous to admit that there is anything wrong.

Nor does the poet mean to treat Job's complaints as obviously false and negligible. One can be really tempted to think of God as pure power or as hostile or as lacking in moral discrimination. As Job says, the problem is not solved by lies about the world. This contributes to his main purpose, which seems to be to make people aware of the reality and the urgency of the problem of those who suffer, shall we say, beyond their just deserts. The thesis of cosmic justice simply cannot be supported by experience alone, and the poet felt it necessary not only to say this but also to set forth at length and with feeling the considerations which experience can adduce against cosmic justice. The book becomes anti-wisdom when ultimately the wise men have nothing to say about cosmic justice. If anything is to be said about it, one must go beyond wisdom; and where is one to go?

I believe the context demands that one go to God at this point, and that is where the poet goes; and we must put his paradoxes in their proper perspective. The poet, of course, had no answer either from revelation or from his own wisdom. The speech of Yahweh asks that one have faith in the demonstrated wisdom of the creator. One must believe that the power and wisdom which produced the world are able to sustain it in wisdom, even though God's wisdom is impenetrable to man. Agnosticism rebels against what it cannot understand and denies reality to the unintelligible. Faith does not embrace the unintelligible, but it finds that a world behind which there is no ultimate wisdom is supremely unintelligible. Therefore it will trust the God who could make an ostrich to handle the problem of evil in ways which are not visible. The basic fault of Job's friends is that they rationalize without evidence.

The book of Koheleth (Ecclesiastes) is one of the strangest books of the Bible; and although it is small, it poses a number of exegetical and theological problems which commentators have not solved. That is to say that we do not understand what the book means. It is classified as anti-wisdom because of a number of passages which we shall discuss presently. These are interspersed in passages which express conventional wisdom; when the conventional wisdom is studied closely, however, it is seen to support the themes of anti-wisdom. It is quite difficult to treat the book as a structured unity; but Koheleth is dominated by the conviction that life is uncertain, and that for several reasons. One is the certainty of death which renders any fancied security illusory. Another is that life does not reward men according to their righteousness and wickedness; this is a candid statement of a theme found in several of the speeches of Job. One cannot even evade the certainty of death by preparing for his sons, since life gives no assurance that the treasure will reach those for whom it was gathered.

Yet Koheleth opposes to this uncertainty the certainty of the necessity that all things return to their point of origin (1:5–11), which compels man, whether he knows it or not, to follow paths which have already been trodden. Man cannot achieve anything new or different. Nor can he escape the set times in which events are set (3:2–8); when the set time comes, the destined event occurs whatever man may intend. Thus Koheleth sees no profit in any of man's toil; it is threatened both by the certainty of death and the uncertainty of life.

Koheleth puts on the person of Solomon, the proverbial example of the wisdom which produces success and prosperity (2:1–26).

His conclusion is that even the most glorious successes of wisdom are also vanity; wisdom is no better than folly, and this is the most frank statement of anti-wisdom in all this literature. Wealth is no assurance against pain and vexation (5:10–17). Hence Koheleth seems to turn to a moderate hedonism (2:24, 3:12–13, 4:6, 5:18, 6:9, 8:15), more fully expressed in a passage (9:7–10) which has a remarkable affinity to a passage from the Mesopotamian epic poem of Gilgamesh.[29] We call this hedonism "moderate" because Koheleth plainly offers man no opportunity for excess; when he speaks in the person of Solomon, who in legend enjoyed every pleasure available to man, he concludes that this is vanity. Should it be called "hedonism"? If this extremely vague word is used with any sort of precision, it is not the word to apply to Koheleth. He does not recommend the pursuit of pleasure; he mutes his pessimism by adverting to the simple fugitive pleasures which life may afford, although even these fugitive pleasures are denied to some.

Pessimism seems to be the word for Koheleth rather than hedonism; and most interpreters have found his pessimism so unbiblical that they have wondered whether he was subject to unbiblical influence, such as Greek philosophy. One would have to ask which school of Greek philosophy; and in fact, there is no definite connection with any Greek philosophical school or work which can be established. The irrationality of the human condition is expressed with a sharpness which is not felt even in the book of Job. Job does appeal to God almost constantly, and God himself finally speaks. It is hardly an exaggeration to say that compared to Job, Koheleth is an atheist. The God who walked in Eden, who spoke to Moses and to Israel, who spoke through the prophets and engaged in dialogue with Jeremiah has become remote and almost uninvolved. He has set times (8:11) to which man must fit himself. He is not a God to whom Koheleth prays or speaks in any terms. Job feels that God ought to be concerned, and he complains when God does not show concern; Koheleth seems to expect no concern, and this is no doubt the key to his profound pessimism.

[29] ANET 90.

Shall we say the Koheleth is the last sour apple on the tree of wisdom? Shall we say that once wisdom is conceived as the key to security, it is misconceived, that it is turned to folly by the wise men? The height of wisdom surely is not to achieve success and prosperity but to live with pain. Koheleth may have known this; if he did, he took a remarkably indirect way of saying it, and Job came closer to suggesting it. Some one has to say that human enterprise is vain; Koheleth says it. Does he achieve greater understanding than Shelley—"Look on my works, ye mighty, and despair"? To say that man accomplishes nothing is a statement of pessimism; indeed, it is a statement full of sound and fury, signifying nothing. If what man is and does is not important, any discourse must end with that perception. This is where Koheleth seems to end.

This is not the more common understanding of the book, I am aware. And therefore I hesitate to credit Koheleth with scarcely more insight in one direction than Job's friends had in the opposite direction. It does seem that unless something else happens, Koheleth leads straight to Lucretius and Catullus, to mention two Roman exponents of hedonism and pessimism. If all is vanity, then man will pursue vanity because he has nothing else to pursue. If folly is as good as wisdom, it is less trouble to be a fool and much more fun. Interpreters think that Koheleth sets up a straw man with these implications. But he never knocks the straw man down. If Koheleth has a lasting message (and I know what my colleagues think of "message"), it is that the wise men know nothing about God. We began this treatment with the observation that the wise men really do not engage in God-talk; we close it with the notice that one of the last wise men does not engage in God-talk and that he finds little to say about human life.

3. *A Problem of Personal Morality and Personal Responsibility*

Wisdom literature is the only type of Old Testament writing which attends formally to the morality of the individual person; and even under this heading, it attends actually to the morality of one who is the adult head of the family or who expects to become the head of the family. It is not concerned with the morality of women or of children. In the social structures of the ancient world, this made sense, for women and children did not have that freedom which entails moral responsibility. They enter the view of the wise as objects of the moral decisions of the adult male or as aids or obstacles to his moral decisions. Their own moral decisions will be made for them, normally by the head of the house, otherwise by some adult male.

Outside of the wisdom literature, even the adult male head of the family is hardly attended to as a moral agent. The discourses, warnings, rebukes, and invectives of the prophets are addressed to groups, not to individuals; when the group is threatened, all the individual members fall under the threat. We have noticed in considering the idea of judgment that this understanding of the individual in society raised problems (see Chapter III, Section 5, above). These problems were solved in a way similar to the ideas of Job's friends; reality was affirmed to be in harmony with what sound theology demanded that it be, and no righteous man perished in Sodom and Gomorrah. One must observe that the prophets as a group do not make the exception which was made by the authors of the stories of the deluge and of Sodom and Gomorrah.

To notice this difference sends us back to a point previously noticed, the point that the wise men were concerned less with morality than with success. They presupposed, as we saw, a stable political and social order in which certain results of certain actions were guaranteed. Deviations from the principles of stability were folly; in the schools of wisdom it was understood that this was damaging to the fool himself. But just as the wise man did not establish a stable order, neither did the fool destroy it. The prophets, on the other hand, view folly as the corruption of a whole people, and the results will be the same for the whole people as they are for the individual fool. Behind both the prophetic and the wisdom view is an understanding of social morality so different from the modern understanding that it is difficult to set it forth. At the risk of some exaggeration, it may be said that the individual man was moral only in society and through society. In a certain sense, he had no moral responsibility; moral responsibility fell upon the whole society which created the conditions in which the individual persons lived. They made those moral decisions, and only those decisions, which the society made possible for them. The Israelite and the Judahite were related to Yahweh only through their membership in Israel and Judah. Within Israel and Judah they heard his *torah* and his word and worshiped him in public social cult. Similarly, they knew the moral will of Yahweh only through their membership in Israel and Judah. It was the duty of the community to cut off the unfaithful members. If it failed to cut them off, their guilt fell upon the entire community, which supported them in wickedness by not punishing them. The sinner did not sin for himself alone. The righteous man was not able to escape the taint which wickedness cast upon the community. Whether he was good or bad, the Israelite stood before Yahweh as an Israelite, justified or condemned with the group. I repeat that I know that this may be an overstatement of an idea of collective responsibility which we share only in part; and it is worth our attention that we do share it. We are no strangers to that guilt which is attached to individual persons because of their membership in a nation or a race. Irrational this may be, but it is an irrationality which is universally human. We shall have occasion to return to the tribal basis of this idea in Chapter VI, Section 1; our interest in this context is the problem of personal morality and responsibility created by the great crisis in the history of Israel and Judah. The prophetic response to this crisis joins the wisdom of the sages, for it is addressed to the individual person and not to the social group.

The two prophets who come under consideration are Jeremiah and Ezekiel, both contemporaries of the fall of the kingdom of Judah in 587 B.C. Jeremiah was a witness of the event; the book of Ezekiel as it has come to us removes Ezekiel from Jerusalem at the time of the disaster, but a number of modern critics have argued that Ezekiel too was there.[30] The arguments have not convinced the majority of interpreters, and in any case, the point is not relevant to what is discussed here. It is a rare human experience to have one's world collapse around one; it has, however, happened to millions in the twentieth century. Many of these, if not most, have rebuilt a world in which they could live. When one

---

[30] Otto Eissfeldt, *The Old Testament: An Introduction*, 370–72.

deals with the collapse of the monarchy of Judah, one must bear in mind that strong social bond which we have mentioned in the preceding paragraphs. Society means institutions, and the security of the individual is guaranteed by institutions. Jeremiah announces the end of each of the major political and religious institutions of Judah: the temple and the cult, the priesthood, priestly instruction (*torah*), prophecy, the monarchy of David. The entire structure through which the Judahite was related to Yahweh comes to an end; and why did not the cult of Yahweh in Judah fall into oblivion with the cult of Chemosh in Moab?

We may possibly exaggerate the social character of Israelite religion; perhaps there was more personal religion than the literature discloses. If there was, we cannot reconstruct it; and in fact, the picture which emerges from the Old Testament literature of the worshiping community of Israel is altogether credible and quite intelligible. In the modern world, where the cult of the individual person is far more highly developed than it was in the ancient world, religion is for many people a purely social affair in which they have no genuine personal response and no genuine personal interest. The ancient world of the Near East did not offer the kind of personal fulfillment which is the legitimate ambition of many people in the modern world. As we have observed, the individual person could make only those decisions which his society enabled him to make, and the options were limited. No more did the ancient world offer to the individual person a relation to the deity which was not a social relation. When the society which was the mediator between the deity and the individual person was dissolved, what medium replaced it?

Jeremiah in this crisis had become alienated from his community before the collapse which he predicted came. His predictions were themselves the major reason why his countrymen rejected him; social critics are indeed sometimes accepted, and may even become fashionable, but men who seriously predict the political and social collapse of their community are likely to be reckoned as agents of the collapse they predict. Jeremiah's life was threatened several times, more than once by the royal authority, at least once by "priests, prophets and all the people" (26:7–8) and on some unspecified occasions. Jeremiah finds the whole people, great and small, rich and poor, old and young, men and women, objects of the anger of Yahweh (5:1–5; 6:9–15). Not unreasonably, people hated him as if he were a moneylender (15:10), and Jeremiah withdrew from all the social amenities of community life, from participation in domestic joys and sorrows (16:1–9). Jeremiah's clear attestations that he had become a social leper should be considered when the literary origins and the interpretation of the "confessions" are discussed. The picture which emerges from them seems entirely credible and consistent. For reasons which are not clear, Jeremiah could not even take part in the cult of the temple (36:5).

Thus Jeremiah does exhibit what has often been said about him by some interpreters and denied by others: the development of a personal religion. This is not presented as a prophetic teaching; it is simply a personal experience. Jeremiah has been alienated from the community through which he was related to Yahweh. The personal relation of Jeremiah to Yahweh is the relation of the prophetic mission, and this could hardly be the example of a personal relation for all members of the community. Yet in a passage of disputed authenticity Jeremiah does in fact announce a future in which each man will know Yahweh without a teacher; this may indeed be the work of a scribe reflecting on the experience of Jeremiah, but it is derived from that experience (31:33–34). We shall meet this theme again in treating the future of Israel. For the present, Jeremiah seems to have nothing to say to his countrymen who are about to lose their God with their kingdom. The land which is described in 4:23–26 is chaos before creation upon which the spirit of God has not yet breathed; this is the land of Judah after the Babylonian conquest.

There is in 31:29–30 a quotation of a proverb which is also quoted by Ezekiel and submitted to a much more elaborate discussion, the proverb about sour grapes eaten by the fathers and tasted by the children. This proverb will no longer be uttered "in those days," the indefinite future in which so many "messianic" features are so often placed. It cannot therefore be urged that the author, whether Jeremiah or a commentator, meant that the principle of individual punishment which is stated will be fulfilled in history. In fact it has not, for, as we have seen, collective guilt is still a real factor in human consciousness and human history; and the author may thus be commended for his insight in restraining himself from an unreal prediction. It is not the proverb but the author who expresses implicit dissatisfaction with the principle of collective guilt. A time ought to come, even if it is postponed to "those days," when a man will have to bear nobody's guilt but his own. Must personal religion and personal responsibility go so far that one cannot bear his share of the burden of the human community? It is another statement directed to the problem of the suffering of the innocent; and it may be a desire of the impossible.

The weakness of the statement is more clearly seen in the discussion of Ezekiel, which is preserved in a double recension (18:1–32; 33:1–20). The first of the passages deals directly with the proverb about the fathers and the sons; the second admits one case of shared responsibility, the case of the prophet who fails to warn the wicked man of his wickedness. Both passages discuss the change in the individual from wickedness to righteousness or from righteousness to wickedness. With the exception of the prophet who shares the guilt of the sinner whom he did not warn, Ezekiel insists that each individual case is solved exclusively on the merits of the individual, not on the merits of his father or on the merits of his previous life. The affirmation is so rigorous that most commentators have found it unrealistic. There is, after all, a human community; no man is an "iland," as John Donne spelled it, and we need not ask for whom the bell tolls. According to Ezekiel, it tolls for only one at a time, and indeed according to what he is at the time it tolls. Men harm and help each other, often in ways which are unknown both to subject and to object. Perhaps Ezekiel lacked the resources both of ideas and of language to make the necessary refinements in his argument. The result is a kind of moral atomism. The breakdown of Israelite society leads to no replacement. Yet Ezekiel (the book, not necessarily the man) is not troubled by the problem of social collapse because he expects the Israelite society to be restored. The chariot of Yahweh departs from Zion but it comes to Ezekiel in Babylon. Perhaps it is more important in Ezekiel's argument to remember not his argument but his assertion that Yahweh desires not the death of the wicked but that the wicked turn from his evil ways and live. This statement of personal responsibility and personal religion will stand without the elaborate argument, and in the context of the judgment of Yahweh upon his people it was a meaningful statement. Ezekiel makes a clumsy effort to affirm the importance of the moral decisions of the individual man, and he believes that Yahweh has regard for them, whatever experience may suggest. It is unfortunate that the statement had to be expanded into moral atomism and a distortion or rather an ignoring of the social character of man's moral experience. From this we may conclude that it is impossible to speak to the problem of the suffering of the innocent without contradicting oneself. Ezekiel is closer to Job's friends and their conventional wisdom than he is to Job. A mere affirmation of the moral autonomy of the individual person is not a solution to the problem raised by the collapse of the Israelite political and religious structure. The innocent do suffer because of the sins of the guilty.

VI

Political and Social Institutions

By way of introduction let us recall that the modern secularization of society and politics was unknown in the ancient Near East. That politics and society should be formally religious was not peculiar to Israel, although we hope to show that Israel had its own way of incorporating religion into politics and society. The man of the modern world is always a member of several groups, some of which may meet only in him. The political society of which he is a member is only one of his social relations; it may be the most important relation in his life and the most demanding one as well as the most controlling, but it is rarely the most interesting and hardly ever the most rewarding. In western countries the citizen looks for his personal fulfillment to other social relations which are private, and he prefers that the state allow these private societies freedom to operate. They are at least theoretically societies which one joins by free personal decision; sometimes, as in the case of labor unions, personal freedom is practically destroyed by social and economic pressure. Membership in religious societies, as a result of the religious pluralism which is the lasting fruit of the Reformation in the western world, is also a matter of free personal decision, and in this generation there is no social pressure in this direction.

In contrast to this, the man of the ancient Near East was a member of only one society if the society was tribal and of two, the family and the kingdom, if the society was political. All social relations were found within these one or two societies; and with reference to our interests here, the political and the religious society (or the tribal and religious society) completely coincided. The social or political society was directly and formally a religious society. It was considered to have a religious foundation in the

236 A THEOLOGY OF THE OLD TESTAMENT

acts of the gods and to be religiously sustained by the protection of the gods. As a society, it was a cultic group. Orthodoxy was not imposed by political ordinance or by social pressure; men simply had never known nor thought of a social organization which was not formally religious. In the terms we have been using, man experienced the deity in the political and social institutions in which he lived.

The integration of religion and society was not always perfect, but this was not because the two structures were directed to opposing ends. This modern complication of religion versus politics did not exist in the ancient Near East except in Israel and in one episode in Egypt, and the character of the Israelite exception will be given the close attention which it deserves. The conflict between Ikhnaton and the Amon priesthood in Egypt is not well documented, but it certainly appears to have been a conflict of religion and politics and in fact to have been ultimately the crudest kind of power struggle.[1] Normally, in the ancient Near East, religion was a means by which the ends of state were pursued, and these were fertility and prosperity, internal order and external security. The state which sought no more from the gods than these things did not think of the gods as being excessively demanding.

1. *The Tribal Confederation*

As Martin Noth pointed out, Israel first surely appears in history as a league of twelve tribes established in Canaan.[2] More recent studies may suggest that this should be revised to a league of ten tribes, but for the problem under discussion the number is not important. I accept the hypothesis of George E. Mendenhall that the majority of the members of the Israelite confederation were not immigrants but individuals and groups who had withdrawn from the feudal monarchies of the Canaanite city-states, where they had been subjects and serfs of a landowning military aristocracy based on a divinely established kingship.[3] Wherever

[1] John A. Wilson, *The Burden of Egypt,* 206–35.
[2] "Das System der zwölf Stämme Israels" BeitWissAT (1930).
[3] *Biblical Archeologist* 25, 1962, 66–87.

one is able to make a pointed contrast between the Israelite confederacy and the Canaanite monarchy, the Israelites appear in stark opposition to the Canaanite system. This occurs in so many details that mere coincidence is not an explanation. The Israelites appear to have formed a society which was deliberately a rejection of the basic principles of Canaanite society and religion; and this new system was placed under the patronage of Yahweh, an entirely new god. We have already touched upon certain details of the Israelite system such as covenant and covenant law in Chapter II, Section 2. We now discuss the experience of Yahweh in the institutions of the confederation, even at the risk of some repetition; for the experience of Yahweh in the confederation was the constitutive religious experience of Israel, never entirely lost in the centuries which followed.

First of all, the early Israelites rejected kingship, and with it they rejected any kind of public authority whatever. The league was a purely religious union and in no way a political union. It had no structure and no central authority. The name "tribal" is apt not only because it was a league of tribes, but also because the entire structure was tribal, which means familial. No Israelite could hold that kind of authority over other Israelites which we call "political," and which they knew only as the absolute power of the ancient king. Nor could there be an aristocracy; no Israelite was better than another, whether because of birth or wealth. The Israelites overturned the Canaanite city-states, but they did not replace them with other states. They created a political vacuum.

Socially this meant that the security of the individual person rested in his kinship group and in no public authority. The union of the tribes in covenant meant that all Israel became a vast kinship group. Although the title of *go'el* (avenger), is rarely given to Yahweh in early literature, the idea of the Great Kinsman who defends the life, liberty, and property of his kinsmen is very probably a reflection of an early idea of Yahweh; it can scarcely be anything but an archaism in Second Isaiah, the biblical writer who uses the term most frequently. The Canaanite kings had not furnished to their subjects the kind of security of which Hammurabi boasts in the prologue and the epilogue of his code.[4] In fact the

4 ANET 164, 177–78.

kind of serf of which Mendenhall speaks was not even in the
system; he was, rather, beneath it, sustaining it by his underpaid
production.

In this social context, the cultic recital of the exodus acquires a
new and vitally important dimension. Yahweh is saluted as the
liberator of the oppressed and the scourge of oppressors. Students
of ancient Egypt notice that the conditions which the exodus narratives describe as the slavery of the Israelites in Egypt were
normal conditions of the life of the Egyptian peasants. In fact,
these conditions have not changed substantially in the twentieth
century; but the Egyptian peasants did not rebel against Ramses II,
and they did not rebel against Nasser. The Israelites, whose god
had delivered the oppressed from Egypt, were alone in affirming
that the condition of the peasant deserved the compassionate attention of God, and they alone produced a society in which no
man was above another. It did not endure, as we shall notice.

The political vacuum created by the rejection of kingship was
filled by Yahweh. We have already noticed that the treaty covenant
formula suggests the idea of Yahweh as overlord, and we noticed
also that this is not explicit in the literature early or late. In the
political system of overlords and vassals, the suzerainty of the
overlord did not remove the vassal king from his throne. The
submission of Israel to the covenant law of Yahweh left no room
for human authority. If the functions of the ancient king are correctly described as war and law (Mendenhall), covenant law removed one of them. As we shall see below, the idea of the holy
war removed another. Nothing was left which the elders of the
clan or tribe, village or town, were unable to handle.

It seems clear beyond doubt that the Israelite theory of land
tenure was based on the donation of Yahweh the overlord. Land
tenure in feudal monarchies means the donation of land to the
vassal, who in return promises military service to the overlord.
The Canaanite vassals of the local kings comprised the chariot
aristocracy; and it is not merely coincidental that the Israelites
not only repudiated chariots, but even the quite innocent horses
which drew them. The Deuteronomic criticism of kingship includes
the acquisition of chariots (1 Sam 8:11), and both Joshua (Josh
11:9) and David (2 Sam 8:4) are said to have hamstrung cap-

tured horses. These episodes bear witness to the deep Israelite revulsion against the monarchy supported by the military aristocracy which the earliest Israelites knew in the Canaanite city-states; as we shall see, this is exactly the kind of monarchy which arose under David and Solomon.

The Hebrew terms for land owned by the individual or the family are *gōral* (lot; cf. the English word "lot," still employed to indicate a piece of land apart from the buildings), *naḥalah* (portion or assignment), and *ḥēlek* (portion). It is possible that the account of the division of the land (Josh 13–19), which can scarcely be historical, is a narrative constructed on the idea of "lot." De Vaux points out that in the ancient Near East feudal holdings were sometimes assigned by lot.[5] Joshua acts as the agent of Yahweh the overlord, and he assigns the land to the tribes. It is not indicated that the land was assigned to individual families in the same way. There is in fact nothing in the Israelite laws governing the ownership and transfer of land, but the practice can be reconstructed. De Vaux suggests that the practice was governed by public feeling and custom. In any designation, the practice seems to have been that land remained in the kinship group. If the owner could not retain his land, the nearest of kin had the obligation of buying it. This was an instance of the *go'el,* but unlike the obligation to avenge murder or injury, the purchase of land became an option rather than an obligation. The obligation or option was passed along the line of kinship until a purchaser was found. Evidently the observance of this law or custom would prevent land monopolies from arising. The existence of this law or custom is deduced from the episodes of Naboth (1 Kings 21), of Jeremiah and Hanamel (Jer 32) and of Boaz and Ruth (Ruth 3:12–13, 4:1–12). In each of these episodes, there is clear reference to an unformulated obligation to buy and sell land within proximate kinship. Probably the law of the jubilee (Lev 25:28), again scarcely historical, is an obscure allusion to the ancient custom of holding land within the family. In this form of land tenure, the individual Israelite as well as the tribe was a liegeman of Yahweh.

[5] Roland de Vaux, *Ancient Israel,* 164–67.

The holy war and its association with the land have already been treated (see Chapter III, Section 4, above); and it remains to point out in this context that the holy war can be considered as the service due to the overlord from the vassals in return for the donation of the land. It is not the only form of service; we have already noticed that the stipulations of the covenant, while they cannot be defined exactly, must include the basic principles of Israelite law. I have suggested that the holy war was waged only in defense of the land of Yahweh; and this limitation fits very well the pattern of feudal service. The holy war is also fought by Yahweh as the major combatant; the Israelites are no more than his auxiliary troops, and victory is assured. Whether Yahweh was thought of as fighting the gods of other nations cannot be shown from even older texts. But since the gods of nations were utterly powerless, they were meaningless, whether they were real or not. The only real resistance to Yahweh was furnished by human military resources.

The individual member of the tribe felt no security except in the tribe. For the Israelite the tribe included the Great Kinsman, Yahweh. Corresponding to collective security was collective guilt; the wrongdoing of members of the tribe rubbed off even on those tribemen who had no share in the wrongdoing. The topic deserves attention if for no other reason than that it has often been adduced as an example of primitive thinking which is altogether repugnant to modern civilized ideas of justice and personal responsibility. We have already touched upon the problem of personal and collective responsibility in Chapter III, Section 6, and Chapter V, Section 3, and we return to it now as it is an effect of tribal society. But it is altogether false to label the idea of collective guilt as either biblical or primitive. The twentieth century, the most militant of centuries as well as the most civilized, has experienced horrors due to modern belief in collective guilt which exceed anything known to us from "biblical" or "primitive" peoples. The psychology of modern warfare demands that the combatants be trained to hate men whom they have never seen before, for very few men can kill without hating the victim. This cannot be achieved on a large scale except by identifying each individual enemy with a guilty group. The moral level of warfare is well below the "biblical" and "primitive" level of Ezek 18:20—"The wickedness of the wicked shall be upon himself." That particular type of community which is called solidarity is neither primitive nor biblical; and it is very doubtful that man will ever outgrow it. It is, as we have noticed, the reverse side of collective salvation; the Christian belief in salvation through the saving act of God in Christ is based on the same belief in solidarity which is expressed in the belief in collective guilt.

An almost stock example of collective guilt is the execution of Achan and his entire family for the theft of devoted goods from Jericho (Josh 7). Here it is not a question of the historical reality of the event but of the belief expressed; and clearly there is a belief that the entire family should be executed for the crime of its head. It is the same logic which is expressed in the total destruction of Jericho, Ai, and other cities. There may, however, be a genuinely primitive idea of solidarity in the story which the scribes no longer recognized. I have elsewhere expressed this theory in these words: "The idea of collective guilt also runs through much of the Old Testament. The group maintains good relations with Yahweh only if it preserves its integrality. The holiness of Yahweh will not tolerate individual deviations. That the group is unaware of the erring member is not relevant. In ancient Israel the individual member was not capable of a fully independent decision. Unless the group rejected the offender from the community, it shared his guilt as long as he remained unpunished . . . The use of the lot to discover the culprit is likewise a piece of primitive thinking . . . its use as a substitute for investigation to determine guilt is revolting to the modern reader. Primitive thinking, however, has a logic of its own. As we have noticed above, the guilt falls first upon the group; the duty of bearing the guilt is not dissimilar to military service or any other community service. In the original conception of the lot, the individual was not punished; someone had to bear the guilt of the group, and since it was indifferent whether it was one person or another, the lot could be employed. The logic of collective guilt is no longer seen in the story of Achan."[6]

[6] J. L. McKenzie, *The World of the Judges*, 55–56.

Primitive this view of collective guilt may be, but it is rational compared to the later scribal belief that the entire family could be justly executed for the crime of a single member. In the primitive logic, Achan and his family were not "punished," for they were not "guilty"; the community was guilty, and guilt demanded expiation from the community. This is where the modern man finds it difficult to follow the reasoning; he does not think of guilt as something which must be eradicated. Better to let the guilty escape, he thinks, than to risk punishing the innocent. The primitive tribal thinking which imposes expiation by lot as a community service believes that it is punishing the guilty—the community— and not punishing the innocent—for the donors of their lives are not being punished. The modern man claims that he does not believe that the innocent person should share the responsibility for crimes committed by a member of his group; I say he "claims" he does not believe this, for the history of the wars of the last sixty years show that modern man may very well believe it, and when he is in a position to deal with his conquered enemies on this principle, he does so deal with them. He would be less barbarous sometimes if he selected atoning victims by lot like Achan— and in fact, modern reprisals in war have sometimes been made by this method.

Primitive belief in collective guilt should not be confused with a more recent fallacy that society is the criminal and the actual agent of the crime is innocent, himself a victim. Neither in the more primitive belief in expiation as a community service nor in the later Israelite belief that a group could be justly exterminated for the guilt of some of its members was there any room for such nonsense. They never doubted that there were individual guilty persons. The community was guilty only because the guilty individual survived within it, and it seems to have been irrelevant that he was not punished because his identity was unknown. To find him or to offer a substitute was the duty of the community. A similar rationalization can be seen in the execution of an entire group; the group had not dissociated itself from the guilty member nor had it furnished a substitute expiation.

The tribal league was the first—and so far the last—human community which its members believed was established by the direct and positive act of God with all the resources it needed to sustain a full human life for each of its members. By its rejection of monarchy, it was, as we have noticed, a nonpolitical community. It was a formal return to the more primitive tribal association, a kinship group in which God was the Great Kinsman. This involves a certain narrowness by definition; nothing in early Israel suggests that tribalism could be the seed of a view of humanity as one great kinship group. But its denial of politics as the ancient Near East knew politics was quite explicit and not an unconscious response to abuses. Early Israel believed that political structures came between man and God. It replaced political structures with political anarchy, confident that God would accomplish what was needed in crises. Nothing was envisaged in daily life which was beyond the competence of the elders of village and tribe, who were themselves kinsmen to those who had disputes or problems and bound not to some abstract justice but to help the kinsman in need. As long as the elders rendered judgment according to the terms of covenant law, the member of the tribe had nothing to fear. If an entirely new situation arose, the Israelites believed that the elders, not without a charismatic impulse like the impulse of the judge who delivered them in war, could devise a new law to meet the new situation. God could be experienced in law, in cult, in deliverance from enemies, in prosperity on one's own land, in peaceful cohabitation with one's neighbors, as long as the apparatus of false gods, kings, and landowning military aristocracy was totally and effectively removed.

We have described, here and in preceding discussions of the relevant topics, a social ideal which is simple but not ignoble. We advert to the narrowness and even vicious xenophobia which the community manifested, and we can observe that they were not notably more anti-social in these respects than other human communities. Yet we know that the tribal league endured at most from 1200 to 1000 B.C., and we do not know how successful it was in furnishing its members that security which they expected Yahweh to grant them in terms of the covenant. The scribes who have preserved a very sketchy record of the downfall of the tribal confederation were content to say that Israel went whoring after other gods. This may and possibly ought to be enough for the theologian, but it is not enough for the historian. In terms of the discussion which we have mounted, to go whoring after other gods is to return to the Canaanite way of life. The scribes do not give us details; and when we come to David and Solomon we shall learn what a return to the Canaanite way of life was. The historian may in addition venture other hypotheses, more historical and less theological. He may wonder whether a nonpolitical group was capable of sustained military resistance to the Philistines, a much smaller but much more disciplined group, better equipped for war. He may wonder whether a nonpolitical and purely religious unity could be sustained for so many people over so extensive a territory. He may wonder whether the tribal confederation was a victim of the march of history, of progress. The Israelite scribes would say that it need not have been a victim if it had maintained its integrity as the people of Yahweh. The statements of the historians and of the scribes do not cancel each other out. The narrowness of the league, it seems, kept it from being a permanent social form. Its principles did not demand that it remain narrow and viciously intolerant. It experienced the benevolence of Yahweh; becoming unfaithful to his will as they knew it, the confederacy had to experience his judgment.

2. *The Monarchy*

The biblical account of the origins of the Israelite monarchy is found in 1 and 2 Samuel. Although a full critical presentation should be presented, such a presentation does not lie within the scope of biblical theology. I work on the assumption that these books, in a form substantially identical with their present form, were first prepared by the scribes of David to explain how the monarch chosen by Yahweh attained and held the throne of the people of Yahweh. This critical assumption demands detailed argumentation which lies outside the scope of this work. I refrain from giving it also because in the present state of the criticism of the books of Samuel any position would be hypothetical. No one disputes that the purpose of the history of David is as I have described it; and this purpose is sufficient to justify the theological use I make of this history. I add only the assumption that the founder of the dynasty is more likely than any of his successors, none of whom distinguished themselves either as politicians or theologians, to have seen the need for a theological justification for his politics and to have taken action. This is an important critical hypothesis; for, as will appear in the following discussion, the books of Samuel as well as a number of other passages were the creations of the Jerusalem dynasty, produced in order to furnish a theological justification for the monarchy.

The importance of the monarchy in the messianism of the New Testament needs no discussion. While Jesus fitted no Jewish category exactly, the numerous allusions to his descent from David show that many of his contemporaries and many early Christians thought of him as the Davidic Messiah. It is significant that Jesus himself never certainly claimed this title. In the one passage in which he is said to accept the title of king (Jn 18:33–37), Jesus defines his kingship in a purely religious and nonpolitical sense; the claim is made in a context in which Jesus is reduced to utter helplessness. The Davidic kingship, when examined more closely, in no way fits the role of Jesus. It seems better to say this; for our treatment of the messianic kingship of David will contain numerous reservations. In fact, it may seem that we do not regard the Davidic kingship as an authentic experience of Yahweh.

To this point it may be remarked that we have just noticed that the tribal confederation, which was a rather quick failure, must still be treated as an authentic experience of Yahweh. To return to our Introduction, it is not proposed that the Old Testament anywhere presents a pure experience of Yahweh. Every experience is mediated through some vehicle of revelation. Just as the prophet does not lose his personal and cultural identity when he utters the word of Yahweh, so the media of cult, of history, of nature, of wisdom—the categories in which we have thus far dealt with the experience of Yahweh—always remain to some degree opaque. The reality of Yahweh is seen but veiled. These remarks seem necessary in view of the fact that the reservations which I am about to make in the theme of messianic kingship have not been made by very many Old Testament interpreters.

It has already been noticed that the tribal confederation was a nonpolitical society. It is at least a legitimate conjecture that this rejection of a political system was deliberate and not merely coincidental. Such a deliberate rejection seems to be expressed in the words of the Israelites in 1 Samuel 8:5, asking for "a king to govern us like all the nations." The scribe who wrote this was well aware that the monarchy was an assimilation of Israel to Canaanite society, the society which the tribal confederation had removed. While we cannot be sure that these words were written in the period of the foundation of the monarchy, it seems that the attitude they express was quite at home in early premonarchic Israel. The line is an example of the "anti-monarchic strain" in the traditions of the foundation of the monarchy. This strain is found in 1 Samuel 8 and 1 Samuel 10:17–27. One may add to this in theological character, if not in literary origins and style, the law of the king in Deuteronomy 17:14–20. This last passage is certainly critical of the monarchy, although it is not as sharply critical as 1 Samuel 8, and seems to suggest that the Deuteronomic law will protect the monarchy from the faults which the author clearly sees and hints at.

Literary criticism has generally located such passages in the later monarchy and interpreted them as reflections of the unhappy experience of Israel and Judah with most of its kings. One can hardly dispute the thesis that the passages, especially such explicit passages as 1 Samuel 8, are indeed history rather than prediction. On the other hand, there are excellent reasons for thinking that anti-monarchic convictions were a logical result of the amphictyonic creed and amphictyonic institutions, which, as we have seen, move directly against the society, politics and theology of the Canaanite city-states. It was precisely the belief that Yahweh was experienced in the institutions of the tribal confederation which led Israelites to think that he could not be experienced in monarchic institutions.

In opposition to the anti-monarchic strain is the "pro-monarchic strain," which appears clearly in 1 Samuel 9:1–10:16. This has often been called the "early source." I have suggested reasons why the anti-monarchic strain is at least equally early; and I have elsewhere argued that a number of features in the pro-monarchic source suggest a later date for its composition.[7] But since the pro-monarchic strain in spirit and content must be as early as the reign of David, we are not dealing with a critical problem which involves a long period of time. And it is the pro-monarchic strain which dominates most of the Old Testament view of the monarchy; it is our purpose here to examine the theological basis of this strain.

It must be noticed that in spite of 1 Samuel 8:5, Saul does not appear as "a king like the nations." Of the two functions of the ancient king, war and law, nothing is said of any activity of Saul in law. It is possible that in the community of covenant law (see Chapter II, Section 2) it was not thought that the king would have a function in law. The law was maintained by the tribal elders and the tribal assemblies. Saul is described as a military chieftain. It seems also that he formed a corps of professional soldiers, free-booters; David was such a freebooter, as we shall see. Such a corps seems to be implied in the remark of 1 Samuel 14:52 that Saul attached to himself any strong or valiant man whom he saw. Pro-fessional soldiers also are implied in the rewards which Saul sees David promising in 1 Samuel 22:7—promotion and the donation of land. Saul himself had no other rewards to promise his warriors. In fact, when the Israelites first chose a king, it seems that they appointed a professional warlord. Such warlords flit through the Amarna letters in the fourteenth century B.C.; they were called Habiru.[8] Warlords with their professional personal armies—per-haps gangs is a better word—appear in the book of Judges: Gideon, Abimelech, and Jephthah can be clearly identified as such warlords. It is not without interest that the stories of Judges describe the Israelites as extending to Gideon and Jephthah the same request for a temporary emergency which they extended to Saul as a perma-nent commitment; but Gideon, it seems, accepted a permanent commission to furnish a garrison for the city of Shechem.

That the installation of a warlord as head of the people of Yahweh demanded some theological justification hardly needs ex-planation; and it is the very obviousness of the problem which makes it easier to believe that the problem was recognized at the very beginning of the monarchy. The solutions which the text offers

[7] "The Four Samuels," *Biblical Research* 7(1962), 3–18.
[8] M. Greenberg, *The Hab/piru*, 32–50.

us were the divine election of the monarch and his charismatic endowment. Divine election or approval of the monarch was such a commonplace in ancient Near Eastern theopolitics that it is hardly necessary to cite parallels from inscriptions. Whatever may have been the sincerity of these beliefs, neither the king nor his subjects felt at ease without explicit declarations that the king was the god's man. In the pro-monarchic narratives the choice of God is made known by revelation to Samuel (1 Sam 9, 16). In the anti-monarchic narrative the candidate is chosen by lot (1 Sam 10:17–27). This is not an affirmation that the lot is oracular: the author means that it is not important who is chosen king. He did not believe that the king was divinely elected. The assertion of the divine election was a part of the ritual of coronation, as we shall see below.

The charismatic endowment of the king, however, has no clear parallel in other ancient Near Eastern sources. The term "charismatic leader," coined by Max Weber, has become a commonplace in Old Testament theology.[9] In the broad sense it includes Moses and Joshua and the prophets. More accurately it includes men who receive the spirit of Yahweh, for this is what the Israelites believed the charism was. The typical charismatic figures first appear in the book of Judges; they are all heroes, most of them military leaders, who deliver Israel from its foes. The spirit is said to come upon Othniel (Judg 3:10), Gideon (Judg 6:34), Jephthah (Judg 11:29), and with strange frequency upon the most unlikely of the judges, Samson (Judg 13:25, 14:6,19, 15:14). Possibly the unsavory character of Samson was felt to demand more of the spirit than the other heroes received. When the spirit came upon Saul in 1 Samuel 11:6, it is altogether in character with the spirit of the book of Judges; Saul is moved to summon the Israelites to defend their brothers against enemies. The spirit which fell upon Saul in 1 Samuel 10:6,10 and 19:23 (and upon his messengers in 19:20) is quite another matter; this is the spirit which inspires ecstatic worship (Chapter II, Section 3), and it has nothing to do with charismatic leadership. The spirit which fell upon these heroes is unpredictable and comes from no visible source; it is

[9] Gerhard von Rad, *Old Testament Theology*, I, 93–102.

like the wind, which is signified in Hebrew by the same word which we render "spirit." When Yahweh blows his breath upon a man, the hero is inspired to do the unlikely and the unexpected, to rise to sudden heights of personal achievement out of harmony with his own resources or with normal human resources. In the book of Judges it indeed comes and goes with the wind. In the king it becomes a permanent possession. The ritual by which the spirit was conferred was anointing, and this happens both to Saul (1 Sam 9–10) and to David (1 Sam 16). As it happens, neither of these chapters is rigorously historical. That David was anointed king of Judah in Hebron (2 Sam 2:4) and later king of Israel in the same city (2 Sam 5:3) is much more rigorously historical. One cannot doubt that David made much of the charismatic ritual of anointing; but as a theological and ritual undergirding of kingship, one cannot deny that it was used also for Saul. Again, the anti-monarchic narrative (1 Sam 10:17–27) omits the anointing. As the king was not chosen by Yahweh, so he does not receive the spirit of Yahweh.

To these two primitive elements found in the books of Samuel we must add a third, the covenant of Yahweh with David and his house.[10] This is found in 2 Samuel 7:5–16, to which Psalm 89:19–37 is closely parallel, very probably a poetic form of the text which is summarized in prose in 2 Samuel 7. I have argued elsewhere that this oracle goes back to the time of David, an opinion which is supported by several recent commentators.[11] The same theme is stated in Psalm 132:11–18 and 2 Samuel 23:5–7; these last two passages are important, for in them the word "covenant" appears. In all of these passages, an eternal dynasty is promised to David, and its eternity is not even conditioned by the fidelity of his descendants to the will of Yahweh. Obviously, the prophet went beyond the possibilities of history; the dynasty of David ended in 587 B.C. and has not been restored. There is no possibility of "fulfillment" of this covenant except in Christian messianism, and I do not believe that this is a legitimate interpretation of the oracle. When David united the kingdoms of Judah and Israel under a

[10] A. R. Johnson, *Sacral Kingship in Ancient Israel* (Cardiff, 1955), 1–30 and 136–41.
[11] ThSt 8(1947) 187–218.

single ruler, he transferred to the throne the covenant relationship of Yahweh with Israel (into which he incorporated Judah). The eternity of the covenant of David is the eternity of the covenant of Yahweh with Israel; but of this covenant David has become the medium. The prophets and poets who formulated this covenant did not have in their horizon any view of the voiding of the covenant either with David or with Israel; the problem raised by the fall of Israel and Judah was solved by eschatology (see Chapter VII, below).

The covenant with David and his house corresponds to the cultic position of the king in other ancient Near Eastern states—with proper reservations, of course; the Jerusalem king was not a god, as the king was in Egypt. But the Jerusalem king became the representative of Israel before Yahweh, the leader of his people in cult and the recipient of the divine oracles by which the will of Yahweh was communicated to Israel.[12] We shall see below how several of the royal psalms present the king as the medium through which Yahweh saves Israel, whether in war or in its cultivation of the soil. We know of no such total mediator in the tribal confederation; and the suggestion recommends itself that the covenant role of David was formed in imitation of the role of the Canaanite king, using Israelite patterns into which the king was intruded.

The covenant with David leaves no room for a covenant with the kingdom of Israel after the schism of the kingdoms, and we do not have enough literature from the kingdom of Israel to know how this problem was solved. Nor do we know how the kingdom of Israel after Rehoboam was theologically grounded. Presumably, the traditions of covenant law flourished better in Israel than they did in Judah; we shall see shortly how the monarchy affected these traditions. Albrecht Alt asked whether the kingship in Israel was charismatic in the sense of the older traditions as opposed to the kingship of Jerusalem, which was dynastic throughout its entire course.[13] In any case, he believed that the kingship of Israel became dynastic with Omri and remained dynastic until the collapse of the northern kingdom. If his interpretation is correct, the charis-

[12] See the full treatment of the role of the king in H. Frankfort, *Kingship and the Gods* (Chicago, 1948).
[13] *Kleine Schriften* II 121–34 (Munich, 1964), 3rd ed.

matic principle appears as a principle of instability; the history of the kingdom of Israel is a nearly uninterrupted history of conspiracy and assassination, in which even Elijah and Elisha appear to have taken part. The installation of Jehu (2 Kings 9) has all the appearance of a purely charismatic accession: the divine election announced by a prophetic oracle, the secret anointing like the anointings of Saul and David. One sees the theological undergirding of the rejection of the dynasty of Omri and the choice of a new ruler faithful to Yahweh. But neither the dynastic principle nor the charismatic principle produced kings who were sincerely religious and minimally competent; and it appears that neither principle was intended to produce these results.

The sacramental character of the king was manifested in the ritual of accession.[14] The ritual of accession is described only for Solomon (1 Kings 1:32–40) and for Joash (2 Kings 12:9–12). De Vaux enumerates as components of the ritual the sanctuary, the investiture with the insignia, the anointing, the acclamation, the enthronement and the homage. The insignia included the crown (and probably the scepter) and the 'ēdût (testimony). De Vaux has compared the testimony with the "protocol" of the Egyptian Pharaoh, a document containing his regal names and titles and his legitimation as a god, Horus the son of Re: it was written by the hand of the god. De Vaux suggests that the same document may be meant by the "covenant" of Psalm 89:40 and the "decree" of Psalm 2:6–7. We have mentioned that the two qualities of the king, divine election and the charismatic spirit, were ritually conferred. Psalm 2:6–7 suggests that the declaration of divine election was a declaration of divine adoption. Israel is sometimes called the son of Yahweh (e.g., Hos 11:1), and while this is later than the origins of the monarchy, it is possible that adoption, like covenant, was transferred to the Davidic king from Israel. In any case, the adoption of the Jerusalem king (see also Ps 89:26–27) is clear.

The adoption of an individual man is much more discordant with rigorous Israelite monotheism than the adoption of a people; and since the adoption of the king leaves no repercussions which

[14] S. Mowinckel, *He That Cometh*, 62–69; R. de Vaux, op. cit., 102–7.

we can find, it appears that we must put the adoption of the king into the pattern which H. Wheeler Robinson defined as corporate personality.[15] The king was not merely a representative or a mediator; he actually incorporated into his person the totality of Israel, whom Yahweh now reached through the king. The adoption of the king does not raise him above the level of humanity (2 Sam 7:14). He is still subject to judgment. He takes on no superhuman attributes nor even heroic attributes. In 2 Samuel 7 and Psalm 89 the emphasis does not fall on godlike qualities but on the permanence of the covenant love of Yahweh; it is as permanent as the love a man has for his son. The qualities desired in a ruler do not come from adoption but from the charismatic spirit.

The ritual by which the spirit was conferred was anointing. Near Eastern parallels to this are uncertain.[16] Other persons or objects anointed in Israel—such as priests, the tent of meeting and its furniture, the ark of the covenant—were consecrated by the rite. The sacredness of the person of the king is clearly seen in David's reverence for Saul (1 Sam 24:7,11, 26:9,11,23; 2 Sam 1:14). The king is the Anointed of Yahweh, the Messiah. Evidently this sacredness did not protect the king from assassination; we should hardly expect it to do this. The king was better protected by the royal palace guard. The spirit, however, appears only in the stories of Saul and David; we have noticed that it is part of the legend of legitimation that the spirit passed from Saul to David when David, still a boy and some years removed from the kingship, was secretly anointed. In the theology of this scribe, the spirit, once given to the king, could not float around with no person on whom to rest. Solomon does not receive the spirit, but wisdom, which is another charism (1 Kings 3; see Chapter V, Section 1). After Solomon there was no successor of David, with the possible exceptions of Hezekiah and Josiah, whom even the scribes of the Jerusalem palace could have considered charismatic in any but the purely technical sense. The belief that the king was charismatically endowed could not have been a vital factor in the kingdoms—that is, the people no longer experienced Yahweh in the king, as the institutions of David and Solomon had been devised to accomplish.

[15] BeihZATWiss 66 (1936) 49–62.
[16] De Vaux, op. cit., 104.

The question has often been raised whether the king took an accession name or throne name when he was installed. There is no evidence that this happened in Israel; but there is no indication that any of the Jerusalem ideology was retained in Israel. The conclusion of De Vaux[17] is that it is probable but not certain that the kings of Judah took a throne name. The practice was known in Egypt, not certain in Assyria, and unattested elsewhere. It survives in the Roman See. The assumption of a new name most obviously signifies the emergence of a new person; the role was thought to effect a true inner personal change. We may associate the throne name with the adoption of the king by Yahweh and the conferring of the spirit. When the spirit comes upon Saul, he is said to be turned into another man (1 Sam 10:6). The conferring of a new name was a rather realistic expression of this belief.

A. R. Johnson has discussed the royal ideology in a number of psalms.[18] Many previous commentators had not identified all these psalms as royal, and it is the particular merit of Johnson's treatment that he presents an intelligible pattern into which these psalms fall. This is the pattern of the messianic ideal; "messianic" here has no reference to the messianism of the New Testament and of Christian interpreters, but to the presentation of the king as King Messiah—literally, as one anointed who has received the charismatic spirit, as a King Savior through whom Yahweh delivers, as a wise and righteous judge who saves the poor and needy. Some of these psalms, it seems, must be early, perhaps as early as the beginnings of the monarchy. As such they would be witnesses of the serious effort of David and his theologians to create a pattern of kingship acceptable in Yahwism. Later psalms, as we have noticed, could have been applied to almost all kings of the Jerusalem dynasty only in a quite conventional sense. Yet some one thought that this ideal should not only be preserved but be given new literary expressions. If Yahweh's covenant with David was to be meaningful, an ideal king ought to be expected. This ideal figure we shall treat in Chapter VII below.

A few remarks on the situation in life of these psalms may help to their understanding. Psalm 72 is a ritual prayer for the king.

---

[17] *Ancient Israel*, 107–8.
[18] *Sacral Kingship in Ancient Israel.*

Psalm 132 celebrates the transfer of the ark to Jerusalem by David and may have been used in the commemoration of that event; see the discussion of the royal and enthronement festivals in Chapter I, Section 1, above. Psalm 89 may be a psalm with an appendix; if it is, the original psalm celebrates the covenant of Yahweh with the house of David and belongs to the royal or dynastic festival. Psalm 101 is a ritual profession of royal integrity; it could be a part of the enthronement anniversary festival. Psalm 18 is a thanksgiving for victory and a profession of integrity; it would also suit the anniversary. Psalm 118 is similarly a psalm of thanksgiving. Psalms 2 and 110 are clearly psalms of accession; Artur Weiser places them in the enthronement festival.[19] Psalm 21 is a thanksgiving for victory and possibly was written for no festival but rather for the return from war. The last words of David (2 Sam 23:1–7) could have been included in the psalms but were not. They belong to a literary form which appears in the Bible and in Jewish apocryphal literature (*Testaments of the Twelve Patriarchs*). Another set of David's last words appear in 1 Kings 2:1–9; it is certainly much less edifying than 2 Samuel 23:1–7. Such poems are also attributed to Jacob (Gen 49), Moses (Deut 33), and Balaam (Num 24:15–19), and a prose exhortation is attributed to Joshua (Josh 23). These last words of the founder of the dynasty would be well in place in the ritual of accession.

We have here a collection of ten poems; and it seems worthy of remark that they contain a number of recurrent themes. The king is a righteous ruler and judge (Ps 72, 18, 118; 2 Sam 23), the defender of the poor and helpless (Ps 72, 101), a ruler of moral integrity (Ps 101, 18), the avenger of crime (Ps 101). Yahweh grants Israel victory over its enemies through him (Ps 72, 132, 89, 18, 118, 2, 110, 21; Gen 49:8–10; Num 24:17–19; 2 Sam 23); this theme recurs in almost every poem and illustrates war as one of the two functions of the king. His reign brings prosperity, of which he is at least implicitly the mediator (Ps 72, 132; Gen 49:11–12; 2 Sam 23). He is endowed with the spirit (2 Sam 23). His special relations with Yahweh are described as the oath of an eternal dynasty (Ps 132, 110), a covenant (2 Sam 23; Ps

19 *The Psalms* (Philadelphia, 1962).

89, 110), election (Ps 89), and blessing (Ps 21). As Yahweh chose David, so also he chose Zion, the site of the palace and the temple, as the place of his dwelling (Ps 132; see Chapter I, Section 3, above).

From these themes there emerges a consistent theology of the monarchy. It corresponds to nothing in historical reality, not even in David and Solomon, the only two kings who ruled over the dual monarchy of Israel and Judah. We have observed that it left no visible trace in the kingdom of Israel after the schism. We see it as an effort to incorporate into Yahwism that political structure which in its origins Yahwism rejected. As a theory it was successful; as a program it meant nothing. The kings at whose festivals these psalms were sung were effectively Canaanite kings. The city of Jerusalem and the city of Samaria, as Albrecht Alt has shown, were the personal properties of the kings; they were in no tribal territory nor indeed in "government" territory; it is difficult to translate these ancient structures into modern terms.[20] Alt indeed argued that Samaria was the Canaanite capital of Omri as Jezreel was his Israelite capital. Such theses probably can never be demonstrated in the rigorous sense of the term. They do, however, suggest to the student that he should look at the pomp, power, and circumstance of the Israelite kings and notice the signs that the kings adopted the only external structure known to them, the structure of the Canaanite city-states. If one looks, one notices that David selected a non-Israelite city for his dwelling and that Omri selected a virgin site. One sees in Jerusalem a royal guard of professional soldiers and a priesthood headed by Zadok, a man whose name is associated with an ancient divine name in Jerusalem (Melchizedek, Adonizedek). The ultimate response to the monarchic theology of Jerusalem is found in the prophets Micah, Isaiah, Jeremiah, and Ezekiel, and to the monarchy of Samaria in the prophets Amos and Hosea.

Albrecht Alt devoted a lengthy article to the part of the kings in the social development of the kingdoms of Israel and Judah[21] though "development" is hardly the word for what Alt discusses. He opens his article by declaring, on the basis of the words of

[20] Alt, *Kleine Schriften* III (Munich, 1959), 243–302.
[21] Ibid. 348–72.

Amos, Micah, Isaiah, Zephaniah, and Jeremiah, that the kingdoms of Israel and Judah experienced profound social disturbances within the few centuries of their existence. We have already noticed the institutions of the tribal confederation and their theological bases (Chapters II, Section 2, III, Section 4, and VI, Section 1), and we are now engaged in a study of the theological basis of the social-political system which overthrew the tribal institutions. Two results of the royal system must be noticed: the rise of a ruling class and the growth of a landowning class. No doubt we are dealing with the same class under different aspects.

The ruling class was the class of royal officers and administrators generally included under the designation of *sarim*.[22] In the tribal confederation the cities and villages were administered by the elders, the adult male heads of families. The *sarim* were royal officers, not necessarily members of the communities which they administered. There are indications that the cities and villages were organized according to the military structure and that the *sarim* dealt with the men of the communities according to the military units of thousands, hundreds, and fifties.[23] The worst example of such centralization and the corruption which it made possible is the seizure of the vineyard of Naboth by Ahab and Jezebel (1 Kings 21). The scribe did not intend to relate this episode as typical, but rather as an example of what could happen under centralized royal authority. In fact we do not know that the elders of the towns were above corruption, but at least they were neighbors and kinsmen of such as Naboth.

The corruption of justice under the royal administration is a complaint of many of the prophets (Amos 5:12,15; Mic 2:8-9, 3:1-3 and 9-11; Is 1:23, 3:13-15, 10:1-2; Zeph 3:3; Jer 5:26-29). The same prophets attest to the rise of a class of landlords and to the breakdown of the ancient Israelite system and the acquisition by the ruling class of vast landed estates.[24] The mass of the Israelites were reduced to the condition of peasants who were perpetually in debt (Amos 2:6-7, 4:1, 5:11-12; Mic 2:2; Is 5:8-10). The restoration of the chariot aristocracy of Canaanite feudal-

[22] De Vaux, op. cit., 69-70.
[23] Alt, op. cit., 352-56.
[24] Ibid. 369-72.

ism is also attested (Is 2:7). One sees here the conditions mentioned in Samuel's "way of the king" (1 Sam 8:10–18) and Saul's quarrel with his own professional soldiers (1 Sam 22:7). The king could create and maintain a loyal staff of civil and military leaders only if he rewarded them with land. This meant the destruction of local and tribal power and the delivery of all administrative and judicial power to the *sarim*. The king did not need to enrich them directly; he merely needed to allow them to serve in positions where they could enrich themselves. The narrator of the story of Naboth relates, somewhat naïvely, the childish grief of the king when his will is frustrated. It is unlikely that the king and the *sarim* very often had the time or the need to shed tears when ancient tribal institutions stood in the way of the enrichment of the monarchical establishment.

We dwell on these considerations, which are sociological rather than theological, because these passages show what was created by the royal messianic theology of Jerusalem which we meet in the Psalms. They show us what the King Savior upon whom the spirit rested really was. We have theology bound to the service of politics and indeed to a remarkably low level of politics. Whatever may have been the future of the idea of the King Messiah— and we shall discuss this in Chapter VII below—for the kingdoms of Israel and Judah, it accomplished nothing from every point of view.

3. *The Community of Law*

The wars and conquests of the Assyrian and Babylonian empires ended the political life of all the small kingdoms and city-states of the ancient Near East. What happened to the kingdoms of Israel and Judah was no different from what happened to the kingdoms of Ammon, Moab, and Edom, to the Aramaean kingdoms such as the kingdom of Damascus, and to the Phoenician city-states. These had no prophets to render a theological interpretation of their political history, but to others than prophets, the fate of Israel and Judah was in no way different from the fate of its neighbors. And if there arose a continuation of Israel and Judah, were there

258   A THEOLOGY OF THE OLD TESTAMENT

not also successor communities of the neighbors of Israel? Indeed
there were, but as far as we know, none of them took the particular
form which Palestinian Judaism took; for from the restoration onward, it is correct to speak of Judaism, the Jewish people, and
the Jewish religion. In the terms in which we have defined our
study, this restored community was a revival of that communal
experience of God which is recorded in the earlier books of the
Old Testament. We have already seen (Chapter II, Section 3,
above) that it was the restored community which produced the
Bible, in the sense that it collected and preserved writings which
it believed were in some sense the word of God. This community
also contributed biblical literature of its own.

The Babylonian conquest of Judah, which terminated in the sack
of Jerusalem in 587 B.C., had wrought severe damage on the towns
and countryside of Judah. The land was depopulated to a degree which cannot be determined, and archaeology attests that a
number of urban sites were abandoned. It would be inaccurate
to think of the country as reduced to an uninhabited desert (like
that poetically described in Jer 4:23–26); but the capacity of ancient military tactics to wreak permanent damage on dwellings,
agriculture, crafts, and commerce should not be regarded as trivial.
There is no reason to doubt the biblical tradition that Jerusalem
was an uninhabited ruin from 587 B.C. to its resettlement in 537.

The resettlement of Jerusalem was accomplished by a band of
Jews from Babylon with the encouragement and the assistance of
the Persian government in 538–537 B.C. in the reign of Cyrus
the Great.[25] As related in Ezra 1:1–3:7, the narrative implies
that the party of exiles moved into a vacuum, much as the narrative
of the book of Joshua implies that the Israelites occupied an entirely empty country; the similarity in conception may not be purely
accidental. Without the panoply of conquest, which historical reality did not permit for the restoration, the establishment of the Jerusalem community was a return by Yahweh of the donation which
he had once made to the ancestors. It was a very small return,
for the nation had been subjected to a searing judgment and punishment for its sins. But this small beginning was certainly seen by

[25] John Bright, *A History of Israel,* 360–73; M. Noth, *The History of
Israel,* 300–16.

some as rich in promise. We do not gather from the narrative of
Ezra that the men of the new Jerusalem saw themselves re-enacting
the exodus, as a number of texts of Second Isaiah suggest (see
Chapter VII, Section 1, below). What Ezra tells us is that they
had a mandate from Cyrus to settle in Jerusalem and rebuild the
temple where prayers could be offered for Cyrus.

This royal edict probably would not have been issued without
the request of Jews. At the same time, it is now known that tolerance and encouragement of local diversity of religion and culture
was a part of Persian imperial policy.[26] The effect of the act of
Cyrus was to produce a cultic community (see Chapter I, Section
7, above). What ultimately emerged was much more than a cultic
community, and what emerged was the product of theological
thinking as much as of the processes of history. Unfortunately,
the chronicler to whom we owe the books of Ezra and Nehemiah
was not contemporary with the events; possibly he wrote as late
as 250 B.C. And while he did preserve contemporary documents,
the consensus of modern scholars that he confused the chronological order of Ezra and Nehemiah casts sufficient doubt on his com-
prehension of the events which he recorded. In addition, he was
clearly tendentious; and for a theological examination of the postexilic situation, his tendencies are of interest.

We have already noticed that he implies that the landscape was
entirely deserted. Historical reality compels him to abandon this
fiction. Both Nehemiah (13:23ff.) and Ezra (9–10) complain of
mixed marriages with women who were not of the "holy seed"
(Ezra 9:2). The "foreign women" are identified in Ezra 9:1 as
"the Canaanites, the Hittites, the Perizzites, the Jebusites, the Ammonites, the Moabites, the Egyptians, and the Amorites." These
appear to be clearly unhistorical designations derived from the
Pentateuch and the book of Joshua. In Nehemiah 13:23 they are
identified as women of Ashdod, Ammon, and Moab; this is not
as obviously unhistorical as the verse of Ezra. One observes that
Nehemiah's adversary, the governor of Samaria, has the surely
Akkadian name of Sanballat (Sin-uballit); the Elephantine documents tell us that his sons had the equally surely Jewish names

[26] Noth, ibid., 304–8; Bright, op. cit., 361–63; A. Moortgat, *Ägypten und
Vorderasien in Altertum* (Munich, 1950), 464–69.

Delaiah and Shelemaiah.[27] Another adversary of Nehemiah, Tobiah, usually called contemptuously "the Ammonite," had as good
a Jewish name as Nehemiah; and the author of Nehemiah admits
that he was a kinsman of many of the "holy seed" (Neh 6:18).
Then we consider the genealogical list of the returned exiles, given
twice (Ezra 2:1–70 and Neh 7:6–73), and a pattern begins to
emerge. The group of exiles asserted that they and only they were
the "holy seed," the remnant of the true Israel, the living heirs
of the chosen people. Sanballat and Tobiah and others unnamed
were descendants of Israelites and Judahites who had not been
transported by Nebuchadnezzar. They were perpetually disquali-
fied from membership in the "holy seed." In this dispute we see
the antecedents of the Samaritan schism; but we see even more
clearly the definition of the "holy seed," the people of Yahweh,
the chosen people, as a purely ethnic group. It is impossible to
tell how well this ideal was implemented in postexilic Jerusalem;
but that it was proposed and cherished seems to be reasonably
clear.

It is also reasonably clear that the cultic community which aimed
at ideal ethnic purity by excluding all but Babylonian exiles and
their descendants did not produce a sturdy social group. The history of the community after the rebuilding of the temple in
515 B.C. is quite obscure, but everything points to a prolonged
period of difficulty and hardship. The need to which Nehemiah
responded in 445 B.C. is not clearly known. He responded by using
his personal influence with Artaxerxes I to get himself appointed
governor of what was very probably the newly established province
of Judah. His most celebrated achievement, the building of the
walls of Jerusalem, did not really solve the problems of the community. Other achievements mentioned in his memoirs were ultimately assertions of the ethnic exclusiveness mentioned above.

The next and the decisive step was taken under the leadership
of Ezra. The date of this step unfortunately cannot be decided
exactly.[28] The chronicler set him in the seventh year of Artaxerxes
I (458 B.C.). There are many difficulties in this date, so many
that modern scholars believe that it must be the seventh year of

[27] ANET, 492.
[28] Bright, op. cit., 386–403.

Artaxerxes II (398 B.C.) or—by conjectural emendation of the text—the thirty-seventh year of Artaxerxes I (428 B.C.). For our purposes, the exact date is not important. For the theological examination of the postexilic community it is important that Ezra came after Nehemiah and was not contemporary, and we adopt the later date.

Ezra was "a scribe skilled in the law of Moses" (Ezra 7:6), devoted to the study and teaching of the law of Yahweh (Ezra 7:10). He went to Jerusalem under a royal commission (Ezra 7:12–26, a document which is accepted as authentic by both Bright and Noth). In this document Ezra is called "the scribe of the law of the God of heaven" (Ezra 7:12). Both Noth and Bright see here an official Persian title, paraphrased by Noth as "state commissioner for the law of the God of heaven" and by Bright as "minister of state for Jewish affairs." It is noteworthy that the mission of Ezra, like the rebuilding of the temple, was accomplished by the mandate of the Persian imperial government. We may suppose that both missions were initiated by Jewish petitions to the imperial court, but the documents do not mention such initiative. Ezra, like Sheshbazzar, was granted subsidies of hard metal from the imperial treasury, to be used at his discretion after he has purchased sacrificial victims, the right to draw upon the treasuries of the province of "Beyond the River," and immunity from local levies for the temple and its personnel. One can hardly fault the generosity of the Persian government. Historians note a similar concern of the Persian government for Jewish religious affairs in the documents of Elephantine in Egypt. In 419 B.C. Darius II authorized the celebration of the Passover for the Jewish garrison of Elephantine.[29] When the Jewish temple in Elephantine was destroyed in a riot (407 B.C.), a petition was presented to the imperial government to authorize its rebuilding.[30] The outcome of this petition is not known; its interest for the present discussion is that the petition presupposed the active concern of the Persian government for local religious problems.

The closing sentences of the document (Ezra 7:25–26) impose the "laws of your God" upon all the people of the province of

[29] ANET 491.
[30] Ibid. 491–92.

"Beyond the River"; this, of course, means the Jews of the province. Ezra was empowered to appoint magistrates to administer justice under this law and to teach the law to those who did not know it. The law was sanctioned by full legal penalties including the capital sentence. The Chronicler, according to the consensus of modern historians, has misplaced the execution of Ezra's commission in Nehemiah 8 and has associated Nehemiah with the promulgation. Ezra read the entire law to the assembly. The first presentation went through a good part of two days; the reading was then interrupted to celebrate the feast of Sukkoth, and the reading of the law was continued through the week of the festival. As the law was read, the Levites explained it, which very likely included a paraphrase of the text into Aramaic. It is impossible to arrive at an educated guess on the amount of text which was contained in Ezra's document.

Two questions arise from this narrative: what was the law which Ezra read and how was the text produced? The story, as we have noticed, does not permit a meaningful conjecture on the volume of the material. It must have been all or some of the five books of Moses; that it was all the books is most improbable and this view is supported by nobody. They do seem to comprise too much text to be read aloud in the situation described, although no one has made the experiment of reading the entire Torah aloud in Hebrew. If it was some of the Torah, we run into the critical question of whether the final redaction of the Torah had been made by 400 B.C. If it had been, it was all done in Babylon. If Ezra read only part of the Torah, what parts did he select and on what basis? The Torah is now all "law," and Ezra may not have thought of it all as "Torah," although this is no doubt what the Chronicler thought. If one assumes that Ezra read only "law," we must ask further how much of the laws of the Pentateuch was contained in his collection. If we accept as a genuine historical record the notice that they discovered in the law the prescriptions for the celebration of the feast of Sukkoth (Neh 9:14–17), they found the feast under this name and with prescriptions for its celebration in the Holiness Code (Lev 23:34–36, 39–43, the latter section being probably a later addition) and Deuteronomy (Deut 16:13–

15). In the covenant code (Ex 23:16) and the Yahwist decalogue (Ex 34:22), the autumn feast is called the Feast of Ingathering, and no prescriptions are given for its celebration. The only answer we can find for the first question is that there is no sure way to determine what was in Ezra's book of the law.

The question how the law was produced is a part of the question of the literary origins of the Pentateuch. This is not a problem of biblical theology, and in no way are we obliged to answer it here. We have observed that the narrative of Ezra, if it is taken seriously, implies that whatever Ezra had was produced in Babylon. What can be said about the contents of the law does not exclude the possibility that his law was further elaborated in Palestine. For our present purpose, it is more important that with Ezra there first appears the idea of the law as a compendium of all divine revelation and as a comprehensive guide of a life lived in accordance with the revealed will of Yahweh. We can further ask now whether the compilation of the law was deliberately made with this purpose in mind. We have seen that the Jerusalem community was at first a cultic community; this community was further defined according to rigorous ethnic purity. We have observed that there are signs that these standards did not establish a sturdy viable community. The law of Ezra added to the cultic practices and the ethnic requirements a way of life defined according to the law of Yahweh. Those who might plead that they met the ethnic standards had in addition to profess belief in the law of Moses. We can see in Third Isaiah as well as in the books of Ezra and Nehemiah signs of deep and embittered divisions in the postexilic community.[31] We also see signs that the immigrant group from Babylon refused to recognize descendants of those Judahites who had not been exiles as genuine Jews. The historian cannot say that the law was compiled and sent to Jerusalem with the sanction of the Persian government in order to set a standard by which all those who claimed to be Jews could be determined; the historian can only say that the law would suit this purpose admirably. But the Samaritan schism, whenever and for what reasons it occurred, was not a division over the law; the Samaritan community

[31] McKenzie, *Second Isaiah*, lxx–lxxi, 198–201, 203–4, 207–10.

accepted the law. It seems far more probable to have been a division over the cult of the Jerusalem temple.

The cultic character of the Jerusalem community is seen in the fact that the high priest was the officer with whom the Persian government dealt.[32] We have next to no information on the administration of the Jewish community, which was purely local. The work of Ezra created the class of the scribes, the doctors of the law, so well known to readers of the Gospels. They had no official rank; their unofficial influence was great, for they were the interpreters of the revealed will of Yahweh. The ideal of the scribe as a scholar and a man of influence, in government as well as in the daily life of his fellow Jews, is set forth in Sirach 39:1–11. The scribes were far more important in determining the character of postexilic Judaism than the priests were.

The account of the work of Ezra is a much more genuinely historical account of the promulgation of the law than the account contained in the book of Exodus. And the Chronicler makes no effort to clothe his narrative in the element of wonder. The wonder lay in the remote past. Yahweh had once given his people his law in clouds and thunder and lightning; it was the same law which was now read by a scribe in the temple courts. Between Moses on Sinai and Ezra in Jerusalem there lay centuries of sin and judgment. The postexilic community received the law with a deep sense of guilt which their ancestors had not felt. The law was a sign that the covenant with Israel endured, as the covenant with David had not. The law was given to a community which would not take its place among the nations; it was a small province of a great empire, with no power of self-determination. It celebrated annually its ritual recitals of repentance and prayer for forgiveness. Fidelity to the law would protect it from the guilt which the fathers had incurred. It gave a sense of security which nothing else had ever given or could ever give. From such sentiments arose the long and tedious Psalm 119, which can be sympathetically read only by one who has the feeling about the law as salvation which the postexilic community had. Other readers must simply endure Psalm 119. More briefly and with more literary merit the law is

[32] Bright, op. cit., 378; Noth, op. cit., 315–16.

celebrated in Psalm 19:7–14 as life, wisdom, joy, and light. Such praises of the law are more common and more extravagant in rabbinical literature;[33] but these sources do not belong to Old Testament theology. Later scribes identified wisdom with the law, personified as a pre-existent being who chose to dwell upon earth in Israel (Sirach 24).

The achievement of Ezra was to establish for the first time in recorded history a religious community. This statement is a commonplace in works on biblical religion and theology; it seems to need some qualification in view of the indications that ethnic purity was an important factor in establishing the Jerusalem community. Yet it was by no means a purely tribal group; the sophistication of fifth-century Palestine had moved far beyond tribal culture. It was not a political society. Its internal cohesion was based on a common religious belief and a common way of life, religiously motivated, which was articulated in a document. This document was produced and interpreted by learned specialists. They were spokesmen for God of a new type, quite distinct from the prophets and from any other spokesmen for the deity in the ancient world. They were the successors of Moses, whose mythological portrait was largely influenced by the ideals of the scribes who produced the portrait.

Thus the experience of God in the postexilic community was mediated through an authoritative document in which his revealed will was finalized and crystallized. It was an experience of security; no Jew need any longer doubt what the will of God was. The document or its interpreters had a response for every situation. It was no longer a theme of promise and fulfillment but rather of fulfillment pure and simple. In the Torah, Yahweh had given Israel all he had to give. This implies a certain messianism of the Torah which we shall discuss in Chapter VII, Section 7, below. The possibility of infidelity to the Torah, like the infidelity of the Israelites and Judahites of the monarchy, was not entertained. Prophecy was not needed, for the Torah and the scribes left nothing for a prophet to say. Political inactivity was accepted not only as a ne-

[33] Strack-Billerbeck, *Kommentar zum NT aus Talmud und Midrasch* II (Munich, 1965), 353–58, and see further Register s. v. *tora.*

cessity imposed by world history but also as a blessing which spared the postexilic community the risk involved in political activity. Ultimately one can compare the postexilic community to the phenomenon of withdrawal, not unlike the withdrawal of the Christian monastic movement or to the withdrawal of the Qumran group from Judaism. The Qumran group seem to have felt that the Judaism of their period had been unfaithful to the ideal of withdrawal from the world. Life under the law was not possible except in a separate and self-sustaining community which jealously preserved its distinct identity.

VII

The Future of Israel

1. *General Remarks*

In this section we shall discuss a number of topics which are usually included under the rubric of "messianism." I shall not use this term, nor do I agree with the presuppositions which the use of this term imply. Since this is somewhat divergent from the more common approach, and certainly from the traditional approach, some words of explanation are in order.

The term "Messiah" represents the Hebrew word *māšîaḥ,* which means "anointed." Without qualification, the word generally means the Judahite or Israelite king; but priests also were anointed. The Hebrew word was rendered in Greek by *christos,* from which we have the English "Christ" (and corresponding words in other modern languages) as a title of Jesus of Nazareth. This title is given him in the New Testament and is itself a confession that he was the expected King Savior (see Chapter VI, Section 2) who would restore Israel to its political independence and lead it ultimately to a position of world dominance. It lies outside the scope of this work to show that this is precisely the role which Jesus of Nazareth, as far as we know him at all, made every effort to avoid; certainly the writers of the New Testament made every effort to avoid it, and the Savior who created the new Israel in no way resembled the King Messiah of Israel and Judah. In any sense in which King Messiah is understood (see again Chapter VI, Section 2), there is no messianism in the New Testament which is derived from the Old Testament.

If we consider merely the element of language, the messianism of the Old Testament is the christology of the Old Testament. I realize that I lay myself open to the accusation of playing with words, which is the occupational vice of theologians; but surely no theologian will rashly accuse a colleague of doing this. There is indeed a messianism of the Old Testament, already treated in Chapter VI and to be discussed again here (Section 2); the judgment of it rendered up to this point has been generally unfavorable. But there is no "christology," by which I mean exactly that the theology of the Old Testament in no way predicts or leads one to expect the historical reality of Jesus of Nazareth nor the saving act which the disciples of Jesus proclaimed as accomplished in him. The study of the theology of the Old Testament has never been advanced by the Christianization of the Old Testament— which, again from the point of view of language, could be called the "messianization" of the Old Testament. Messianism as a theme belongs to the theology of the New Testament and not to the theology of the Old Testament; and it is my personal opinion that it should be studied in the theology of the New Testament with extreme caution.

On the other hand, Jesus of Nazareth was a figure who emerged in Judaism; and we should not leave the impression that as a religious figure he was entirely unrelated to the Old Testament. This was first stated by Marcion in the second century, and the church rejected the teaching of Marcion. In modern times Rudolf Bultmann has at least approached neo-Marcionism. At the same time, the Judaism from which Jesus emerged is a larger and more complex historical reality than the Old Testament. In writing a theology of the Old Testament I do not pretend to write either a history or a theology of Judaism. But Judaism cannot be understood without reference to the Old Testament. As a religious figure, Jesus can be grasped only as a man who arose in Judaism and therefore to some degree from the Old Testament. He certainly cannot be conceived as a product of Hellenism or of the Oriental cults of the Hellenistic world. Once this is said, one must recall the gospel figure that Jesus put new wine into new flasks (Mk 2:22; Mt 9:17; Lk 5:37–38); he shattered the categories of the Jewish religion and culture from which he emerged.

For reasons such as this, I have chosen to deal with the topic of "the future of Israel" rather than with "the messianic hope" or some similar title. The future orientation of much of the Old

Testament and Judaism is a manifest and really unparalleled fact. We have already referred to the Israelite sense of history (see Chapter III, Section 1). The Israelites, at least most of those who wrote the books of the Old Testament, thought of the people of Yahweh as moving through history—but towards what? This objective, always dimly perceived, took various forms in different books and at different periods; it is part of our purpose in this section to explore these forms. The New Testament writers, using a term which is attributed to Jesus himself, sum up the term of history in the phrase "the kingdom of God" (more properly, "the reign of God"). This is really not an Old Testament phrase; and the content of the New Testament reign, itself for many years an object of intense discussion and dispute among New Testament interpreters, can scarcely be found as an Old Testament theme.[1]

But there is more to the Old Testament than future orientation. We see in most of the books a conviction of the indestructibility, the eternity of Israel. The eternity of Israel is the created reflection of the eternity of Yahweh, who has joined Israel to himself by covenant and promise. This conviction does not give any definite form to the term of history mentioned in the preceding paragraph; the form is less important than the belief that there cannot be a Yahweh without his people Israel. This union is founded on the free election of Yahweh and not on a mythological structure of the cosmos as in other ancient Near Eastern religions (see Chapter IV, Section 1). Obviously, this belief in the eternity of the people of God has been inherited both by Judaism and by Christianity; and it will be our purpose to keep the Old Testament belief distinct from its successors.

We have had occasion to point out that the belief in the eternity of Israel was not shared by all the writers of the Old Testament. Among these should be included Amos and the Deuteronomic historian and very probably Jeremiah (see Chapter III, Section 5). Even J could conceive the possibility of the destruction of Israel and the raising of a new people of Yahweh (Ex 32:10; Num 14:12). The New Testament belief that the church is the new

[1] R. Bultmann, *Theology of the New Testament* (New York, 1951), I 4–22; A. Richardson, *Introduction to the Theology of the New Testament* (New York, 1958), 84–102.

Israel is the legacy of this theme rather than the theme of the indestructibility of Israel.[2] Yet the Church has retained the theme of indestructibility at the same time as it has profited by the theme of judgment and rejection.

The classification in the treatment which follows attempts to sort out elements in the future hope of the Old Testament according to different emphases, not according to historical periods and literary authorship. But historical events had everything to do with the development of different forms which the hope took, and we shall try to give attention to the influence of events upon belief. In some instances the classifications overlap; this is unfortunate, but it seems impossible to avoid this in any effort at synthesis. In other instances the classification may seem so broad as to become nearly meaningless; this is especially apparent in the first classification, the national hope, and we shall discuss this immediately in the following paragraphs.

2. The National Hope

Under this rubric, I include passages which have no obvious religious implications apart from the fact that the survival of Israel depends on the will of Yahweh to save. In general, then, these passages express a political rather than a religious hope; and I admit that these words contain a distinction to which nothing in the Hebrew text corresponds. The distinction is valid for us who read the Old Testament, however; and the modern Christian in particular, if he is familiar with the history of the Christian church, knows all too well the failures of the historic Christian churches to distinguish between religion and politics. In the passages to be considered here, the survival of belief in Yahweh, indeed, the very reality of the effective power and will of Yahweh, are seen as connected with the existence of the people of Israel in some distinct form. This is not equally obvious in all the passages considered; the texts vary between a rather crass nationalistic view

[2] Abbott and Gallagher, eds., *The Documents of Vatican II* (New York, 1966), "Dogmatic Constitution on the Church" II.9, 24–26; "Declaration on the Relationship of the Church to Non-Christian Religions" 4, 663–65.

of religion—what we have elsewhere called "theopolitics"—to a much more subtle identification of Yahwism with Israel. The reader of the Old Testament may be surprised to see Second Isaiah bracketed with the oracles of Balaam or Third Isaiah under the same rubric; a difficulty of such attempts to synthesize lies in the fact that Second Isaiah does not appear entirely under any rubric. But I include him here because Second Isaiah has elements of the national hope in the sense described above, although he is certainly the most elevated of the writers who are included here.

We distinguish as well as we can between pre-exilic and post-exilic expressions of the national hope; critical problems arise here, but generally the content of the texts easily discloses whether the writer is thinking of a restoration of the nation or not. This is the major difference between earlier and later texts. In the texts which we judge early there is an unspoiled optimism and a naïve faith in the saving will of Yahweh for Israel. The texts which speak of restoration exhibit a keen sense of guilt and an awareness of the reality of judgment. They do not share the pessimism of Amos and Jeremiah; faith in the saving will of Yahweh has survived judgment. But the texts which are included here do not exhibit the theme of moral regeneration, which we treat below under its own classification.

We have already dealt with the theme of promise and fulfillment (Chapter III, Section 1). It must be mentioned again under this heading, for it is certainly an expression of future orientation in the terms of the national hope. These texts very probably belong to the early dual monarchy. They represent the possession of the land as the term of a divine plan made and announced in centuries long past. The peaceful possession of the land is first achieved under David. We encounter here a theme which C. H. Dodd identified in the New Testament and called "realized eschatology." The national hope of the future goes no further than dwelling peacefully in the land which Yahweh had promised the fathers and given to their descendants. There is no international or cosmic dimension to this hope, no "world to come." The will of Yahweh for Israel is fulfilled when each man dwells under his vine and under his fig tree, with none to terrify—to borrow a phrase from a later writer (Mic 4:4; see below). Peaceful possession of the land was a form of the national hope which never entirely disappeared from Israel's future ideal, and it is even reflected in Matthew 5:5.

The number of certainly pre-exilic passages which express the national hope is not large in any critical hypothesis; and I limit myself to four poems whose antiquity scarcely any critic denies. The oracles of Balaam (Num 23:7–10,19–24, 24:3–9,15–19) probably come from the early monarchy; chapter 24:17 may refer to the monarchy of David. The theme of the union between Yahweh and Israel runs through all the poems. Because of this union, no hostile power can succeed against Israel. There are allusions to victories, but not to the Davidic empire; the most numerous and most explicit references are to the exodus of Israel from Egypt. There is no reference to covenant or to the promise of the patriarchs. Israel is in possession of its land, and there is no greater threat to it than Edom; the direction of the oracles to the king of Moab may not have been a part of their original composition. Some obscure oracles which have been appended (Num 24:20–24) may contain references to Assyria; but this people certainly does not appear in the threatening character which it has in Isaiah. In summary, then, the oracles center upon the peaceful possession of the land, promised in antiquity (here attributed to Balaam) and realized under the monarchy. The oracles belong in the category of realized eschatology.

The two tribal poems of Genesis 49 (the blessing of Jacob) and Deuteronomy 33 (the blessing of Moses) are clearly parallel; and since all critics regard Genesis 49 as the earlier composition, it seems unlikely that Deuteronomy 33 has no reference to the earlier poem. It was a common ancient belief that old wise men at the time of their death were endowed with insight into the future; and these poems are examples of the "testament," in which the patriarch predicts the destiny of his children. Both poems are addressed to the tribal structure; we have seen that under the monarchy this became something of an archaism (see Chapter VI, Sections 1–2). The blessing of Jacob emphasizes both Judah and Joseph, the blessing of Moses the house of Joseph. "The house of Joseph" was the largest and strongest component of the northern tribes; the tribe of Judah was the tribe of David and Solomon. The words of the blessing of Moses concerning Judah suggest that the poem was composed after the schism. The praise of Judah in the blessing of Jacob certainly refers to the dynasty of David, and the poem most probably comes from the dual monarchy. In both poems the theme of peaceful possession of the land is dominant, the theme which we have designated as realized eschatology.

The song of Moses (Deut 32) is in the judgment of critics later than the blessing of Moses, and it is clearly a more sophisticated composition. The song shows an awareness of the sin of Israel and the judgments of Yahweh, both already rendered and still to be feared, which is entirely absent from the blessings of Jacob and Moses. But these judgments are not terminal; they are medicinal, and it is expected that Israel will respond to them. The author's vision of the future (Deut 32:34–43) is a vision of the vindication of Israel, manifested in the total defeat of the enemies of Israel. The poem could in this respect be classified with the postexilic prophecies treated below. This critical question cannot and need not be settled here. There is ample pre-exilic literature which shows a consciousness of the danger of judgment and a hope that the judgment will not be final. Not all prophets had the austerity of Amos. The poem is not concerned with the peaceful possession of the land nor with the restoration of the land after it has been lost. Its emphasis is on the defeat of the enemies of Israel, emphasis which we shall meet with increasing frequency in the exilic and postexilic periods.

The other texts which we shall discuss are classified as exilic or postexilic. Some readers may feel that this classification is sometimes arbitrary. They may be right, but we assume that when a writer speaks of the restoration of a fallen people or of the return of a people to their land or of the re-enthronement of a dynasty, he is alluding to a historical experience and not a vision. Most of these passages are found in the books of pre-exilic prophets. It is a general critical assumption that these texts were added by editors and that they express a belief in the national hope which the pre-exilic prophets did not have, or at least did not express with the same clarity. It is further supposed that these editors felt that the somewhat grim prospect of the will of Yahweh for Israel —in Amos, at least, unrelieved by any softness—was not a complete picture of the relation of Yahweh to Israel. This usually took the form of the "happy ending" of a prophetic book. The principle of the happy ending is most obvious in the book of Amos, which critics suppose ended at chapter 9:9a. The effect of what was added can be seen if we read it. The theory is generally valid, but not easy to apply to such complex collections as the books of Isaiah and Jeremiah. Isaiah at least may have several happy endings, one for each of the various phases of the collection. The work of the scribes shows the strength of the belief of the eternity of Israel, once it took form.

Of the exilic and postexilic prophecies we shall first consider Second Isaiah, not only because he is clearly exilic, but also because it is possible that the theme of the restoration of Israel was first expressed by him. This cannot be demonstrated, and I propose it as no more than a suggestion. It takes a little historical imagination, however, to understand how radical and incredible the proclamation of the restoration of Israel was. Other nations which fell under the Assyrian and the Babylonian military machines did not survive. Israel, in the theology of Second Isaiah, survived because it had a mission; of this theme we shall speak below in Section 5.

The restoration of Israel is a new exodus; and this is as close as Second Isaiah could come to saying that it was a new birth—effectively, a new nation. The theme of peaceful possession of the land is implicit rather than explicit. The restored Israel has no temple and no monarchy; Second Isaiah is indifferent to its political and religious institutions. I have argued elsewhere[3] that the single mention of the temple in Second Isaiah is editorial. The Judahite Second Isaiah speaks expressly of the restoration of Zion and not of Israel; it is not clear that he, like other prophets, envisaged the restoration of the twelve tribes in the entire land of ancient Israel. In this respect, he was more realistic than other visionaries. His restored Zion is not a political power and there is no hint of conquest. These traits of his restored Israel, together with the theme of the new exodus, suggest that we should not think of the restoration of the old Israel but of the creation of a new people. Continuity is maintained by the return of the Babylonian exiles; like Ezra and Nehemiah, Second Isaiah treats the

[3] John L. McKenzie, *Second Isaiah*, 74.

land as empty, much as the authors of Joshua viewed the land as emptied by the conquests of Joshua.

The restored Israel has experienced the forgiveness of Yahweh in a new and unparalleled way, as the old Israel experienced his judgments in a new and unparalleled way. Second Isaiah attaches no merit to Israel which deserves forgiveness; Yahweh is as free in restoring Israel as he was in creating it. Nor is Israel active in its restoration. The human agent of restoration is not the King Messiah of Israel but Cyrus of Persia, to whom Second Isaiah attaches titles which in pre-exilic literature belonged to the King Messiah.[4] One may see here an insistence that the restored Israel has no political power or activity; its mission is to be accomplished on another level. The modesty of the vision of the restoration becomes apparent when it is compared with the vision of Third Isaiah. Other writers who gave expression to the national hope did not imitate the restraint of Second Isaiah.

Babylon plays in the new exodus of Second Isaiah the role which the Pharaoh played in the first exodus. It is a symbolic figure which represents the worshipers of the false gods. When these people set themselves in opposition to the saving will of Yahweh, they are not only defeated but destroyed. Since they are all symbolic figures, it is idle to compare the oracles of Second Isaiah or the narratives of Exodus with known history, which records no fall either of the Pharaoh or of Babylon which corresponds to the symbolic fall of these figures.

The collection called Third Isaiah (Is 56–66) is not as easily dated as Second Isaiah; elsewhere I have located this collection (from different authors) in the period 537–450 B.C.[5] It is hardly possible to locate the Zion poems (Is 60–62) very precisely within this period; the affinity of the poems with Second Isaiah and their optimism suggest an earlier rather than a later date. The restraint of Second Isaiah, mentioned above, has nearly disappeared. Jerusalem becomes the world capital, the one point of light in a cosmic darkness to which all the nations stream. They bring all their

4 Ibid. 73–74, 76–79.
5 Ibid. xviii–xxiii.

wealth so that Jerusalem becomes the economic as well as the political capital. The nations and their kings adopt the abject posture of slaves. In this new world commonwealth, Israelites occupy the privileged position of priests, the established mediators between mankind and Yahweh, supported by the contributions of those whom they represent. The author resumes the theme of marriage between Yahweh and Israel, already employed by Hosea, Jeremiah, and Ezekiel; in these prophets it was a marriage which ended in divorce. Third Isaiah alludes to this (Is 62:4), but the union which he now sees is indissoluble.

The vision is presented in terms which approach grossness; the restoration is described in terms of power and wealth, and the theme of moral regeneration (see Section 8, below) is missing. The author, in spite of his affinities with Second Isaiah, does not introduce the idea of mission (see Section 5, below). He frequently uses the term "righteousness," but in these passages the word normally means "vindication" or "victory" rather than moral probity. It is fruitless to attempt to allegorize the power and wealth described by the author as tropes for "virtue" or "spiritual" goods. For this writer, wealth and power were the concrete attestations of all the "spiritual" goods he knew. He is content with the indestructible union of Israel with Yahweh, from which he deduces what Yahweh must do for his people, and that is to make them the greatest of nations.

The book of Jeremiah contains some extended sections which express the national hope (Jer 30–33). Many modern critics accept the bulk of chapters 30–31 as original; they assume that these sayings, originally scattered, dealt with the restoration of northern Israel and were affected by Josiah's program of restoration.[6] As they now stand, they have been worked into a context of restoration after the exile, a context which was produced by Jeremiah's editors and not by the prophet himself. The same is to be said of chapters 32–33; in each chapter a saying of Jeremiah has been expanded. I have already stated my view that Jeremiah thought of the judgment of Yahweh as final (Chapter III, Section 5); if

---

[6] Otto Eissfeldt, *The Old Testament: An Introduction,* 361–62; Bright, *Jeremiah,* 284–87.

these sayings are to be attributed to him, we must suppose that his awareness of finality was mitigated by some hope of the future. This development of his ideas and of his faith is not impossible nor incredible. It seems most unlikely, however, that a man who announced the end of all the political and religious institutions of Judah should so casually announce their coming restoration. It is at this point that we may see the hands of the scribes who had a clearer and firmer belief in the eternity of Israel than Jeremiah had.

For a statement of parts from which the collection was assembled and the provenience of these parts, one may consult Bright's commentary. The collection contains both clear threats and clear promises of restoration. The threats seem to have been edited in such a way that they are turned into promises; see, for instance, the endings of chapters 30:7,11, and 30:16–17. Some of the promises, especially chapter 31:2–6,15–22 are most easily understood as addressed to northern Israel and can be dated early in the career of Jeremiah (Bright). Such a theme belongs in a consideration of the national hope, which in this interpretation of Jeremiah meant a reunion of the divided monarchies. The realization of such a hope demanded the active interposition of Yahweh in history, for the kingdom of northern Israel was hopelessly destroyed by the Assyrian conquest. The hope itself is again the hope of the peaceful possession of the land in prosperity. Some parts of the chapter have affinities with Second Isaiah (Bright). It is much easier to attribute these to an editor who belonged to the school of Second Isaiah, rather than to look for a contrived explanation of how Jeremiah may have shared both the style and the ideas of Second Isaiah. These affinities can be seen in chapters 30:10–15 and 31:7–14; and the editor intended by these expansions to apply the sayings of Jeremiah concerning the reunion of Israel and Judah to the restoration of all Israel. The words concerning the reestablishment of the temple and the monarchy are in obvious contradiction to Jeremiah's announcement of the fall of both these institutions and should not be attributed to him. Neither should the most explicit declaration of the eternity of Israel in the entire Old Testament (Jer 31:35–37). The national hope of Jeremiah was most clearly expressed in the prophecy of the new covenant

278   A THEOLOGY OF THE OLD TESTAMENT

(Jer 31:31-34); I treat this passage not under the theme of national hope but under the theme of moral regeneration (see Section 8, below). That it is a saying of Jeremiah has been disputed by many critics; this does not alter our treatment of its content. But it may be pointed out that a prophet who announced that Yahweh was destroying all the religious and political institutions of Judah is a likely candidate for the authorship of a relation between Yahweh and his people which is totally noninstitutional.

The majority of critics believe that very little of the expressions of the national hope in chapters 32-33 can be attributed to Jeremiah.[7] My own inclination is to assign only chapter 32:6-15 to Jeremiah. To this passage two long speeches from Jeremiah and from Yahweh have been added. The symbolic action of Jeremiah in purchasing the field is significant enough as a witness that there is a future. But what is this future? I have remarked above that the national hope of Jeremiah cannot be considered as a restoration of the past without falsifying all the beliefs which Jeremiah not only proclaimed but suffered for. Yet these long speeches contain the hope of the restoration of just those elements of Judahite life and society of which Jeremiah announced the end: the city, the monarchy, and the priesthood. The writer of chapter 33:24 might have been parodying Jeremiah himself. Jeremiah indeed had a hope for the future, but it cannot be called a national hope. Historic Israel and Judah in his proclamation were over, ended and done. Obviously the spokesmen for the national hope, when it did arise, not only had to bypass Jeremiah, they had to rewrite him.

As expressions of the national hope in Ezekiel, I include most of chapters 34, 36-37, and 40-48. It is impossible even to dip into the critical problems of Ezekiel; hardly any book of the Bible has been submitted to more intensive discussion in the last sixty years, which sometimes seems to threaten the annihilation of Ezekiel both as a book and as a person. Recent criticism has tended to return to a more conservative, or at least a less radical, position.[8] Fortunately, it is not vital for biblical theology that we solve these problems here; in any hypothesis, the passages are clearly passages of restoration which presuppose the fall of Judah

[7] Bright, op. cit., 297-98.
[8] Eissfeldt, op. cit., 365-82; Fohrer, *Ezechiel* (Tübingen, 1955), VII-XII.

and the exile. They are collections of sometimes quite disparate sayings.

The sayings about the shepherds (Ezek 34:1–10) and the sheep, rams, and goats (34:17–22) appear to be doublets. In all probability they are directed against the oppressive ruling classes of the monarchy; there will be no such oppressors in the restored Israel. The rest of chapter 34 expresses the themes of peaceful possession of the land, prosperity and security from external enemies; these themes, we see, become commonplace in the national hope. The apostrophe to the mountains of Israel (36:1–15) bears upon the theme of fertility, especially in chapter 36:13–14, which is probably a rare allusion to the harshness of the land of Palestine.[9] The sayings in chapter 36:16–38 introduce the gratuitousness of the restoration, a theme which Ezekiel shares to some extent with Second Isaiah. The restoration is done because of nothing in Israel which deserves it, nor even out of the compassion of Yahweh for those who suffer—is it not a righteous judgment? It is done because of Yahweh's holiness, which here means his zeal for his name; and this in turn means that he must safeguard the recognition of his divinity. How much this idea had to do with the whole hope of restoration and of a glorious future—which we shall consider below—cannot be argued from the texts. I suspect it is implicit almost everywhere and that the dominant base of the hope for the future was the thought that Yahweh owed it to himself to restore Israel. This idea overcame the possibility that he might destroy Israel and create another people, which we discussed above in relation to the eternity of Israel.

The vision of the dry bones (Ezek 37:1–14) is an assurance that Yahweh will restore Israel, even though the task seems impossible. The passage is not even an implicit profession of belief in the resurrection of the body, and no modern commentator takes it as such. The vision of the two sticks (37:15–28) is a statement that the restored Israel will be a reunion of the two parts of the divided monarchy, a theme which we have seen in Jeremiah 30–31. Once the idea of a restoration had been formed, it was no more difficult for Yahweh to restore the ideal Israel, defined by the

9 Ibid.

boundaries of the kingdom of David, than it was for him to restore the kingdom of Judah. The oracle of the reunion is filled out by the commonplaces of the restoration—peaceful possession of the land, covenant, monarchy and temple. As we have noticed in discussing Jeremiah, these commonplaces are less a vision of a new Israel than a vision of the old Israel restored.

The vision of Ezekiel 40–48 will be treated below in Section 4, under the classification of the worshiping community.

There is little critical doubt that the prophecies of Zechariah 1–8 belong in the period indicated by the book itself, 520–518 B.C. The prophet communicates his message in the form of visions, each of which contains a symbolic figure which must be interpreted by an angel. He sees the rebuilding of Jerusalem (1:13–17) and the overthrow of the hostile nations (1:18–21). The same themes are repeated chapter 2:1–5,6–13, with the added note that Jerusalem rebuilt will be much larger than historic Jerusalem and that hostile nations shall not only be overthrown but shall be subjected to Judah. The priesthood will be restored (3:1–10). The dirty garments of Joshua which are replaced by clean garments are clearly interpreted (3:4,7) to signify the past sins of the priestly house. The high priest is associated with Zerubbabel, the descendant of David who was appointed governor of Jerusalem by the Persians; see Section 3, below. The flying scroll and the woman in the ephah symbolize the moral regeneration of the people; see Section 8, below. For the episode of the coronation (6:1–15), see Section 3; for chapter 7:1–14, see Section 8. The themes of peace and prosperity are resumed in chapter 8:1–13 and are joined to the theme of moral regeneration (8:14–17; see Section 8); mourning shall be turned to gladness (8:18–19) and Jerusalem will be the world capital of the worship of Yahweh (8:20–23).

In Zechariah we meet the themes which had by his time become well established; he adds nothing new to them. In spite of the references to moral regeneration, which we have noticed and shall discuss below, he is probably the most candidly nationalistic of the postexilic prophets. He does not even share with Jeremiah and Ezekiel the vision of a reunited as well as restored Israel; like Ezra and Nehemiah, he treats the northern tribes as having ceased to exist. In this he is, like Second Isaiah, more realistic.

His nationalism is redeemed by a sense of mission (8:20–23; see Section 5, below). If the interpretation proposed by many modern scholars of the coronation is correct (6:9–14; see Section 3, below), he was an active nationalist. The number of cross references which we have given to other themes of the future hope show that it is imprecise to classify him simply as a Zionist; but it seems obvious where his interest lay. The indissoluble union between Yahweh and Israel he takes for granted; it is not the object of question or doubt and seems to be subject to no qualification. Yahweh had restored his people, and the rebuilding of the temple had begun. To some this might have seemed "small things" (4:10), but the incredible had happened; the dry bones of Ezekiel had come to life, even though that life was faint, not yet a mighty host. The reference to "small things" most probably suggests that some of Zechariah's contemporaries were disillusioned; see Haggai 2:3. It is hardly possible that most of the people of restored Jerusalem shared the optimism of Second Isaiah or Zechariah.

The texts discussed hitherto we have classified as obviously exilic and postexilic and formally concerned with the idea of national restoration, either as shortly to be expected or as already being accomplished. This theme was also inserted into the collections of pre-exilic prophecies as glosses. These glosses were intended to mitigate the austerity of the pre-exilic prophets; and this is said with no implicit acceptance of the principle proposed by older critics that the pre-exilic prophets were all prophets of doom (*Unheilspropheten*) with no announcement of salvation. I believe that Amos was such an *Unheilsprophet;* I cannot be equally sure of any other pre-exilic prophet. The glossators felt that the pre-exilic prophets took little or no account of the possible survival of Israel in judgment and had no awareness of the dogma of the eternity of Israel. These glosses, they felt—I am reading their mind, but what else is interpretation?—filled in what the pre-exilic prophets did not know because they had no experience of the saving acts of Yahweh in the restoration of Israel.

The conclusion of Amos (9:9b–15) illustrates very well the work of the glossators, especially since it stands in flat contradiction to the previous line (9:9a) as well as to the thrust of the whole book. The assertion of destruction is negated by the insertion of the superlative of the infinitive absolute; this is the only way in which the two lines could be joined. The glossator then adds the commonplace of the ingathering of Israel, the restoration of the dynasty of David, and the prosperity of Israel dwelling peacefully in its land. What I have called the "commonplace of the ingathering of Israel," not yet noticed in the texts, appears mostly in the glosses; and Isaiah 11:10–16, appended to the messianic oracle of chapter 11:1–9 (see Section 2, below), has the ingathering as its main theme. The author also sees the reunion of the full Israel and victory over the traditional enemies, mostly the immediate neighbors. The victory over Egypt is a re-enactment of the exodus. The isolated saying of Isaiah 11:10 sees Judah as a world capital. The theme of the ingathering appears also in Isaiah 27:12–13; here it was very probably added to soften the severity of 27:7–11, which speaks of the destructive judgment inflicted upon Israel. The closing oracle of the ingathering is matched by the statement of renewal in 27:6, so that the oracle of judgment has been completely wrapped in promise.

We have already noticed expressions of the national hope in the book of Jeremiah. Glosses of the type we are concerned with appear in chapter 23:1–4,7–8. These contain the theme of the ingathering of Israel, the replacement of unfaithful shepherds by true shepherds (see Ezek 34), and the restoration as a new exodus (see Second Isaiah). These are obviously derived. Likewise derived are most of the themes in the gloss in Joel 2:18–29, although it may be a question whether this passage should be called a gloss. As it stands, it is a response to the prayer which precedes it. But it contains the commonplaces of victory over enemies and prosperity. The new feature in this saying is the diffusion of the spirit upon the whole people. We have discussed the spirit in Chapter VI, Section 2, above; there we saw that it was a charismatic impulse which fell upon religious and political leaders. The casual way in which Joel confers this upon each individual Israelite is more surprising and more revolutionary than appears at first glance. In such a charismatic society, where is there room for the charismatic leader? One may compare this idea with Jeremiah's idea of the new covenant (see Section 8, below). It is also a part of the postexilic refusal of prophecy; see Zechariah 13:2–6, in which the traditional title of the prophet, *nabi',* is no longer accepted.

The critical problems of the book of Micah sometimes seem to be beyond rational solution; but there is no doubt of the presence of postexilic nationalistic glosses of the type we are considering.[10] Perhaps the scribes thought that a book which contained a saying like Micah 3:9–12 needed such glosses. In any case it has them in chapter 4:6–13, the ingathering of Israel and victory over enemies; chapter 5:5–9, victory over enemies and the pre-eminence of restored Israel among the nations; chapter 7:11–20, forgiveness of national sin, the ingathering of Israel, prosperity, the new exodus, submission of the nations. These we have now come to recognize as commonplaces. A similar gloss appears at the conclusion of Zephaniah (3:11–20). This gloss contains the theme of the moral regeneration of the survivors (see Section 8, below) and the lowly people, which suggests Third Isaiah (see Chapter VI, Section 3, and Section 6, below).

A last expression of the national hope may be seen in Daniel 2, now generally dated in the second century B.C. during the oppressive rule of the Seleucid kings. The vision is interpreted unambiguously to signify the ultimate supremacy of the kingdom of Judah over all the kingdoms of the world. Here we verge upon apocalyptic (see Section 6, below); but this passage suits the description of national hope as well as any we have mentioned.

The texts which we have classified under the national hope have, it will be admitted, a remarkable community of content and mood. I have suggested that they derive from the sayings of Second Isaiah. But when one classifies Second Isaiah as a spokesman for the national hope, one is immediately aware that he breaks out of the category. He will come up again under the classification of the mission of Israel, where he has very few companions. In Second Isaiah the national hope is accessory to the idea of mission; in the other texts cited, the idea of mission generally does not appear.

The national hope does not exclude the idea of moral regeneration, nor does it of necessity include it. We shall study this category below (Section 8). I do not believe that it can be assumed to be implicitly present in the texts where it does not appear, just as I do not assume that the idea of mission is present where it does not appear. We have had occasion to refer to passages in which the national hope, as far as we can read, is no more than a restoration of the national reality which came under judgment. This hope does not preclude the necessity of moral judgment. We shall see that this unsatisfactory belief drove the school of Third Isaiah to the edge of apocalyptic.

The national hope, if it follows its own inner logic, attaches to the nation the same necessity which it declares of Yahweh. We have already observed that even the J narrative of the Pentateuch rose above this necessity. What is implied is that Yahweh needs Israel in order to survive—in the theology of Ezekiel, that he seems to be a failure as a God if he does preserve his own. What he might do after judgment is his decision, not the decision of prophets or priests of the chosen people.

I have adverted to the preservation of the national hope in Christian belief and doctrine. I have adverted to an inner contradiction which may lurk in the belief in the indefectibility of the church. The contradiction becomes explicit if the necessity of the church is identified with the necessity of God. Actually, belief in the necessity of the church has always meant belief in the necessity of contingent forms of the church—which is as clear a contradiction in terms as one can manage.

Let us return once more to the commonplaces of the national hope. They are peace, prosperity, security from enemies or, better stil, victory over enemies. These are the goods which a government is expected to give its citizens. They are really not the works of God. An assurance that they cannot be achieved as lasting goods without the act of God is a belief which Christians share with the ancient Israelites; but one misses in the national hope a belief that God by his intervention will establish these goods for others besides Israel. The national hope, again if it follows its own inner logic, is essentially ethnic. It seems of value to point this out, since Jews and Christians have so often taken the national hope in isolation from other elements of the biblical hope of the future. If we did not have six other themes to discuss under this topic, we would do well to omit this one entirely; for taken by itself it is not theology.

3. *Royal Messianism*

We have already dealt with the theopolitics of the Israelite monarchy (see Chapter VI, Section 2). This political theology was directed to immediately practical ends in the present, and therefore I separated the consideration of the monarchy from the hope of the future. This meant that I divided into two parts a collection of texts which is often studied as a unit.[11] As suggested before, the Davidic monarchy was proposed by its prophets and scribes as a kind of realized eschatology; Yahweh had brought Israel to the end which he had designed for it, and there was no further advance to be expected. After the schism of Israel and Judah, the united monarchy was still treated in prophecy and liturgy as the ideal towards which Israel might hope to return. In many passages of the national hope (see Section 2, above), the monarchy is included in the idea of the restoration. Several of these are merely conventional and need no comment; the monarchy was a component of the old Israel which is to be restored, and there is no emphasis on the King Savior theme. In most of the national hope passages, the monarchy is not even mentioned.

We consider here those texts in which the monarchy is a part of the future hope and more than a merely conventional feature. It is not altogether sure that all these texts have a futuristic outlook.

We may begin with a text which is a remarkably simple expression of a hope of a future for the monarchy. The books of Kings conclude with a notice that Jehoiachin, the exiled king of Judah, was restored to favor by the Babylonian king Amel-Marduk at his accession in 562 B.C. (2 Kings 25:27–30; Jer 52:31–34). The authors of the Deuteronomic history were historians of judgment, and it is not improbable that they regarded their history as a closed book; if they did, their theology would have been the theology

[11] McKenzie, "Royal Messianism," CathBiblQuart 19(1957), 25–52.

of Amos rather than of Second Isaiah. Thus the conclusion of 2 Kings may be an instance of the "happy ending" mentioned above, appended to the history by a scribal editor.[12] It is of interest because it calls attention to the one surviving element of monarchic Israel and Judah, the monarch himself. Possibly the scribe thought this was a witness to the eternity of the dynasty of David.[13] In Jehoiachin the people of Yahweh survived.

Isaiah 9:1–7 contains an oracle about a future king which has long been intensely discussed, and the divergence of opinions forbids any apodictic interpretation.[14] Certainly, a future king is mentioned; the question is how far into the future Isaiah intended to point. Many critics have insisted that the future king meant is Hezekiah, the successor of Ahaz. If this is correct, then the passage should not be included in the consideration of the hope of the future. Other interpreters feel that Isaiah could hardly have seen such an ideal figure as he describes on the near horizon. Actually, he does not go far beyond the ideal king of the royal psalms (see Chapter VI, Section 2). Many of the older critics denied the poem to Isaiah himself and treated it as we treated the glosses of the national hope; they thought it was an exilic or postexilic gloss in which the national hope of the future would be centered upon the Messiah King Savior of the dynasty of David. The critical question cannot be settled here; unfortunately, the theological significance of the passage here depends on the critical question. There is no other royal text in which the King Savior has such a prominent role in the future; the ideal king here is much closer to the King Messiah of the psalms (see Chapter VI, Section 2) than he is to the national future considered in Section 2 of this chapter. This by itself is not enough to turn the balance of opinion in favor of a historical interpretation of the text.

There is less critical doubt concerning Isaiah 11:1–9,[15] but O.

---

[12] J. Gray, *I and II Kings* (Philadelphia, 1963), 704.

[13] G. von Rad, *Old Testament Theology*, I, 343.

[14] Eissfeldt, op. cit., 318–19; F. L. Moriarty, *Jerome Biblical Commentary* (Englewood Cliffs, 1968), I, 270; J. Lindblom, *Prophecy in Ancient Israel* (Philadelphia, 1962), 249, 368–69; A. Alt, *Kleine Schriften* (Munich, 1964), II, 206–25.

[15] Eissfeldt, op. cit., 319.

Kaiser has recently spoken in favor of authenticity.[16] This is generally regarded as an exilic or postexilic expansion; chapters 11–12, the conclusion of the first collection of Isaiah, are entirely secondary. It may indeed have been the presence of the oracle of the child king in chapter 9:1–7 which led the editor to insert this royal oracle. The dynasty of David has fallen ("stump," ch. 11:1), but a new king will arise. He will have the charismatic spirit which was attached to the dynasty. Conquest is not a theme of this ideal ruler, and this deserves emphasis. His attributes are righteousness and fidelity. How he achieves universal peace is not described; the universal peace is a restoration of the paradise of Genesis 2. The picture is obviously more idealistic than the features of the national hope; more is expected of the King Messiah than presiding over Israel dwelling in peace and prosperity in its land, with his foot firmly planted on the neck of a prostrate ancestral enemy.

The image of King Messiah, long and justly popular in Christian devotion as an image of the future for which Christians hope, has no echo elsewhere in the hope of the future. The other texts in which the king plays a part in the hope of the future barely escape conventionality. Such a text is the gloss repeated twice in Jeremiah (23:5–6 and, with some verbal variations, 33:14–16). The work of the king is righteousness, justice, and security—the qualities signified by his throne name which were so notably lacking in the historical dynasty of David. There will be a king in the restored Israel, and he will be what a king ought to be; this is what I mean by a merely conventional view of the monarchy. Micah 5:2–4 is most easily understood as a postexilic gloss; the obscurity of 5:3 does not prove this, but neither does it disprove it. A new David is expected who will create security; no more details are given. Ezekiel 34:23–24 is probably a gloss; the king occupies a small place in Ezekiel's future. He is described simply as shepherd.

The royal messianism of Zechariah is unique. In the first place, he joins the king and the high priest in a new way (Zech 3:6–10, 4:6–14). He does not call Zerubbabel king, but to an understanding audience he would not have to use the term. Joshua the high priest and Zerubbabel the governor, the descendant of David,

---

[16] *Isaiah 1–12* (Philadelphia, 1972), 152–55.

are joined as the two anointed. Zerubbabel has founded the temple
and will complete it (Zech 4:9); in this he re-enacts the role of
Solomon in the building of the first temple.

In spite of the intense discussion of the problem, I am satisfied
that the name of Zerubbabel has been replaced by the name of
Joshua in Zechariah 6:9–14.[17] In the first place, we have no evidence that the crown was ever worn by a priest; Zechariah did
indeed introduce some novelties, but not this one. The name of
"Branch" is elsewhere borne by the descendant of David (Jer 23:5,
33:15; Zech 3:8). Furthermore, Branch will have a priest by his
throne—strange, if addressed to Joshua. In this hypothesis, Zechariah actually reinstalled Zerubbabel a king in Jerusalem. Whether,
as many scholars have thought, this elicited the intervention of
the Persians, I am not prepared to say. Such a theory explains
why the name of Zerubbabel was replaced by the name of Joshua.
But the change of the name does not demand such an explanation.
In fact, there was no installation of a successor in the restored
community, and the high priest during the Persian and Greek periods was the representative of the community with the imperial
power. John Hyrcanus of the Hasmonaean dynasty united in his
own person the offices of king and high priest.

I have removed most so-called "messianic texts" to the discussion of the historical monarchy of Jerusalem (Chapter VI, Section
2). The reasons alleged for this treatment are probably not convincing, but they deserve consideration. The main result of this
distribution of material is to destroy much of traditional Christian
"messianism," as I have indicated. Once this reclassification is
made, it is apparent that the monarchy occupies a very small place
in the hope of the future. Reflection suggests that this is altogether
probable. In the postexilic community, memories of the monarchy
must have been a memory of a ghastly failure. The monarchy failed
to exhibit precisely those qualities which are mentioned in such
texts as Isaiah 11:1–9 and Jeremiah 23:5–6. It offered no hope
of producing a King Savior. The dominant expression of the national hope, limited as its horizons are, is non-political. There was
no reason to think that a restored dynasty of David would be any

17 M. Noth, *The History of Israel*, 312.

better than the dynasty which had perished. If Yahweh was indeed to work something new, he would have to go beyond the establishment of the dynasty in Jerusalem. Other features of the hope of the future, to which we must now turn, indicate the directions in which the work of Yahweh might be expected to turn.

4. The Worshiping Community

Under this rubric we take account of some texts which compel the conclusion that at least some members of the exilic and post-exilic communities looked to a future which was religious and in no way political. The Babylonian wars had destroyed Judah as a political entity. These Jews accepted this as a judgment; if they had collected the writings of the prophets, they had ample evidence for this conclusion. They seem to have been satisfied that Yahweh would not again create a people with political independence. His will would be found in a community which lived quietly in submission to the Persian Empire. They had no plans for anything beyond the Persian Empire, but the plans they had could survive any empire. The destiny of Israel was to worship Yahweh in a fitting manner—that is, in the manner which he himself had revealed.

Such a cultic hope is expressed by Haggai (2:1–9). Haggai utters his conviction that the erection of the temple is the primary task of the restored community. He does not know what Yahweh will do in the future; he does know that whatever it is, Yahweh will do it in his temple, the place of revelation. In fact, Haggai seems to have shared the royal messianism of Zechariah for Zerubbabel (Hag 2:20–23). But nothing will happen until the community has restored a fitting house of worship. Probably Haggai had apocalyptic hopes concerning the act of Yahweh, but they have not been left us under his name.

Malachi was entirely concerned with cultic rectitude. The faults which he criticized in the postexilic community, with the exception of failure to observe the marriage laws (Mal 2:10–17), are all in the area of cultic regulations and priestly instruction (torah). In the future he sees proper sacrifice offered to Yahweh all over the world (1:11), and he hints that the faithless priests of Jerusalem will have no part in this universal sacrifice. It is in the temple that the "messenger" of Yahweh will appear (3:1-4). This messenger is not derived from any other biblical passage; but as a precursor of judgment he reappears in the New Testament (Mk 1:2; Mt 11:10), where he is identified with John the Baptist. The work of the messenger is to purify the priesthood and restore the proper cult; in the context (which is not necessarily original) he is mentioned before the apocalyptic judgment of Malachi (see Section 5, below).

The Old Testament contains two major literary monuments to the worshiping community as the hope of the future. The first of these is found in Ezekiel 40-44. The literary origins of this passage are complex and need not be discussed here; the passage certainly belongs to the theology of restoration.[18] The rebuilt temple is clearly the center of the restored Israel; and the whole section of Ezekiel 40-48 really describes the restoration of the worshiping community rather than the national hope treated in Section 2, above. The author clearly means to represent the new temple as built according to divine specifications and thus perfect, free of every blemish. But why the author goes into such detail about its dimensions escapes the reader. Possibly there are implicit references to the pre-exilic temple, destroyed by the Babylonians, which we are unable to grasp. It has been thought that the author intended this description as a realistic and practical plan for the rebuilding of the temple. In fact, it is not complete enough to be a practical plan of construction; and while the author may have meant the distribution of the land (chs. 47-48) as a practical plan, it could be such only in the hypothesis of a miraculous recreation of the topography. It seems that the whole scheme is better treated as imaginative, no more realistic than the new river which springs from the temple mountain (ch. 47:1-12). This does not mean that the author may not have meant his vision realistically; we are approaching apocalyptic literature, and the capacity of these writers to believe in the realism of their fantasies should not be underestimated. If the author was not Ezekiel, he was Ezekiel's

[18] Fohrer, op. cit., 219-20.

literary heir. Where other poets were satisfied with a blurred image of the chariot of Yahweh, Ezekiel gives nearly a draughtsman's sketch of the vehicle (ch. 1). Similarly, the new temple, which others would have left outlined in a rosy glow, has a complete ground plan.

The ideal temple is served by an ideal priesthood (Ezek 44). This is the family of Zadok, the same priestly family which served the pre-exilic temple. This author, like the author of the first part of the book, is aware of the profanations of the temple committed by the priests themselves (ch. 8). Yahweh destroyed the temple because it had been profaned. The new temple must be kept holy; and the author, not really an apocalyptic writer, sees the possibility that profanation can happen again. There is no "king" in the restored community, but only a "prince" (*nasi'*); this word is probably an ancient designation of a tribal chieftain. The author is interested only in the cultic functions of the prince, which are minimal; but he is also aware of the history of the oppressive ruling classes of the monarchy, which will not recur in the restored community (45:8-9). There is very probably an implication that the kings of Judah, who owned the temple as a royal chapel, were responsible for many of the abuses which the author wishes to prevent. The new temple is entirely in the custody of the Zadokite priests, the only trustworthy class.

Whether it is symbolism or naïve realism, it is from the temple mountain that the stream rises which will regenerate the land (Ezek 47:1-12). The imagery of water in the Bible is rich and varied and best appreciated when one has experienced, either in Palestine or elsewhere, the importance of water in semiarid or marginal areas. Water is often in the Bible identified with life; in the new Israel the new life comes from the temple where Yahweh dwells among his people. It is a refinement on the commonplaces of prosperity in the national hope (Section 2, above).

The second major literary monument of the worshiping community as the hope of the future is found in the books of Chronicles. This work, now generally grouped by scholars with Ezra-Nehemiah as the Chronicler's history, is a rewriting of the history of Israel from Adam to the fall of the monarchy of Jerusalem. The history up to David is sketchy; possibly the writer or writers belonged to the same scribal tradition which produced the priestly history incorporated into the Pentateuch. From David to Zedekiah the main source is the text of the books of Kings, which is largely copied word for word. The omissions and additions—from unknown sources—of the Chronicler reveal an astonishing idea of history and an unreserved readiness to rewrite the record according to what the Chronicler thought was the true theology of history. Israel as a kingdom is simply excluded as far as possible and treated as a foreign nation. Virtue is rewarded and sin is punished; the climactic advance of judgment in Kings is not found in Chronicles. David is purged of his sins by silence about them and endowed with an oversized halo. All this can be explained as the Chronicler's theological evaluation of the pre-exilic history of Israel; to him it was a preparation for the establishment of the temple community of the restoration. This was a nonpolitical community, and the history of the politics of the monarchy to him is simply irrelevant as anything except examples of judgment. The great achievement of David was the preparation of the building of the temple (1 Chron 22–26). The Chronicler did not have much use for Solomon, who simply executed the will and plans of David with the materials which David had collected. Interpreters generally agree that the Chronicler was a member of the temple choirs, if his interest in this feature of worship is any clue to his identity. David is not yet the author of the Psalms, but he is the patron of those who wrote and sang the psalms. All the saving and judging acts of Yahweh in the past and even the prophecies (in which the Chronicler shows no interest) have left only one enduring reality: the temple in which Yahweh dwells and in which alone he is worshiped. Yahweh destroyed the temple of Solomon, and the Chronicler is not even very clear as to the reasons. It does not make much difference, because the new temple is a better temple. He did not have to be convinced of this, as Haggai had to convince his contemporaries.

The future of Ezekiel 40–48 and the Chronicler is certainly theocentric, to say the least. For them the destiny of Israel is to give Yahweh the worship which he desires and which is worthy of him. This future contains no dreams of world or even local conquest, and no saving victories of Yahweh are expected. The worshiping community has no political structure. The theme of prosperity is muted, and there is no expectation that the wealth of nations will flow to the temple. There is simply no attention paid to the world outside the restored community and no questions concerning the relations of Yahweh to the nations. The future hope of the Chronicler is another example of realized eschatology. Once Yahweh has restored for himself a worshiping community, there is nothing else which he is expected to do. The future hope must be called ingrown. The community has nothing to say to the nations. No idea of mission (see Section 5, below) is apparent. The Persian Empire (or the Greek Empire of the Ptolemies, depending on when one dates the Chronicler) protects the community both from the attacks of enemies and from the temptations which accompany political independence and responsibility.

Yet the Chronicler built soundly. The theology of the temple community was able to withstand the attacks of the Seleucids on the worshiping community; and when the Romans took away the independence which the Maccabean wars had briefly won, the ideal of the worshiping community survived in the Sadducees. The ideal was not able to survive the destruction of the temple by the Romans in 70 A.D.

5. *The Mission of Israel*

In contradistinction to the idea of the worshiping community, which we called ingrown, the idea of a mission of Israel to the nations sees the entire future of Israel in relation to the outside world. It will become apparent that there are not many texts which contain this theme. Once the theme is established, one may find it implicit in other texts or, by the use of a somewhat strained typology, see it expressed in other themes where it is not at all on the surface. We shall not deal with such texts—those of conquest of the nations, for example—for we take them to mean primarily what they say; and we have classified them under the national hope. The mission is quite explicit in the texts which we mention.

We may begin with a text found in two prophetic books, and

possibly original in neither book.[19] Isaiah 2:2–4 (=Mic 4:1–3)
is doubtfully from either prophet, if for no other reason than the
tag line, "It shall come to pass in the latter days." The "latter
days" were not seen in pre-exilic prophecy. The eminence of Zion
and the concourse of the nations to Zion in no way express the
idea of conquest. The nations come to Zion to learn the ways of
Yahweh; and only from Zion can they hear the "law," more properly the revealed teaching, and the word of the Lord, the inspired
utterance. If this text is as late as it appears to be, the word of
the Lord has become synonymous with the *torah,* the law. From
the union of all peoples in the teaching and the word, the prophet
sees the end of war. The vision of universal peace is founded in
the vision of the unity of all peoples in one faith. It must be admitted that Christians have sometimes attempted to hasten both
the unity of faith and universal peace, but this does not invalidate
the vision of the prophet; the Christians did not lead in beating
their swords into plowshares.

Much the same theme is expressed, with less poetic imagery,
in Zechariah 8:20–23. The idea of "mission" is somewhat dim;
actually, the nations shall come to Jerusalem to seek the favor
of Yahweh. But they shall have to go to the Jews to find him;
and it is assumed that the Jews will make him known when they
are asked. It is somewhat remarkable to find this idea in a book
which otherwise, as we have noticed, is an outstanding example
of national and royal hope for the future. We may regard this
passage as a universalist gloss of the same type as Isaiah 2:2–4 =
Mi 4:1–2. A longer universalist gloss appears in Isaiah 19:18–24;
here both Egypt and Assyria, the traditional enemies of Judah,
become worshipers of Yahweh in fellowship. These foreign nations
even receive the designations which originally belonged exclusively
to Israel as the people of Yahweh (Is 19:25).

Second Isaiah made the theme of mission dominant in his prophecy; it explains why Israel has been restored—or rather created
anew.[20] Second Isaiah, we have already noticed (Section 2,
above), is not really a spokesman of the national hope. His use
of the imagery of the exodus suggests the creation of a new Israel

[19] Kaiser, *Isaiah 1–12,* 24–30.
[20] McKenzie, *Second Isaiah,* lvii–lviii, lxv.

rather than the restoration of the old Israel. This may seem to press the point with excessive subtlety; but we have observed that where other prophets and glossators are quite explicit about the restoration of ancient institutions, Second Isaiah is silent about them. The fallen institutions of the past will not serve the mission of the new Israel; in fact, they would be obstacles to the mission.

The mission of Israel is simply to proclaim to the nations that Yahweh alone is God. Israel proclaims this by its very reality; it is a "witness" to Yahweh (Is 43:10–13, 44:8). Here the Hebrew word which is translated "witness" rather means "evidence"; Israel does not have to speak. It is a living example of the righteousness of Yahweh. His righteousness is first seen in his judgment of Israel, and it is further seen in his restoration of Israel. Righteousness is the attribute both of the judge and of the savior, and Yahweh has proved himself fully righteous. Righteousness is also the quality of the victor; and only Yahweh can emerge victorious from what seems to be the total destruction of the people of his own creation. He was not, like the gods of the nations, defeated in the fall of his people; he has shown that he is the only god who is master of the destiny of peoples. This is possibly an implicit allusion to the annual determination of the fates by the gods in the Mesopotamian New Year festival.[21] But Israel is not struck dumb; presumably it is the spokesman of the instruction and the way of life (Hebrew, mišpaṭ) which will issue from Yahweh to the nations. Israel will proclaim the praise of Yahweh (Is 43:21). The mission receives its fullest expression in chapter 45:14–25. Here the nations come to Israel (what moves them to come is not stated) and offer themselves in a submission which is purely religious; they come to worship Yahweh, the one and only god whom Israel alone worships. In a rare phrase, the prophet makes Yahweh say that he did not create the world to remain a chaos (45:18). It may be a fanciful interpretation, but the prophet seems to say that the chaos from which creation emerged is not entirely overcome until every knee shall bow and every tongue shall swear in attestation that Yahweh alone is God.

I have expressed elsewhere my opinion that the Servant Songs

[21] Saggs, *The Greatness That Was Babylon,* 382–83; A. L. Oppenheim, *Ancient Mesopotamia,* op. cit., 201–6.

contained in the book of Second Isaiah are from an author different from the anonymous writer whom we call Second Isaiah.[22]
In the same work I have discussed at length my interpretation
(in no way original) of the Servant Songs and the identity of the
Servant.[23] Since I have not revised my ideas in the interval, I may
be excused from repeating this discussion here. I believe the Servant cannot with satisfaction either be entirely identified with Israel
or entirely distinguished from Israel. This means that I have
adopted a somewhat fluid interpretation of the Servant as an ideal
figure and a "corporate personality," to borrow the classic phrase
of H. Wheeler Robinson. For the purpose of theological interpretation, these problems of criticism and exegesis, as obscure and
as warmly discussed as in any passage of the entire Bible, are
mere house cleaning. Whomever the author meant by the Servant
and whatever he intended the relation of the Servant to Israel to
be, there can be no doubt that the Servant is a figure with a mission in which Israel is somehow deeply involved. Interpreters differ on the manner and the depth of the involvement.

In the first Servant Song (Is 42:1–4) and the response
(42:5–9), the Servant is seen as a new Moses.[24] He reveals
"judgment" and "instruction," the traditional terms for the revelation of the "law." This is the revealed will of Yahweh giving
directions for a way of life. But where Moses spoke to Israel, the
Servant speaks to "the earth" and to the "coastlands." In the
response he becomes a "covenant" of peoples and a "light of
nations." The contrast between the mission of Moses and the
mission of the Servant seems clearly established: the Servant is to
do for the world what Moses did for Israel.

In the second Servant Song (Is 49:1–6), the world-wide scope
of the Servant's mission is equally clear (49:6); and the contrast
between the limited scope of a mission to Israel and the scope of
a mission to the nations is clearly expressed.[25] Yahweh intends
much more than merely the restoration of Israel. The response
(49:7–13) does not echo the theme of mission with any clarity.

[22] McKenzie, *Second Isaiah*, xli–xlii.
[23] Ibid. xlii–lv and comments on the Servant Songs.
[24] Ibid. 36–41.
[25] Ibid. 104–9.

The third Servant Song (50:4–9) and its response (50:10–11)[26] do not allude explicitly to the mission of the Servant, but to the difficulties which he encounters in doing whatever it is he has to do. He still appears in the role of teacher (50:4).

The fourth Servant Song (Is 52:13–53:12)[27] is the major *crux interpretum* of the Old Testament. As we have remarked, the idea of mission is clear; but we need very much to know who is the subject of the mission and to whom the mission is directed. It is the very ambiguity of these questions which permitted Christian interpreters beginning with the New Testament to affirm that the passage is a prediction of the redeeming death of Jesus Christ. Modern Christian interpreters cannot accept this simplistic view; but it is obvious that the primitive Christian community, and in the opinion of many Jesus himself, interpreted his role in terms of the suffering Servant. For the mission of the Servant in the fourth poem is achieved through vicarious atoning suffering. The innocent through his suffering secures the deliverance of the guilty from punishment. The idea is clear in the poem; its application in detail is not clear. The author of the Targum of Isaiah did not think it was applicable to Israel, or indeed to any situation which he could think of, for he transformed the passage into a statement of the victory of the conquering King Messiah.[28] No doubt many others shared his problem. The idea of mission as a proclamation of revealed doctrine could be understood and accepted; mission as the acceptance of undeserved judgment was too much for this scribe, as indeed it has been too much for most readers of the Servant Songs and of the Gospels.

In treating Second Isaiah, I treated this passage not as opposed to the national hope and the King Messiah theme but simply as a parallel and nonconverging line. I said this because the Song does issue in a triumphal conclusion. I do wonder, however, whether Isaiah 53:10–12 may not be the response to the fourth song; we find responses to the other three. In this hypothesis, the fourth song would be in rather clear and probably deliberate opposition both to the national hope and to the idea of King Messiah. It is

26 Ibid. 115–17.
27 Ibid. 129–36.
28 J. F. Stenning, *The Targum of Isaiah* (Oxford, 1949), 178–81.

a completely new interpretation of the saving power and will of
Yahweh. I can present this only as a suggestion which my colleagues will probably reject. In any case, the fourth song suggests
that the theme of salvation and victory is not at all simple; that it
is much more than the restoration of the exiles to their land and
the rebuilding of Jerusalem and the temple; that it is even much
more than the establishment of a worshiping community which
lives under the Law. When we deal with the theme of the future
of Israel, we have to set this text aside as without parallel, even in
the texts which conceive the future of Israel not as national or
political but as missionary. The scribe of the Targum of Isaiah
was not the earliest example of triumphalism; this term probably
belongs to the glossators of the national hope and the royal hope.
But he did see that this song was in deadly opposition to any
national-political messianism. He believed in this messianism, so
he rewrote the song to suit his belief. His successors live to this
day.

6. *The Apocalyptic Future*

The name "apocalyptic" (from Greek *apokalypsis,* revelation)
is applied to a type of literature which flourished in Judaism after
200 B.C. and in Christianity until A.D. 200.[29] The name is derived
from a common feature of these writings, the claim that they are
secret revelations delivered to some ancient hero to be revealed
at the time of the author, who masks himself under the name of
the ancient hero. This merely external trait is joined with other
traits which identify the type. The central feature of apocalyptic
writings is the vision of a world catastrophe; the powers of evil,
generally identified with the great political powers of the world
contemporary with the author, align themselves for a massive struggle against God in which they are totally and finally defeated.
This initiates the rule of the saints, identified with Israel or the
church. This cosmic combat is normally described in highly symbolic language which often becomes grotesque, as in the monsters

[29] E. Kautzsch, *Die Apokryphen des Alten Testaments* (Tübingen, 1900),
XX–XXIII; S. B. Frost, *Old Testament Apocalyptic,* 1952.

of Daniel 7–12 and the Revelation of John. The symbolism is generally transparent; in the same two books, interpreters have never been puzzled by the identity of the Beast which comes from the sea or the Scarlet Woman. It was not the purpose of the writers to be obscure in their imagery, and they are obscure only when we do not know enough of the contemporary period to be sure of the identification.

Whether the Old Testament actually contains apocalyptic literature could be disputed. The element of pseudonymity, for instance, is not as clear as it is in the apocryphal books. I treat certain passages as belonging at least to the beginnings of apocalyptic; and it should be apparent from the discussion that these passages are not in the same line of theology or of literary form as the prophets, whether pre-exilic or postexilic. Below I shall try to point out what appear to be the roots of this development of belief. One may indeed quarrel with the use of the term "apocalyptic"; I do not believe one can quarrel with the distinct classification of these passages nor their relatively late age, nor with their close relations with literature which any one would call apocalyptic.

Apocalyptic literature is clearly eschatological, if we mean a terminal state in which history ends; it is so clearly eschatological that one may easily wonder whether the term should be applied to anything else. We have observed above (Sections 2–5) that the future considered up to this point in our exposition is not eschatological in the way in which modern theologians use the word. In these passages a further development of history is not expressly excluded; history rather comes to a rest, like the Sabbath rest of creation. But when the heavens collapse and the earth bursts into a cosmic flame, the author is doing his best to show that he is talking about the end of history. It does not seem to be an idea which man has often reached. Thus the P version of the deluge approaches apocalyptic, for he describes the world as relapsing into the chaos which preceded creation; it is not eschatology, for Yahweh restores what he had destroyed, substantially unchanged. But P, who was not far removed in time from the earliest biblical apocalyptic, wanted to show what Yahweh could do in judgment if he wished.

I have said, following the critical consensus, that these passages are late, and I mean well into the postexilic period. Daniel 7–12 is certainly from the second century B.C., and Zechariah 9–14 cannot be much earlier. The apocalyptic passages of Third Isaiah could come from the middle of the fifth century B.C.; and we may take these as terms within which we locate the passages. There are some scattered apocalyptic glosses in the prophetic books which can without difficulty be located in this period. It should be noticed that this is the least known period of Jewish history; this gives critics a certain freedom in suggesting the period as a date for uncertain documents, but there is also some risk in doing it. It is tempting to locate a text we do not understand very well in a period which we do not know very well.

It is probable that the development of apocalyptic eschatology is related to the protology of creation (see Chapter IV, Section 2, above), which we have attributed to Second Isaiah. Before him, it seems, creation was an annual event, a renewal. Corresponding to creation was the annual collapse of nature, the return to chaos. As creation becomes an absolute beginning, so the annual collapse turns into an absolute end, to be expected at some time in the future. The end is still seen in mythological terms as the final combat of Yahweh and the dragon, who is now identified with the great world powers; the diabolism of the author of Revelation is not evident in the apocalyptic passages of the Old Testament. The mythology of the end is the counterpiece to the mythology of the beginning; and the end is really the fulfillment of creation, the production of a new heavens and a new earth.

The passage called the "apocalypse of Isaiah" (Is 24–27) is clearly a postexilic appendix to the book.[30] One may observe why this is classified as apocalyptic and Isaiah 13 is not; Isaiah 13 speaks of an expected historical event, the fall of Babylon (which actually never occurred as the prophet describes it), using the imagery of apocalyptic poetry. In Isaiah 24–27, on the other hand, the world catastrophe is described as clearly as the author knew how. He speaks of the earth, never designated as a particular land. The city which perishes is "the city of Tohu," never identified with any known city. The collapse is indeed the collapse of the heavens,

[30] Eissfeldt, op. cit., 323–27.

but it is explicitly described as the earthquake, a phenomenon quite familiar in Palestine. There is also a social collapse; there is no longer any distinction of classes, commerce ceases, and the normal joy of life disappears from the earth. No one escapes from this except the people of Yahweh. The judgment reaches not only human kings but "the host of heaven," the cosmic forces (probably identified here with the gods of the nations). The author (or a glossator) identifies this event with the final victory of Yahweh over the monster of chaos, here given the name of Leviathan, a dragon found in the Canaanite myths of Ugarit. It is scarcely coincidental that the epithets given Leviathan in chapter 27:1 are derived word for word from a Canaanite mythological poem.[31] An additional argument for a late date for at least part of the passage is a probable allusion to the resurrection of the dead in chapter 26:19; there is no other clear allusion to this belief in the Hebrew Bible outside of Daniel, which belongs to the second century B.C.

There are apocalyptic elements in Third Isaiah 65–66.[32] We have already mentioned the dualism of the true and the false Israel which appears in these portions of Third Isaiah. No such dualism appears in the pre-exilic prophets; all Israel is the false Israel, and all Israel falls under judgment. The authors of Third Isaiah did not foresee in the future a repetition of past judgments; no biblical writer did. These authors could hardly have been unaware of the question of personal freedom and personal responsibility (see Chapter V, Section 3, above). A judgment which must come upon the false Israelites ought to spare the true Israelites. The judgments of nature and of history do not make such distinctions. Such a discrimination has to be apocalyptic. Only sinners shall perish. The righteous will live in a new Jerusalem in a new heavens and a new earth. They will enjoy mythological peace and prosperity, in an image (Is 65:25) obviously borrowed from Isaiah 11:9; indeed, much of the eschatological imagery is derived from earlier portions of Isaiah. Immortality is not yet within the writer's view, but he seems to envisage longevity comparable to the longevity of the antediluvian patriarchs (65:20).

[31] ANET 138.
[32] McKenzie, *Second Isaiah*, lxx–lxxi, 197–210.

The same themes are continued somewhat incoherently in chapter 66, which is a montage of fragments and glosses. The most obviously and offensively apocalyptic verse of the whole collection is 66:24. Such "morose delight"—as early moral theologians described this type of feeling—is quite common in the apocalyptic books. The modern Christian may feel that he has risen above the joy of contemplating the pain and death inflicted upon sinners; he is probably not as far above it as he likes to think. In fifteenth- and sixteenth-century Catholic Europe the public attended the burning of heretics on Saturday afternoons as we go to college football games.

Ezekiel 38–39 contain a somewhat contrived version of the apocalyptic battle; it is doubtful that this passage comes from the same literary source as most of the book of Ezekiel. G. Fohrer[33] defends the originality of a "Kernel." The author uses real geographical names and possibly real personal names; but if the origin of Gog is Gyges of Lydia (about 650 B.C.), the author uses names sufficiently removed from his own place and time to make them equivalently imaginative. It is not a real historical nation and king but "the world" which the author has in mind. It is possible that this is not genuine and fully developed apocalyptic. The author need not be thinking of "the end of days," but of restored Israel living in peace and quiet in its own land. Should the restored Israel be attacked by great powers such as Assyria, Babylonia, and Persia—all, even Persia, probably extinct at the time of the writer—they will be utterly defeated, and the Jews will not have to make a single movement in self-defense. Yahweh will accomplish the victory without human aid. Indeed, this passage might be included under the category of the national hope; but it does illustrate the imagery of the apocalyptic battle and may be considered a primitive example of apocalyptic thinking.

The book of Joel is by general consent located well into the postexilic period, later than Nehemiah.[34] This critical consent is largely based upon the apocalyptic character of the book and thus is not entirely free from the charge of a circular argument. It is not even sure that the first part of the book (1:1–2:29) is apoca-

[33] *Ezechiel,* op. cit.
[34] Eissfeldt, op. cit., 394–95.

lyptic. The majority of modern interpreters think that the locust plague is a real event; the view that the locusts symbolize the army of evil from which the people of Yahweh are delivered by his intervention does not enjoy much favor. Whatever is to be said of the first part, the apocalyptic character of the second part is clear, so clear that the unity of the book has been questioned.[35] Here the great army of evil matches itself against Yahweh. The scene of the conflict, "the last judgment," is Zion, the valley of Jehoshaphat (not otherwise mentioned) is "the valley of decision." The author uses and alters passages of earlier prophets (Joel 3:10 = Is 2:4; Mic 4:3; 3:16; Amos 1:2). The result of the apocalyptic victory is the secure establishment of Zion in prosperity. Again we are dealing with primitive apocalyptic; in spite of the judgment of the nations, the vision ends in something which is more like the expressions of the national hope (Section 2, above). The theme of apocalyptic judgment of the nations is briefly expressed in the apocalyptic gloss of Zephaniah 3:8–10. Another apocalyptic gloss in Malachi 4:1–5, however, is more probably derived from the judgment between true and false Israelites in Third Isaiah. There is no explicit reference to the nations, and the reconciling mission of Elijah is most obviously directed to the Jewish community. From this passage, however, Elijah became the precursor of the apocalyptic day both in the apocryphal books and in the New Testament (Mk 9:11–13; Mt 17:10–12).

Two major collections of apocalyptic writing, II Zechariah and Daniel, are by general agreement located in the Greek period (after 330 B.C.). This agreement is less massive for Zechariah 9–14 (Deutero-Zechariah); some scholars have argued an earlier date for these chapters, even a pre-exilic date before Zechariah 1–8.[36] The book of Zechariah is so remarkably free of concrete historical allusions, though full of a number of cryptic allusions to events which cannot be identified, that no one can be assured about the date of the book. As we said for Joel, Zechariah is

---

[35] Ibid. 393–94.

[36] Most recently B. Otzen, *Studien über Deuterosacharja* (Copenhagen, 1964).

regarded as late because apocalyptic literature is late—again, an argument which appears circular.

The apocalyptic element in Zechariah is not present throughout the whole collection; chapters 9–12 express the national hope, with nothing added to the content of this hope as already outlined in Section 2, above. These elements include the restoration of Israel in its land and the city of Jerusalem, the ingathering of the exiles, the defeat of traditional enemies whose territories lay adjacent to Israel and Judah, and the reunion of Israel and Judah. There is also royal messianism; but the house of David, like the house of Israel, is not beyond criticism. "The Messiah of the poor" (9:9) has no parallel in other royal sayings. Those who locate the book in the Greek period are compelled to take some of these allusions as cryptic designations of peoples of that period: Egypt, for instance, means the Ptolemies, and Assyria means the Seleucids. The other ethnic names are not so easily identified; but it is characteristic of later literature to be often archaic in the use of geographical and ethnic names.

The apocalyptic themes are clearer in Zechariah 12–14, most of all in chapter 14. Chapters 12 and 13 contain some of the most obscure passages of the book. The exaltation of Judah and Jerusalem is clear; the occasion of the mourning of the land is not. The explicit declaration of the end of prophecy must arise from a situation which we cannot reconstruct. The apocalyptic of chapter 14 is nearly pure and unalloyed. There appear the cosmic battle and the defeat of the nations, accomplished by Yahweh without human aid; the end of winter and of night; water rising from Jerusalem, with an improvement on the spring of Ezekiel, which flowed only to the east—this stream flows to both east and west; the removal of the mountains of Palestine, except the mountain of Zion; the gathering of the wealth of nations. The defeat of the nations is described with vindictive glee (14:12–15). The slaughter, however, is not so whole that there are no survivors of the nations. Those who do survive will make an annual pilgrimage to Jerusalem to worship Yahweh. Unlike some glossators (see Section 5, above), this author does not see them united with Israel in one people of Yahweh.

I call this nearly "pure and unalloyed" apocalyptic. The event is as clearly final as the author could make it; he expects no further history after this judgment. It is conceived and described in the geography of Palestine and the history of Israel, but the author does succeed—not perfectly—in giving this geography and history a cosmic dimension; it is within the terms of this geography and history that the history of mankind and of God's saving acts and judgments reach their fullness. That apocalyptic such as this does not break out of the limits of the national hope is obvious, and we shall return to this consideration below.

The apocalyptic of the book of Daniel is found in chapters 7–12. The author's pseudo-prediction of history (11) enables us to date at least this part of the book between 167 and 164 B.C., the dates of the profanation of the temple by Antiochus and of his death, which had not yet occurred when the passage was written. The form of the apocalyptic is the vision of monstrous beasts, symbolic of historical figures; the use of symbolic numbers, by which the time of the announced event can be calculated; the exact pseudo-prediction of events (which had already occurred when the passage was written); the interpreting angel who explains the vision (a feature which already appeared in Zechariah). These are common features of the apocryphal books.

The vision of the four monsters (Dan 7) is very nearly the classic sample of apocalyptic symbolism. Interpreters have no difficulty identifying the monsters as the empires of the Babylonians, the Medes, the Persians, and the Greeks. The fourth monster is the great conqueror Alexander, the horns are the successors of Alexander; the little horn with a big mouth is Antiochus IV Epiphanes (175–163 B.C.), the Seleucid king who became the great persecutor of the Jews. Actually, modern historians understand his persecution as an effort to strengthen his unwieldy kingdom by imposing Hellenistic culture upon all his subjects.[37] The Jews regarded this correctly as a move which would assimilate Judaism out of existence. The resistance which will overcome Antiochus (the author wrote before his death) is not human but divine; "the Ancient of Days" (Yahweh) will sit upon the throne of judgment and will deliver the government of the world to "the

[37] W. W. Tarn, *Hellenistic Civilisation* (Cleveland, 1961), 214–16.

son of man." This phrase has a celebrated history in Jewish apocryphal literature and the New Testament which lies outside the scope of the theology of the Old Testament. Whatever is to be said of the phrase in later literature (and almost everything has been said), in Daniel 7 the literal translation "son of man" represents the Aramaic phrase which means a human being. This human being who receives world dominion from the Ancient of Days is the people of Yahweh, the Jews. Here apocalyptic merges with the expressions of the national hope; and perhaps we are over-precise in classifying this vision under a different head from the vision of Daniel 2 (Section 2, above). As an interesting footnote to the author's knowledge of history, we may note that a distinction between the empire of Medes and the empire of the Persians is known only to the author of Daniel among the extant ancient writers.

The vision of the ram and the goat (Dan 8) is parallel to the vision of the monsters. The ram is the empire of the Medes and the Persians (two horns) and the goat is Alexander; the four horns represent the Diadochi, the four successor kingdoms of Alexander. The little horn is, of course, Antiochus IV; he was still trying to subdue Judea at the time of the writing. But the author, in both visions, makes use of the data which he had. The numbers of a time, two times, and half a time (7:25) and 2,300 evenings and mornings (= 1,150 days; see 8:14) represent the interval between the profanation of the temple by Antiochus in 167 and its purification by Judas the Maccabee in 164.

The vision of the seventy weeks (Dan 9) is difficult to interpret in any hypothesis. The author begins from the seventy years dominion of Babylon of Jeremiah 25:11–12 and 29:10. In Jeremiah this number signifies the greatest span of the individual human life; no one living at the time when the oracle was delivered would survive to see the fall of Babylon. The actual interval between the date of the oracle—605 B.C.—and the fall of Babylon to Cyrus of Persia in 539 was sixty-six years; but this is merely coincidental. The author of Daniel knew that the fall of Babylon had not meant the liberation of the Jews; and he asks, rather obscurely, what the number means. The answer of "seventy weeks of years" (seventy times seven) is actually a way of signifying an indefinite number, like the saying of Jesus that one must forgive his brother "seventy times seven" times (Mt 18:22)—that is, there is no limit at which the duty of forgiveness ceases. The author of Daniel, however, attempts to put some order into the "seventy times seven" by inserting into the period recent and contemporary events. Our inability to identify these allusions precisely makes it difficult to grasp his meaning. But the key to the interpretation of the passage is the recognition of the fact that the author did not know the number of years which lay between Jeremiah and his own time. The passage is an early and excellent example of the tinkering with numbers which becomes characteristic of subsequent apocalyptic literature. As Daniel 12 shows, the author did not mean "seventy times seven" as an indefinite number; he believed he and his contemporaries stood on the brink of the apocalyptic event.

The vision of Daniel 10–12 is a fictitious forecast of the events between the later Persian Empire (the author mentions the four last kings of Persia, but we cannot be sure his knowledge was accurate) and 164 B.C.; Antiochus IV is still living when the author wrote. This kind of forecast, we have noticed, is frequent in later apocalyptic literature. There is scarcely any parallel to this detailed exposition, which can be checked out with a handbook of Hellenistic history. The forecast comes to a sudden end when the writer reaches the time of his composition. So does the world of the writer. He sees no solution to the conflict of the people of Yahweh with the hostile world, symbolized by Antiochus, except the intervention of Yahweh which brings history to an end. In the apocalyptic event, the dead saints will rise and the kingdom of the people of Yahweh will be established. Some further numerical calculations at the end of the book suggest that the period of time indicated in Daniel 7:25 and 8:14 had passed when the book was completed.

The allusion to the resurrection is the only clear allusion to this belief in the entire Hebrew Old Testament, although it is very probable that the belief is reflected in Isaiah 26:19. I have not included this belief for discussion in the theology of the Old Testament because it can be proved only for the end of the Old Testament period and because it simply is not a component of the theology of the books of the Old Testament. Any hope of the future is expressed in terms of the enduring group, not of the individual person; and it is in these terms that I have discussed the hope of the future. Attempts to find this belief in earlier books have not been favorably received by interpreters.[38] The question can never be settled with the kind of conviction which one may seek in the natural sciences or history or even theology. If one presupposes that the Israelites believed in the resurrection of the dead, one can interpret some passages as expressions of this belief. If one presupposes that they did not so believe, the passages make excellent sense, but a different sense. Belief in the resurrection of the body is sufficiently rare in the history of religions to justify a demand for a clear and unambiguous statement of the belief. We have such a statement in Daniel 12:2, probably in Isaiah 26:19, both surely quite late in the postexilic period. We do lack any history of the development of the belief, and this is vexing; but the history need not be supplied by creative interpretation of the texts. Except in the Greek period and in a few texts, the relation of the individual person to Yahweh after death is simply not a matter of belief or of concern. Koheleth, probably from the Greek period himself, said there is no work or thought or knowledge or wisdom in Sheol, to which you are going (Eccles 9:10). I think this justifies me in excluding this consideration from theology, which I defined in the beginning of this work as "God-talk."

This review of Old Testament apocalyptic passages permits some remarks by way of summary. One cannot fail to notice the contrast between the pre-exilic prophets and the apocalyptic writers in one respect: the pre-exilic prophets address a people who have freedom and responsibility for their collective decision. They threaten Israel and Judah precisely because it is in their power to avoid the judgment which they deserve. The apocalyptic writers address a people who have neither freedom nor responsibility. Political decisions are made by the nation and their kings; the people of Yahweh are simply passive in history. And the apocalyptic writers have no program except to remain passive; action will come from Yahweh when it comes. He alone can match power with the nations. And when he does act (with rare exceptions noted above), the judg-

[38] M. J. Dahood, *Psalms* (New York, 1970), iii, xli–lii; F. B. Vawter, JBL 91 (1972), 158–71.

ment will be inflicted on the nations, not on his own people. The line in apocalyptic is clearly drawn between the good people and the wicked people, and there is no question on whose side Yahweh is to be found.

One can hear in apocalyptic literature the eternal voice of the oppressed; possibly they were not as oppressed as they thought they were or no more oppressed than any one else. We have noticed that in the theme of the exodus the Israelite poets describe as slavery what was the ordinary life of the Egyptian peasant. The Jewish struggle against Antiochus was a cultural battle as well as a religious battle; religious wars have always been such, and if the elements could have been sorted out, there need not have been any religious wars. If war is always basically irrational and immoral at best, what words can be found for religious wars? But the author of Daniel is truly passive. He does not mention the Maccabees more than once (they are probably "the little help" of 11:34). When Yahweh is going to intervene, what use is there in guerrilla warfare? If he is not going to intervene, then—depending on one's objectives—there may be a great deal of use in it. The Maccabees, W. R. Farmer has maintained, are the legitimate ancestors of the Zealots of Roman times.[39] If this be accepted, one has to say that the line goes on from the Zealots to the more recent Stern Gang and the Irgun Zvai Leumi. One does not go in this line from the essential passivity and historical helplessness of the apocalyptic writers. But the apocalyptic view of the world—meaning here the Gentile world—is that it is we and Yahweh against them. Judgment, as we have already observed (Chapter III, Section 5, above), is vindication for us, condemnation for our enemies. One may say that the apocalyptic writers and the Maccabees agreed in principle and disagreed in tactics; and the principle on which they agreed was that those who worshiped Yahweh could do no wrong. It would be hard to bring Amos and Jeremiah under this principle. And to return to the voice of the oppressed, however much one can and ought to feel sympathy for the oppressed, their voice, when they can get away with it, is usually the voice of vindictive hatred. The apocalyptic judgment is a dream of how the oppressed become the oppressors.

[39] W. R. Farmer, *Maccabees, Zealots and Josephus* (New York, 1956).

These must be called crude features in an image which attempts to express the conviction that the righteousness of Yahweh demands some explicit act of cosmic justice that will be recognized as such. There have to be and there are better images; and one thinks that one can see the petty vindictiveness of the oppressed creeping into the image. Surely Yahweh is, from Genesis to Malachi, the patron of the oppressed; we have seen the opinion that this quality of Yahweh is at the root of the Israelite covenant (Chapter II, Section 2). It was in other ancient Near Eastern cultures that the gods were the patrons of the oppressors. But Yahweh simply can be the property of nobody, not even the oppressed. One wonders whether the scribes who produced apocalyptic literature had in their collection of sacred books the lines of Amos 3:2: "You only have I known of all the families of the earth; therefore I will punish you for all your iniquities."

7. *The Law as Fulfillment of the Future*

We spoke above (Chapter VI, Section 3) of the postexilic community as the first religious community, founded after Ezra upon a document. This document was the Pentateuch of our Bible, known generally among Jews as the Torah, not altogether accurately rendered in English as "Law." The capital letter indicates that there is no other Law. It is, as we pointed out, the revealed will of Yahweh, put in a fixed and unadulterable form, a complete guide to conduct and always capable of clarification and extension by the work of the scribes who interpret it. These scribes in Judaism succeeded to the work of Moses, the author of the Law (see Mt 23:2). The collection was actually the product of the scribal school known to critics under the symbol P (the "priestly writers"); this school was exilic at the earliest, mostly postexilic. One probably does not misread their mind seriously if one supposes that they believed a written code was the best way to assure that the Jewish community would not fall under judgment as their fathers had. I classify them here under the future hope because it seems that they expected their document to produce the future; no further destiny was in view for Israel except to live under the Law, which was to live under the will of Yahweh. This was a

version of the "realized eschatology" which we have encountered
before.

The major difference between the community of the Law (and
the community of worship) and the other forms of the future
hope is precisely that they were "realized," that they were historical
forms. They may not have been awe-inspiring ideals, and they
were hardly saving acts of Yahweh which would cause the nations
to stop their mouths; but they were possible and real. Furthermore,
they were enduring. The community of worship endured until the
Romans destroyed the temple of Jerusalem in A.D. 70; and its
representatives were that "party" in Judaism known in the New
Testament and to Josephus as the Sadducees. The community of
the Law was represented by the party of the Pharisees; and only
Pharisaic Judaism has endured until modern times. It may indeed
appear that to classify Judaism of the Law as "eschatological" is
to stretch the term beyond all meaning; and hence I do not use the
term "eschatological," but speak simply of the hope of the future.
And since Pharisaic Judaism is generally not eschatological in any
usual sense of the term, it appears itself as a terminal state, the
last of the saving acts of Yahweh. The terminal act is the production of a people who live under his revealed will. They are "a light
of nations," in the language of the Servant Songs (Is 49:6), but
no further saving act is envisaged. The people of Yahweh in the
Law has attained its future.

The community of the Law does not so much assert that history
has an end as to say that it is not important whether it does or
not. The community of the Law is not apocalyptic and it expresses
no hope in the cosmic victory of Yahweh over the nations, still
less any hope that the people of Yahweh will be granted world
rule. At the same time, it expresses no hope that the nations will
become worshipers of Yahweh. Yet it did not exclude these themes
from its beliefs. What it rejected, as the New Testament books
relate it, was any revelation above the Law or supplementary to
the Law. I think this shows as well as anything else what I mean
by the belief in the community of the Law as terminal, itself the
end of history. No further saving act of Yahweh could be admitted,
even within the community of the Law, unless it were an apocalyptic saving act. Whether such an event is to occur or not, the community of the Law remains a witness to the unique divinity of

Yahweh, but precisely through the observance of the Law. Its identity somewhat raises it above the course of history—not that it is not affected by this course, but that it is unchanged by it. One must admit, I think, that this is a kind of eschatology.

8. The Moral Regeneration of the Future

This theme is distinguished from the theme of the Law in that it does not depend upon a fixed written code. Certainly, the community of the Law, as we noticed, is intended to secure the people of Yahweh from a judgment like that which the people experienced in the past. The texts included under the heading of moral regeneration are all rather surely earlier than the production of the Torah and do not conceive moral regeneration as fidelity to the Torah. Many of these authors, however, were aware of the tradition of covenant law; and the language of covenant law appears in several of these texts.

Moral regeneration is conceived as a collective regeneration of the people and not of individual persons; and this indeed may be one of the ideas both of covenant law and of the Torah, neither of which is addressed to the individual person. As the judgment falls upon the people as a whole, so the renewal which is hoped is a renewal of the people as a whole. The problem of Third Isaiah concerning the genuine and spurious Israelites (see Chapter VI, Section 3; and Section 6, above) did not fall within the view of those writers who spoke of a moral regeneration of the people.

The earliest expression of this theme is found in the book of Hosea. One passage (Hos 2:14-17) is universally accepted as original. The prophet in this passage does not really speak of judgment as he does in later passages, where his despair is much more in evidence. Here he hopes for another exodus and sojourn in the desert. This is not the image of Second Isaiah; the people of Second Isaiah were effectively dead and a new people is created. For Hosea the exodus was a period of testing from which Israel emerged faithful, the bride of Yahweh's youth. That this could be re-enacted was a paradoxical hope, really not only a hope for a return of love but for a return to youth. In the Gospel of John (3:4), Nicodemus found the saying of Jesus concerning a second birth para-

class of society which needs it most and whose regeneration will most benefit other classes.

One of the most important and at the same time one of the most disputable texts of this classification is Jeremiah's oracle of the new covenant (31:31–34). A fundamental question is whether this is from Jeremiah or from a scribal editor, but for the purpose of theological discussion it is not necessary to solve this question.[42] In contrast to the community of the Law (Section 7, above) the author rejects the law in the restoration which he foresees. There will no longer be a written code of any kind; the author apparently knew the story of the tablets of stone inscribed with the law given to Moses (Ex 32:15–16). By the image of the law written on the heart and not on stone tablets, the author does the best he can to distinguish between external direction and instruction and internal personal motivation. The same image distinguishes direction given to a group and accepted by membership in the group from personal decision. In this image, each individual person has the relation to Yahweh and the responsibility which the people of Israel had to Yahweh in the experience of the exodus. More than this, such a direct personal relationship renders unnecessary any intermediary between the individual and Yahweh; where each man is, so to speak, his own Israel, no instructors are necessary. Jeremiah elsewhere was somewhat hostile to the scribes, the interpreters of the law of Yahweh (Jer 8:8). In his future there is no place for them; and this is in direct contradiction to the community of the Law.

If this text is pressed, it becomes the clearest statement in the Old Testament that there is no future for Israel. The revolutionary implications of the passage are generally not noticed by interpreters; yet we have already observed that the book of Jeremiah is revolutionary in more than one aspect (Chapter II, Section 3.c; Chapter III, Section 5). It is not surprising that the prophet who announced the end of all the political and religious institutions of Judah should have no place for these institutions in the future. To say that he has nothing but an unstructured individualism would be true; but we have no right to impose upon any single prophet the obligation to say everything that can be said. Jeremiah saw

42 Ibid. 362; also Bright, *Jeremiah,* 287, who affirms authenticity without reservation.

doxical. We may read too much into Hosea when we notice
a return to the desert involved an abandonment of the contem
rary culture. Yet it is quite clear that Hosea regarded the c
temporary culture as identical with the culture and religic
structure of Canaanite civilization, although he did not employ su
words. The moral regeneration of Israel demanded its impoveris
ment. Only when it had found Yahweh in the desert could it hop
to have an enduring prosperity based on its enduring union wit
him who gave grain, wine, and oil.

If Hosea 14 is original, which is not certain, Hosea never gave
up this hope of reunion.[40] The image of marriage is so completely
personal that the sayings of Hosea are not governed by terms of
covenant nor even by strict consistency; and a work which exhibits such transparently profound feeling will be no more consistent than the speech of any one who is deeply moved. The book
ends, as we have seen (see Chapter II, Section 3.c, above), with
a complete judgment upon Israel; but Hosea's intensely personal
view of Yahweh allows Yahweh the same inconsistency which
men exhibit in moments of passion. A return to the fidelity which
is owed to Yahweh can restore what has been destroyed, even
though Israel is to all appearances dead. But life returns, not by
the word of the prophet as in Ezekiel's vision of the valley of
the dry bones (Ezek 37:1–14) but in answer to Hosea's invitation to return. It is Israel's decision whether it shall live or not.

The moral regeneration of Isaiah 32:1–8 is generally regarded
as an expansion.[41] The king is mentioned, but his importance is
not such as to justify classifying this saying with royal messianism.
The saying certainly echoes the awareness that the pre-exilic monarchy often failed "to reign in righteousness" (32:1). But the author is more aware of the existence of "knaves," by which he
probably means to designate the ruling classes of the monarchy
(see Chapter VI, Section 2, above). The moral regeneration
which the author sees is the liberation from the corrupt ruling class.
This does indeed suggest a pre-exilic date for this passage; but
for our purposes, the date of the passage is not that important.
The moral regeneration which the author hopes for touches that

[40] Eissfeldt, op. cit., 387.
[41] Ibid. 317.

the fall of Judah as a colossal institutional failure; and his vision is not a vision of new institutions, much less of those institutions which he had seen fall. The point of this saying is that one of the institutions which failed was the Torah. There is, I believe, no way in which one can put Jeremiah's new covenant in the same basket with the priestly writers and the postexilic community of the Law—which means Pharisaic Judaism. There may be no way of putting him in the same package with any institutional religion, including Christianity. The text always remains as a criticism of those who believe that laws written on stone will do what needs to be done. Jeremiah's case, if one insists, is overstated; so was the case of the priestly writers.

A similar, although less powerful, statement is found in that prophetic book which is usually not credited with much profundity, Ezekiel (36:25–27). Here the process of regeneration is the work of Yahweh; the symbolic rite of purification with sprinkling achieves marvelous effects. The new community receives a new heart and a new spirit. The old heart was a heart of stone; and it is hardly probable that the writer knew of the covenant of Jeremiah. A law inscribed on stone could be inscribed on a heart of stone; and we see that the two writers are wholly in agreement on their symbolism. The Israelites of Ezekiel do not need a new law but a new heart, a heart of flesh, sensitive and responsive. They need also a new spirit, that principle of action which from premonarchic times was conceived as an impulse from Yahweh which moved men to act beyond their known capacities and expectations (Chapter VI, Section 2). This charismatic endowment, in early times given to heroes and kings, now becomes the possession of each individual person, a theme found elsewhere in postexilic expressions of the future hope (Joel 2:28–29). The subsequent history of the idea of the universal diffusion of the spirit lies outside the scope of Old Testament theology; but the presence of its roots in these passages should be noticed. The author, probably unconsciously, approaches the language of creation (Gen 2:7).

The theme of moral regeneration is clear in Zechariah 5 and 8:14–17. In Zechariah 5 two images are employed: the scroll which flies over the land containing curses upon those who steal and perjure themselves and the vessel which bears out of the country the woman called Wickedness. That wickedness is a woman is a not uncommon biblical theme which, in spite of certain contemporary urgencies, need not detain us here. The point of the writer is that wickedness must be removed from the land which Yahweh has renewed. The exhortation of Zechariah 8:14–17 is derived from the proclamations of the pre-exilic prophets; they are quite general, but the prophet means that the characteristic national vices which brought the judgment of Yahweh upon his people must not occur in the restored people. These passages do not envisage a genuine internal change of character such as the passages of Jeremiah and Ezekiel cited above suggest; but they carry the same implication, that a mere restoration of what went before the exile is nothing really new.

What is probably a postexilic gloss in Zephaniah 3:11–13 expresses a hope of moral regeneration. The passage is of interest because it sees moral regeneration as the piety of the poor, the theme which we have noticed in Third Isaiah and some other postexilic writers (Chapter II, Section 3.c, above). It echoes the saying of Isaiah 2:10–19, which attacks human pride.

9. Summary

The modern reader is likely to ask himself whether the theme of moral regeneration is not, together with the theme of the mission of Israel, the only expression of a future which offers a genuine hope for mankind. The other themes which we have set forth suffer from nationalistic or tribal or political or secular restrictions which make it difficult to think of them as expressions of hope which could be meaningful to any one except members of the postexilic Jewish community. If we think of the dreams of the national hope or the apocalyptic hope, these could hardly be valid even for members of the postexilic Jewish community. The reign of the saints of Yahweh over the world has never occurred, and the modern reader of the Bible doubts very seriously that it ought to occur or that Yahweh ever intended that it should occur. Enough trouble has been caused, he thinks, by efforts of earlier saints to realize this hope; and if one retains any belief in the Bible as a sacred book, one knows that the Bible never had in mind Oliver Cromwell or the crusade against the Albigensians, however unpalatable Charles Stuart or the Albigensians may have been.

We have given extensive discussion to this theme because it is, in the last analysis, the theme of Israelite belief which distinguishes it from other ancient religions. As far as we know Mesopotamian, Canaanite, and Egyptian religions, they lived in an eternal present. When the political societies which were undergirded by these religions perished, the religions perished with them. The belief of Israel proved itself independent of the political societies of the monarchies of Israel and Judah. Further analysis discloses that this independence was at least implicitly an assertion that the concerns of Yahweh were larger than the concerns of Israel and Judah. It is more than the development of monotheism; it is an understanding that if the nations have no gods, then Yahweh is their god. His future does not depend on the future of the people who worshiped him.

In spite of this, we have given most attention to the national hope, which affirms that Yahweh must have an Israel to believe in him. Yet the writers knew that he did not need Israel. They were faced with the statement that Yahweh had destroyed Israel, a judgment which showed his independence of rather than his dependence on Israel. If he had restored Israel, as he did, there must have been some other purpose than the mere existence of Israel, unfaithful in cult and covenant. We have seen that there was more than one effort to express this purpose. Possibly no one has ever accepted easily and gracefully the realization that his destiny is to live for others.

This is the theological value of the various themes of the future hope, that what we can now see as the genuine hope of the future was not easily reached. It was necessary for at least some to rise above ethnic and national considerations, which come to us so naturally, to a vision of a destiny which was truly human, wide enough to correspond to the vision of one god of all mankind. It is only fair to say that the postexilic Jews as a body did not rise to the level of this vision. It is only candid to say that Christians, who have seized upon an often spurious "messianism" of the Old Testament hope of the future as a vindication of their religious system, have as a body risen no higher. The hope of the Old Testament did see a future which rose above sectarianism; the fulfillment of this hope still lies in the future.

Epilogue

In the Preface I have explained why this Epilogue is necessary. In this instance, moreover, the delays and the prolongation of time compel me to write an epilogue in order that I may speak to some writings which, in the normal and hoped course of development, would have appeared at the time of publication of my book, after its publication, or in any case after its submission to the editor, so they would not have been treated in this book. The number of writings which could be cited are too large for quotation or even for listing, and I have restricted myself to three titles, chosen both because they are recent and because they include summaries of the work of others. They are in the order of appearance, Hans-Joachim Kraus, *Die Biblische Theologie,* Neukirchen-Vluyn, 1970; Brevard S. Childs, *Biblical Theology in Crisis,* Philadelphia, Westminster 1970; and Gerhard Hasel, *Old Testament Theology: Basic Issues in the Current Debate,* Grand Rapids, Eerdman's, 1972. All three of these are "how-to-do-it" books; and while I wish with all my heart that these my colleagues had written a biblical theology instead of directions for the same, frankly I am, as a competitor, happy that they did not. I have in this book given attention to Walther Eichrodt and Gerhard von Rad because their method is clothed in flesh and blood, and it is easier to discern what the method is. Of these three works I must say that I do not know how well the kit of instructions will hold up when the actual work is undertaken. I am reminded somewhat irreverently of the man who built a boat in his basement with no plans for getting it out of the basement. My boat may not float, but it is in the water. And I certainly mean by this no implication that these three colleagues are unable to produce a biblical theology; since I have to pay attention to their work, I observe that they did not, and what they did produce was too late for me to use. And I cannot resist noticing that when I signed the original contract to do this work, biblical theology was in no way "in crisis" and there was no "current debate." Now I see no way of escaping involvement in both.

Let me attend first to the fact that both Kraus and Childs are writing about "biblical theology," by which they expressly mean the theology of the entire Bible, Old and New Testaments. I have written a theology of the Old Testament. I present it with the full expectation that reviewers will be displeased because I wrote it as if the New Testament did not exist. I see now that I must speak to this. I was aware that both Eichrodt and Von Rad gave considerable space to the relations of the two Testaments; I gave nearly none and thought that this treatment would, so to speak, justify itself. In the last analysis, this is the only justification I can expect. But in addition to Eichrodt and Von Rad, Kraus and Childs obviously see the relations of Old and New Testament as the major problem of biblical theology, and Hasel sees it as the major problem of Old Testament theology. Plainly one who sings so far outside the chorus will find it difficult to prove that he is in tune. I must advert to the discord because I believe I have a valid view of Old Testament theology which deserves to be presented.

I said above that I wrote the theology of the Old Testament as if the New Testament did not exist. It seems to me that at least some justification for the procedure lies in the fact that the books of the Old Testament were written when the New Testament did not exist. I fully agree with the statement (which I am unable to trace, although it was probably Adolf Harnack or Rudolf Bultmann) that the Old Testament is not a Christian book. It was written neither by Christians nor for Christians. This rather obvious fact is open to inferences not all of which I accept. It certainly justifies the methodological division between the theology of the Old Testament and the theology of the New Testament. No one has criticized Eichrodt or Von Rad or any other Old Testament theologian for a false methodological division. A theology of the Old Testament written by a Jewish scholar would not be criticized for not treating the relations of Old Testament and New Testament. If the Jewish scholar were to treat this question, I doubt that many Christian scholars would like his treatment. This suggests that the concern about the relations between the Old and the New Testaments comes from something outside the Old Testament itself; and where does that leave the question of method?

I do not wish to imply Marcionism even in the attenuated form in which Harnack and Bultmann have preserved it. I think this book is an attestation of my conviction that all three of them are wrong. The Old Testament is not a Christian book; this book on the theology of the Old Testament is a Christian book, at least in the sense that it is written by a professing Christian mostly for professing Christians, I presume. I make no effort to conceal my Christianity and in some instances I have sat in Christian judgment on Old Testament writers. I expect reviewers to respond unfavorably to this, but the Christian faith makes demands which are incompatible even with the religion of the prophets. I wish to present the truth that the Christian faith has the religion of the prophets as one of its components. It is but one of the components of a theology of the Old Testament, and not all the components are of equal value; and it is time we lost our fear of using this word. I have more or less tried to suggest that the Christian faith arose—or rather erupted—out of a historical experience and not out of a development of doctrine. That historical experience I described by the well-worn tag of "encounter with God."

Granted that the Old Testament is not a Christian book, it has passed into Christianity as a legacy of the primitive Christian church. The members of this church were Jews, and they accepted these books as the only sacred books endowed with divine authority. We shall see shortly that they accepted them with reservations which other Jews found intolerable; these reservations, I think, are not problems of Old Testament theology. With these books the early church accepted patterns of religious thought and religious language which were the major elements in the subsequent development of Christian belief, even after the Hellenization of Christian belief had begun. These patterns of thought and language were not entirely submerged in the Hellenization and Europeanization of Christianity. It can safely be stated that the biblical patterns ceased to be the major factors after the rise of medieval scholastic theology; this, again, seems to lie outside the concerns of Old Testament theology. The Reformation, among other things, was an attempt to restore the biblical patterns to what the reformers thought was their due primacy; at the moment, the success of their effort is less important for us than the fact that they thought the effort should be made. Modern "biblical movements" are similar if less revolutionary endeavors; and they have persisted even though many theologians have called them a flight from reason. In a certain and very proper sense that is what they were.

The indelible imprint of the Old Testament on the Christian patterns of thought and language would of itself be enough to justify an Old Testament theology on a scale as large, let us say, as the study of the mystery religions or the documents of Qumran and Nag Hammadi. I doubt whether it is studied as intensively in the contemporary scholarly scene as these last two sets of documents, which without doubt have the interest and appeal of a brand new set of problems. But such studies, I think, ultimately explain themselves as contributing to the theological understanding of the New Testament; to employ a phrase which I used above, they are not carried on as if the New Testament had never been written. Something more than this has always been sought in Old Testament theology and is clearly demanded in the works of Kraus, Childs, and Hasel. It has taken me a book-size manuscript to state what I understand that "something more" is. With deference to my colleagues, let me add a brief and more precise summary of how this refers to the New Testament, and my points are two.

The first point I have made earlier. The God whom Jesus called his Father and whom he taught his disciples to address as Father is Yahweh of the Old Testament, the God of the fathers, of Abraham, Isaac, and Jacob, who led his people out of Egypt and into exile in Babylon, who spoke in sundry times and divers manners to the fathers and the prophets in times past and in these last days in the Son. It was not necessary for the disciples to ask Jesus, as the Israelites asked Moses, "What is his name?" (Ex 3:13). This fact, so obvious that it approaches banality, deserves more than casual attention. The same God was proclaimed to Gentiles who did not know Moses from Menelaus. This God was not Zeus, the great Olympian lecher who founded his career on the castration of his father. He was not the Canaanite Baal, the one god against whom the Old Testament mounts a sustained polemic; and with the Baal go all the fertility gods of the ancient Near East. He was not the impersonal Supreme Good of whom (or of which?) Plato spoke with such moving eloquence. He was not the Cosmic

Fire, or whatever it was, which the Stoics saw at the top of things; nor was he the sanitized Zeus to whom the Stoic Cleanthes wrote a hymn. It was not of him that Lucretius wrote *Tantum religio potuit suadere malorum*—although I am not sure that Lucretius would have found the Old Testament entirely foreign to his line. The Father whom Jesus proclaimed was, as he is called more than once in the Old Testament, the one God and there is no other. He was not an abstraction created by philosophical discourse nor an element of nature disguised in mythology; he was a person with a history known to the community in which Jesus spoke about him. Without this history one does not enter into the area of discourse of the New Testament.

My second point touches the identity and the role of Jesus, and here I ask pardon for quoting an earlier statement of my own concerning this: "It is the history of Israel that sets Jesus apart from all culture-heroes, king-saviors, cosmic men, and mythological bearers of life; or, in more modern terms, from political saviors, economic prophets, scientific sages, military heroes, psychotherapist bearers of life. It is remarkable, it is even sharply surprising, when one reflects that only as the Savior of Israel can Jesus be recognized as none of these other things."[1] I recall this quotation because the reader may remember that I dealt with the theme of King Messiah as a theological blind alley in Chapter VI, Section 2, and Chapter VII, Section 3, above. There was really no change in my thinking on the subject in the ten years which separate these passages. My point in the earlier passage was that the role of Jesus can be protected from distortion only by holding fast its connection with biblical antecedents; a non-Israelite and nonbiblical Jesus makes no sense, already said by Paul when he said that Christ is "folly to Gentiles" (1 Cor 1:23). My point in the second passages was, to use the words of the same verse of Paul, that Christ is "a stumbling-block to Jews." As he cannot be understood without the Old Testament, so he is not found in his full reality in the Old Testament. I quoted above the texts which allude to pouring new wine in old flasks. Jesus arises from the categories of the Old Testament but he surpasses them; he corrresponds to no religious figure of the Old Testament. He is neither predicted nor foreshad-

[1] B. W. Anderson, ed., *The Old Testament and Christian Faith* (New York, 1963), 109.

owed. He is contained in neither allegory nor type. "Messiah" is not an apt title of Jesus; but no title is apt.

These are my two points of reference between Old and New Testament; but there are other points to consider which arise from the theological discussion of this problem in past and present. They may be called points of nonreference. In my last chapter I drew up a list of forms in which the belief in the eternity of Israel expressed itself in various Old Testament books. I found neither system nor even consistency in these forms and made no special effort to list them in the order either of history or of logic. In drawing up the list of these themes, I made no conscious effort to assert or to imply what finally emerged, that the New Testament rejects almost all of them. In the terms I used, it rejects the national hope, royal messianism, the worshiping community, and the Law as fulfillment of the future. It retains and profoundly transforms the themes of the mission of Israel and of moral regeneration. I deliberately leave the apocalyptic future hanging in the air; it is the function of New Testament theology to define the apocalyptic of the New Testament. I wonder how one can speak of "development" in the face of such remarkable discontinuities. And here we touch upon a key word in all my three writers—"continuity." All believe that it is the office of biblical theology to show the continuity of the two Testaments—or the unity of the Bible; here it means the same thing. I can only submit the opinion—I cannot argue except to repeat the presentation I have given—that the unity which consists in continuity does not exist and cannot be shown. It is a devious and tortuous path through a tangled wilderness that we trace; and I do not know by what assurance the biblical theologian or any theologian can say that we are out of the woods and know where the path leads us. If I say that it is a crooked path, I do no more than echo Ezekiel (18:25-29) and one of the psalmists (Ps 18:26).

I have already implied that I do not agree with Childs's proposal to do biblical theology by studying Old Testament texts used in the New Testament. He gives examples of this method, and I do not deny that it is a way of doing biblical theology. It is not a feasible way of doing a book on biblical theology and still less of doing a book on Old Testament theology. Pursuit of his method on the scale on which he wrote would, I fear, involve a work of

several volumes. Nor do I see how in his method one would achieve
what I said I seek, the insight which comes from a view of the
whole. Indeed, Childs's suggestion may cast doubt on the validity
of the methodological distinction between Old and New Testament
theologies; I doubt that he means this, for this obvious criticism
of most Old Testament theologies he never makes.

In my Introduction I disclaimed any employment of prediction
fulfillment, foreshadowing revelation, allegory, typology, spiritual
sense, fuller sense, or other similar techniques derived from the
New Testament and the Fathers of the Church. There is no doubt
that the New Testament employs some rabbinical and allegorical
exegesis. As an interpreter, it is my duty to explain Paul's use
of the allegory of the slave girl and the free woman, not to employ
it myself. For me this exegetical technique falls in the same basket
with the New Testament view of the three-decker universe; perhaps
this ought to trouble me, but it does not. Manuals of biblical introduction used to tell students of the "accommodated" use of the
Scriptures, by which they meant the application of the text to a
situation bearing only a superficial resemblance to the situation
envisaged in the text. The classical example of such accomoda-
tion (in which Virgil was used, but the principle is the same) was
the application of the shipwreck line in *Aeneid I* to the seminary
oyster soup: *Apparent rari nantes in gurgite vasto.* I fear that this
principle will take care of most of the Old Testament texts quoted
in the New; but perhaps Childs can do more theology out of the
prohibition of muzzling the ox that treadeth out the corn than I
can see. The prohibition is directed at a peculiarly revolting instance of *chutzpah.*

Earlier efforts, from the patristic age onward, to impose a false
unity upon the two Testaments have left me extremely cautious
about finding a nonexistent development of doctrine or an orderly
and coherent historical process which moves sweetly from the good
to the better. I used the example of the battle of Gettysburg, which
exhibited its own inner logic, perceptible only after the event. Battles are not examples of smooth and orderly development; and
they are better analogies of the historical development of the Old
Testament than the evolution of a theological school. I have used
the well-worn phrase "encounter with God" to designate this his-

torical process; it should be recognized frankly that the encounter of man with God is basically hostile. One word for a hostile encounter is "battle."

This was probably a bit of a digression. To return to the main thrust of my argument, I have said in my Introduction that the use of the Old Testament in the New is indeed a theological problem, but not a problem of Old Testament theology. It seems to me that the Old Testament theologian surrenders his freedom if he accepts this as his problem. To accept the problem presupposes a theory of biblical inspiration which is no longer tenable or implies a divine "plan" which the writer knows and can set forth. In a review I agreed with Franz Hesse that it is time to say goodbye to *Heilsgeschichte*.[2] As a principle of unity of biblical theology, the history of salvation is as contrived and strained as any dialectic ever invented. It assumes that the New Testament is a term toward which everything in the Old Testament was directed. Elements of the Old Testament in which this direction cannot be seen must be twisted to fit the scheme or omitted from the history of salvation.

I am fascinated by a fear which I think I perceive in many of my colleagues, and I ask their pardon if I am misreading their minds. There seems to be an unspoken fear that unless we can explicitly and formally integrate the Old Testament into the New, we either surrender the Old Testament to Judaism or we join Marcion. I do not share this fear, and perhaps I ought to share it. I have given what appear to be valid reasons why the Christian must accept this heritage from Jesus and the apostolic church. It is a heritage with which the church has never lived comfortably, and possibly living comfortably is an objective which we should not seek. Possibly the purpose of the Old Testament in the church is to make the church uncomfortable. It certainly has done this; and it has resisted efforts to show that after all it makes good sense. Is this not equivalent to saying that God makes good sense? Eliphaz is not celebrated as the wisest of Old Testament sages, but he spoke for the others when he said that God does things great and unsearchable, marvelous things without number (Job 5:9). This is the limit which every biblical theologian must recognize; but he should not recognize it before he reaches it.

---

[2] F. Hesse, *Abschied von der Heilsgeschichte* (Zürich, 1971).

Index

Aaron, 54, 55
Abbott and Gallagher, 270 n
Abimelech, 247
Abraham, 70, 74, 139 ff., 159, 164, 201
Abschied von der Heilsgeschichte, 326 n
Achan, 241–42
Acts of the Fourth Jewish Congress, 151 n
Adad, 197, 198
Adonijah, 207
Adultery, 104, 112
Ägypten und Vorderasien im Altertum, 162 n, 259 n
Ahab, 91 ff., 100–1, 256
Ahaz, 107
Ahijah, 90
Ai, 151
Albright, William Foxwell, 49 n, 50 n, 74, 78 n, 81 n, 85, 140 n
Alexander the Great, 305, 306
Alt, Albrecht, 75 n, 91, 250, 255–56, 286 n
Altorientalische Texte zum Alten Testament, 80 n
Amalekites, 152
Amarna letters, 247
Amaziah, 94
Amel-Marduk, 285
Ammon (Amon), 151, 164, 236, 259
Amorite, the, 145
Amos, 26–27, 69, 94–95 ff., 102–4, 105, 110, 123–24, 125, 154 ff., 192, 255, 256, 269, 271, 273, 309, 310; and Bethel, 21; and criticism

of cult, 58 ff.; denies he is prophet, 87; and exodus, 145; and faith, 34; and glosses, 281–82; and "happy ending," 274; Joel and, 303; and the nations, 167–68, 171; and nature, 199; and Sabbath, 80
Amphictyony, 81–82
Ancient Israel. See Vaux, Roland de
Ancient Mesopotamia, 295 n
Ancient Near East: Supplementary Texts . . . , The (ANES), 215 n, 216 n
Ancient Near Eastern Texts . . . (ANET), 103 n, 109 n, 178 n, 189 n, 190 n, 194 n, 197 n, 203 n ff., 214 n, 222 n, 226 n, 237 n, 260 n, 261 n, 301 n
Ancient Near East in Pictures, The (ANEP), 50 n, 52 n, 189 n, 196 n
Ancient Records (Luckenbill), 132 n
Anderson, B. W., 323 n
Antiochus IV (Epiphanes), 305 ff., 309
Antiquities of Jordan, The, 53 n
Apocalyptic future, 298–310
Arabs, 153
Aramaeans, 92, 101, 167
Aramaic Inscriptions . . . , 76 n
Aramaic treaties, 76
Archeology of Palestine, The, 50 n
Aristotle, 174, 183
Ark, 42, 48 ff., 56–57, 254
Ark, Noah's, 199
Arpad, 169
Artaxerxes I, 260, 261
Artaxerxes II, 261

244–57, 313–14 (*see also* specific rulers); and New Year, 42; prophets and (*see* Prophets and prophecy)

King Savior; King Messiah. *See* Messianism

Kingship and the Gods, 250 n

Kleine Schriften. See Alt, Albrecht

Koheleth, 34, 210, 211, 218, 225–27, 308

Köhler, Ludwig, 20 n

Kommentar zum Neuen Testament, 43 n, 126 n, 265 n

Königsherrschaft Gottes im Alten Testament, 43 n

Kraus, Hans-Joachim, 43–44, 319 ff.

Kuhl, Curt, 102 n, 112

Lacedaemonians, 134

Lamentations, 156

Land, 83, 150–53, 238–40, 271–72, 273, 290, 291

Language and Myth, 174 n

Law, 70–85, 127, 212–13, 238, 247, 250, 257–66, 314, 315 (*see also* Pentateuch; specific books, laws); as fulfillment of future, 310–12

Levi, 139

Leviathan, 190, 195, 223, 301

Leviticus, 39 n, 41, 45, 47 n, 49 n, 57, 85, 262

Light, 188–89

Lindblom, J., 286 n

Literatur der Aegypter, 208 n

Lods, Adolphe, 102 n

Lot, 201

Luckenbill, D. D., 132 n

Lucretius, 227, 323

Ludlul bel nemeqi, 215

Luke, 81, 121, 122, 268

Maccabeans (Maccabees), 293, 309

Maccabees, Zealots and Josephus, 309 n

McCarthy, Dennis J., 75 n

McKenzie, John L., 69 n, 89 n, 97 n,

101 n, 105 n, 120 n, 137 n, 151 n, 193 n, 196 n, 241 n, 263 n, 274 n, 285 n, 294 n, 296 n, 301 n

Malachi, 119, 120, 123, 127, 289–90, 303

Males, heads of families, 227–28

Manasseh, 139

Manoah, 142

Marcion and Marcionism, 19, 268, 321

Marduk, 189, 215

Mari, 85

Mark, 268, 290, 303

Marriage, 105, 259, 276, 313. *See also* Adultery

Matthew, 121, 198, 268, 272, 290, 303, 307

Matzoth, Feast of. *See* Unleavened Bread, Feast of

Medes (and Median army), 133, 305, 306

Memphis, 189

Mendenhall, George E., 71 n, 75 ff., 81 n, 236, 238

Men of God (Rowley), 98 n

Mesopotamia(ns), 68, 132, 177–78 ff., 185 ff., 198 ff. (*see also* Babylonians); New Year, 39, 41; priests, 55; prostitution, 207; and Sabbath, 80; sacrifice, 45; temples, 48, 51, 52; wisdom, 203 ff., 209, 210, 213, 215, 218, 226

Messianism, 23–24, 28–29, 34, 53, 62, 163, 179, 245, 253, 267 ff., 285–89, 317

Metaphysics (Aristotle), 174 n, 183 n

Micah, 53, 72, 106–7, 123, 155, 157, 255, 256, 271, 274, 283, 287, 303; and exodus, 144, 146; and judgment, 156

Micaiah ben Imlah, 93

Miriam, Song of, 144

Mission of Israel, 293–98

Moab, 93, 151, 164, 171, 230, 259, 272